Rhisome

Crown

Tiller

Stolen

leaf

sheath

Blade

Node

Clum

Mid vein

Inforsence

Practical Golf Course Maintenance

The Magic of Greenkeeping

by

Gordon Witteveen

and

Michael Bavier

Ann Arbor Press
Chelsea, Michigan

Library of Congress Cataloging-in-Publication Data

Witteveen, Gordon
    Practical golf course maintenance: the magic of greenkeeping / by Gordon
Witteveen and Michael Bavier.
        p.   cm.
    Includes bibliographical references and index.
    ISBN 1-57504-047-6
    1. Golf courses—Maintenance. 2. Turf management. I. Bavier, Michael.
II. Title.
    GV975.W58   1998
    796.352'06'8—dc21

                                                                98-9691
                                                                CIP

ISBN 1-57504-047-6

ANN ARBOR PRESS
121 South Main Street, Chelsea, Michigan 48118
Ann Arbor Press is an imprint of Sleeping Bear Press

PRINTED IN THE UNITED STATES OF AMERICA
10 9 8 7 6 5 4

Dedication

To our green chairmen

Acknowledgments

This book had its origin in The Magic of Greenkeeping, a seminar for golf course workers, superintendents, and others interested in golf course maintenance. The book is organized much as the seminar, with the cutting and cultivating operations in the first part, followed by management operations in the back of the book. The seminar is composed of more than 200 slides and many of these are also part of this book. The seminar has been presented to more than 1,300 students in 5 countries. The feedback that we received from our students had a profound influence on the development of the seminar, as well as the book. Our students were a source of inspiration and we thank them for being so open with us about their likes and dislikes, which are reflected in the book.

Most of the book was written during 1996 and completed in early 1997. During that time we received much encouragement from many of our friends, among them Dr. James Beard at Texas A&M, Dr. Jack Eggens at the University of Guelph, and Larry Marty, instructor at Kishwaukee College in Illinois. Our colleagues in Canada and the United States frequently asked how the book was progressing, thereby ensuring our commitment to complete it.

Special thanks to our friends Marie Thorne and Adrian Gallant, both experts in their fields. Marie reviewed the chapter on spraying and Adrian checked the part on fertilizers for accuracy. Larry Longo, a rules official with the Canadian Professional Golf Association and a loyal friend, checked the chapter on rules as they affect maintenance. Superintendent Peter Leuzinger from Chicago supplied us with his equipment inventory and reviewed the chapter on the operation of the Turf Care Center. Paul Voykin, one of the greatest superintendents to have originated in Saskatchewan, helped with information on wildflowers. Tim Hiers, Superintendent at Collier's Reserve in Florida, answered all our questions about Integrated Pest Management, and in the process revealed himself as the quintessential superintendent that he is.

We also received great help and encouragement from Bill Fach, Superintendent at the Yorkdowns Golf Club. Bill is a natural bookworm as well as an outstanding superintendent. We were fortunate to have him read the book in its entirety and make suggestions before it was sent to our publishers. We must not forget Walter Woods, now retired from St. Andrews in Scotland, who helped with bunker rebuilding, and also our colleagues Joe Bedford and Aiden O'Hara in Ireland. Nigel Butler and Pye Bredenkamp helped us while we visited South Africa. In New Zealand we learned greenkeeping from Walter Ward and Bob Bradley. Closer to home, we received support and encouragement from the following: Dr. James Watson, Paul Scenna, Paul Dermott, Keith Bartlett, Ron Craig, Gary Stairs, Cory Janzen, Ken Wright, Oscar Miles, Terry Buchen, Dudley Smith, Bob Heron, Ron Heesen, Grant

Humes, Brent Wadsworth, Doug Anderson, and Bill and Betty Radke, who all helped in their own ways.

Our final thanks must go to the two very special women in our lives: Marilyn and Mary, who were always at hand to assist with the computers, the disks, the e-mail and the faxes. We also thank them for putting up with our frequent absences, all for the sake of spreading the gospel of greenkeeping.

Biographies

Michael Bavier grew up in a small Minnesota town called Willmar. He developed his love for golf as a caddie at the Wilmar Golf Club and later worked on the grounds crew while attending high school. After graduating from Penn State College he did his internship under Warren Bidwell at the Olympia Fields Golf Club in Illinois.

He served with the U.S. Marines in 1964. Later he became Assistant Superintendent at the Oak Ridge CC in Hopkins, Minnesota and soon after served as Superintendent for four years at the Calumet CC in Homewood, Illinois. For the past 28 years he has been Superintendent at the Inverness GC near Chicago.

Michael has always been active professionally, serving as director, secretary, and president of the Mid West Golf Course Superintendents Association. In 1981 he was elected President of the Golf Course Superintendents Association of America. To this day he is active in the Musser Foundation, an organization that raises money for students in their final year of a doctorate's degree in a turf-related field. Together with his friend and colleague Gordon Witteveen he is a frequent speaker on the Turf Conference Tour both in North America and overseas, often presenting "The Magic of Greenkeeping Seminar" to wide ranging audiences.

Gordon Witteveen was born in the Netherlands and attended the Ontario Agricultural College in Guelph, Ontario. During summer vacations he developed a love for golf while working at the Noranda Mines GC in the province of Quebec. Upon graduation from college he became Superintendent at the Highland CC near London, Ontario, and after three years moved on to Toronto as Superintendent at the former Northwood Country Club for 12 years. Since 1973 he has been at the 45 hole Board of Trade course in the village of Woodbridge near Toronto.

Gordon Witteveen helped start the Canadian Golf Superintendents Association in 1965 and served as that association's first secretary. He initiated *The Green Master* magazine and served as its editor for five years. In 1970 he was President of the Canadian group. He has also served on the Board of Directors of GCSAA and is still active in the OJ Noer Turfgrass Research Foundation.

Gordon is well known for his many presentations at turfgrass meetings all over the world. His best known presentation is "25 Years of Mistakes." He writes regularly for several magazines and is a past Leo Feser award winner of *Golf Course Management* magazine.

Foreword

Gordon Witteveen and I worked together when our firm made extensive alterations to the Board of Trade Country Club, near Toronto, where Gordon was the golf course superintendent. I've also had a number of opportunities to play Michael Bavier's course, the Inverness Club near Chicago. I was impressed with Michael's ability to keep his course looking cool and inviting during the heat and humidity of a Chicago summer. Even during the scorching summer of 1995, Michael didn't lose a blade of grass.

Now Michael and Gordon have combined their talents to write an exceptional book of greenkeeping. In it, they share their love for their profession, combining knowledge based on years of experience and widespread travels. I admire what Gordon and Michael have accomplished, and recommend their book as a welcome addition to golf's literature by outstanding practitioners of the greenkeepers' art.

Arthur Hills
Toledo, Ohio

Introduction

We found ourselves on a small, side road about a hundred miles north of Auckland in New Zealand, looking for a golf course. After several turns of the road, the familiar sight of green fairways, tees, and greens came into view and we noticed a small tractor and wagon, parked off to the side of a golf hole. At first sight there was no sign of a living person anywhere near, but closer inspection revealed a man, lying flat on his stomach with the upper part of his body stuck in a hole. An all-too familiar scene: someone fixing a pipe leak! We decided to investigate, and the repairman turned out to be the superintendent! We discussed the pipe problem, offered some advice, and then our newfound friend asked if we cared to have a cup of tea. We accepted, and minutes later we were in a shed with a hard dirt floor, seated around a ramshackle table on rickety chairs, discussing greenkeeping in New Zealand. With the steaming tea between us, we exchanged information on our programs and compared our methods. Our host had only two helpers, a grown man and a young boy to look after 18 holes, so plenty of shortcuts were needed to make the course playable and to get the work done. Each green had three holes but only one flagstick! The golfers were expected to change the stick regularly and thus spread the wear. The holes were changed just once a week, the greens cut every other day, and the fairway mowing completed during weekday afternoons. Rough and bunker maintenance was sporadic. In spite of the abbreviated maintenance program, which we would not dream of implementing in America, the golf course looked inviting, and we enjoyed our game when we played later that day.

Several months later, back in America and again looking for a golf course, we turned our rental car from a busy thoroughfare onto a tree-lined boulevard. The guardhouse, the size of a suburban bungalow, yielded a uniformed man who sternly asked us our business. He seemed somewhat suspicious, perhaps because he was more accustomed to whisking Cadillacs, Lincolns, and even the occasional chauffeur-driven Rolls Royce through with a wave of the hand. We were finally, somewhat reluctantly, given permission to visit the Director of Golf Course Operations. A curbed, asphalt road with ample signs made the large, luxuriantly landscaped building easy to find. We passed several dozen neatly parked automobiles and left our car in a spot designated for visitors. As we glanced through open doors, we saw as much machinery as one would find at a regional turf conference. The Director was in his office in conference with the assistants and we waited politely as an efficient secretary poured us cups of coffee and asked if we would like a muffin. We gladly accepted and settled down in cushioned chairs and air conditioned comfort, waiting for our audience with the Director. Meanwhile the secretary answered all our queries politely and informatively as she worked on one of several computers.

After a short while, the Director appeared and introduced the assistants, took us for a tour of the maintenance facility in the company of a uniformed mechanic, and explained the workings of the operation. All the machinery was in showroom condition and parked in its appropriate place, marked with thick, yellow lines. The cement floor was treated with a special finish that made it shine and easy to clean. The tool benches were as clean as the staff room lunch tables. There was no dust, no grease, and not a single screw driver or wrench out of place. Near the time clock on the staff room wall, we saw the names of the employees and counted them carefully: 37 people were employed here, and it seemed as if there were a golf cart for each and every one.

The greens were cut every day with pedestrian mowers, and they were often rolled as well. The holes were changed and the ball marks repaired. If need be, the greens were syringed. The 63 bunkers were hand-raked. The blocks on the tees were also changed daily, and every divot and scar repaired or replaced. On the fairways, the mowers cut in perfectly straight lines and the clippings were collected in baskets and hauled away to be composted. There were no divots on the fairways. In fact, there was not a blade of grass out of place!

Later, while we golfed in this heavenly valley, we reflected on the superb condition of the course and the magnificent operations center. We could not help but compare it to the modest shed that we had visited in New Zealand just a few months before. And then we began to realize, that although the area of the two golf courses was miles apart, the basics of greenkeeping were very much the same: cutting grass, changing holes, raking bunkers, applying fertilizer, repairing waterlines, and many other chores are all essential operations that take place daily on golf courses all over the world. The size of a golf course's budget largely determines the degree of sophistication that superintendents employ to get the job done. The objective is invariably the same: providing a pleasurable golf course that is affordable for the majority of the golfers.

During our travels in many different countries we have encountered a wide disparity in golf courses and in conditioning, but in conversations with our colleagues, we were always amazed as to how much more we had in common than set us apart. At times language was a barrier, as in continental Europe when we haltingly conversed with Spanish, Italian, French, and German greenkeepers. At a conference in southern France the well-known presentation, "25 Years of Mistakes," was instantly translated by two bilingual superintendents into French and German. In Malmö, a Swedish superintendent provided the same service for his colleagues. While we discussed greenkeeping with a South African Superintendent on that country's east coast, he frequently stopped to instruct his native staff in Zulu, a nasal language that includes many sharp clicks of the tongue. In Kathmandu, Nepal, the course manager, a Hindu who spoke only a few words of English, eagerly asked us questions about greens and grasses. At the time, he was in the process of converting the sand greens to grass. In our communications with non-English-speaking peoples we discovered that although the languages differed, familiar words such as green, fairway, and golf kept cropping up in our exchanges. In addition, we used signs and sounds to make ourselves understood, with gratifying success.

It was by traveling and visiting with colleagues that we discovered that fundamental greenkeeping differed little from country to country and continent to continent. We have learned much from our peers everywhere, and in these pages we share with our readers what we have learned, not only in distant countries but also from old-timers at home, at meetings and conferences. It is the type of knowledge that cannot be learned at school. One can find it in a greenkeeper's shed in New Zealand, in an air-conditioned office in North America, and everywhere else where golf is played and where superintendents sweat and toil and rejoice when they beat all odds and a produce a fine golf course.

We hope that you will enjoy this book and will find the information on these pages useful and the anecdotes entertaining. The essence of our professional lives is spread out over these 21 chapters. As the book progressed, we came to realize that we needed to sharpen up some of our practices. It is all very well to preach and advocate, but it does no good to say one thing and do another. Thus we have become better greenkeepers during the process of writing the book. We have attacked our jobs with renewed vigor and fresh enthusiasm. We hope our book will have the same effect on our readers.

Gordon Witteveen and Michael Bavier
Spring 1998

Contents

Practical Golf Course Maintenance

The Magic of Greenkeeping

1 Cutting Greens

Of all the playing areas on the golf course, none is more important than the green. Fully 40 % of all golf shots are played on and around the green. Golfers may tolerate mediocre fairways, poor bunkers, and sparse tees, but they expect, and deserve, puttable, near-perfect greens. When a golf ball rolls onto the green toward the hole, nothing must impede it from its true path. The factor that most affects the roll of the ball is the smoothness of the putting surface. Only shaving the green with a sharp mower will ensure that the golf ball rolls truly and smoothly.

All other work that is done to a green, such as topdressing, aerifying, fertilizing, spraying, and watering are wasted unless the green is cut to perfection. No matter how healthy the green, no matter its dark green color, no matter its long root system, no matter the absence of disease, if the green is not cut perfectly, golfers will condemn it, and much work is wasted. Cutting the green to perfection is the icing on the cake. Cutting the green is the glorious culmination of all the hard work that has been done before. That is why cutting greens is so very important in maintaining golf courses to perfection.

CUTTING THE GREEN, 10 STEPS TO A PERFECT PUTTING SURFACE

The Rider

Until the mid 1960s, all greens were cut with walk-behind mowers. It was a time-consuming process, often taking three to four persons to cut all 18 greens plus a putting green during the morning. Then came the riding greens mowers, and suddenly it was possible for just one operator to cut all the greens before lunch. Golf course superintendents were ecstatic and the new machines took the golf course market by storm. After a while, smart superintendents discovered that the riders had some serious drawbacks: compaction, the Triplex Ring phenomenon, and hydraulic spills made us realize that all was not well in the land of high-speed greens

Figure 1.1. Cutting a green to perfection is the final and most critical step in preparing the putting surface for play.

cutting! All the same, most greens can be cut to perfection with riding mowers, and the steps to do it perfectly follow.

1. Check the machine for oil and gas. Make sure the seat is adjusted and ascertain that all three cutting units are set at the same height and that they cut well. The cutting height and the sharpness of the unit are checked routinely by the mechanic or his assistant, but even the mechanic is not infallible and operators should be aware that mowers may lose their edge.

2. Inspect the green by walking and scanning the putting surface. Look for spikes, stones, and debris and fix ball marks in the process. Remove the flagstick and place it aside. Some fast operators believe that they can remove the stick as they cut the green by reaching out from the seat, but this is seldom a good idea, and quite often leads to accidents.

3. Select the direction of cut, making sure that it is different from that of the day before. Make the first cut across the hole and then work toward the front of the green, just in case golfers should catch up. With friendly golfers, you may even be able to finish the back of the green while they are putting. The direction of cut is changed every day to help reduce the buildup of grain. The grain on a green is the direction in which the grass leans, much like the nap on a living room rug. Change the cut every day, and ideally, grain will be eliminated or at least reduced.

4. Straight cutting lines are essential. For the first pass, pick a tree on the horizon and keep looking at that tree, not at the green, while mowing across the green. A straight line will result. For subsequent passes it is no longer necessary to look at the tree on the horizon. Instead, focus on the straight line that has been completed at the far end of the green.

5. The overlap: Novice cutters should overlap at least 6" or more. Experienced cutters may reduce the overlap to as little as 2". The markings on the baskets can be helpful in determining the degree of overlap. Missing a small strip of grass because of insufficient overlap is a cardinal sin against good greenkeeping. It results in golf balls jumping on the green and losing their direction.

6. The turn: It is important to make long, wide turns. Short, quick turns tear the turf on the apron. If a sand bunker or other obstruction is in the way of completing the turn, maneuver back and forth, or make the turn in the adjacent rough. Operators should be cautious when making turns on wet aprons. Mowers can slip and slide, and have been known to end up in the bunker or, worse, in an adjacent pond, much to the embarrassment of the superintendent.

7. Check the baskets for clippings while the green is being cut. Clippings tell a story: uneven distribution within the basket means the cutting unit is set improperly. Unbalanced quantities between the baskets may indicate differing heights of cut. If there is a problem, call the mechanic or the superintendent! If you think the green has been cut perfectly and the mowers are as sharp as Gillette, come back in the evening. With the setting sun over one's shoulder, every imperfection on the green is clearly visible and suddenly the perfect green does not look as perfect anymore.

8. Empty the baskets before they become too full. Baskets laden with wet grass affect the quality of cut. If policy dictates that clippings be spread, learn the sweeping, coordinated motion of the upper body, arms, and hips, that result in the perfect dispersal of the grass clippings. The clippings should be spread in the rough behind the green, never on the fairway in front nor in wildlife areas at the back!

9. The cleanup pass is an operation filled with danger. Cut into the adjacent apron and an ugly brown streak will result. Leave a few inches uncut, and the Super's wrath will be upon you. Instead, slow the machine down to a crawl and concentrate on the edge with all your faculties. The cleanup pass may be omitted from time to time to prevent the development of the dreaded "Triplex Ring" phenomenon.

10. Although many operators now use earplugs to protect their ears from excessive noise, it is important to listen to the sound of the mower, especially the sound of the reels touching the bed knives. Maladjusted reels can be detected simply by listening to the whir of the reels. When the green has been completely cut, replace the flagstick back into the hole liner. Take the whipping pole and brush off the clippings that may have fallen off the mower during cutting near the edge of the green and on the apron. Stand back for just a few seconds and admire your work!

**Figure 1.2. Operators must be carefully trained and become skilled at
handling mowers so that accidents will be avoid. Slippery
slopes near ponds are particularly hazardous.**

The Walker

The walk-behind greens mowers have been with us since the beginning of our
greenkeeping days, except that the initial models did not have an engine, and needed
to be pushed! To cut a green with such a push-type mower often took almost an
hour. The small gasoline engine changed all that. With the advent of the triplex
mower, it looked as if the walkers would soon become obsolete, but that has not
been the case. In fact, in recent years the walkers are once again gaining in popularity and are now widely used. Most courses have both walkers and riders in their
maintenance buildings.

1. Check the machine for oil and gas and that the cutting unit is for the
   correct height, and that the reel is adjusted to cut properly.

2. Inspect the green by walking and scanning the putting surface. Look for debris and fix ball marks. Remove the flagstick and put it aside.

3. Select the direction of cut, making sure that it is different from that of the day before. Inexperienced cutters should consider starting along the edge of the green, so a straight line will result. If by chance the line is curved, corrections can be made without any problem and not be noticed.

4. For walker units, it is even more essential that a straight line is created. "Snaky lines" result in a horrible looking, mixed-up checkerboard pattern, just the opposite of what is required: a perfect geometrical formation!

5. The overlap is equally critical when cutting the green with a walker. Too much overlap, and it takes forever to finish the green. Experienced operators will overlap as little as 1/2" and thus cut a green very quickly, but one little slip of the mower, or one brief moment of inattention, results in a strip of uncut grass.

6. The turn can be tricky when using a walker. Novice operators should disengage the traction clutch when turning. Experienced cutters can swing the mower around without damaging the grass and without losing their straight lines.

7. Check the basket for clippings. Clippings tell a story: uneven distribution within the basket means the cutting unit is set improperly.

8. Empty the basket before it becomes too full. A heavy basket affects the height and quality of cut. Learn the proper way to spread the clippings. Clippings can be spread behind the green but never on the fairway in front nor in the wildlife areas.

9. The cleanup pass is very important. Avoid cutting into the adjacent apron. It is best to slow the machine down for the cleanup pass. It is permitted to omit the cleanup pass from time to time in order to avoid the creation of wear patterns.

10. It is essential to use shoes with flat soles that leave no marks on the greens. Walk lightly, with your body weight on the toes and ball of your feet across the green and never lean on the handle of the mower. Rather, lift it up ever so slightly, so that the cutting unit retains contact with the green's surface at all times. Not doing so can result in a rippled or washboard appearance of the green surface.

A well-cut green is a sight to behold. The straight lines that make up the checkerboard are an earmark of perfection. Grass on a putting green can be so perfect that it looks almost artificial. "It can't be real," the uninitiated observer will think. "It must be magic." And it is, it is The Magic of Greenkeeping!

The Sequence of Cutting Greens

A woman golfer once related how she can tell, when she gets to the golf club in the morning, if the superintendent has the interests of the golfers on his mind. "If the putting green has been cut," our golfer said, "it shows that the superintendent cares

Figure 1.3. The cleanup pass requires diligent attention. Care must be taken not to cut into the collar.

about his golfers." We agree, and we strongly recommend that the putting green be among the first greens that are cut in the morning, certainly before the golfers start arriving at the golf shop.

Using riding greens mowers, it is relatively easy to stay ahead of the players. Mowers cut faster than most golfers can play. Superintendents should be aware that some golfers may play from the back nine and the needs of those golfers should be taken into account when the superintendent schedules cutting. When using walker-type greens mowers, three or more operators may be needed to cut all 18 greens as well as the putting and pitching greens ahead of the golfers. The cutting sequence is then determined based on the experience of the superintendent, and the sequence will vary from course to course.

When greens are mowed after play has begun, it is best to change the sequence in which they are cut. Many superintendents will start with the 18th green and work backward, in order to avoid bothering the same foursome more than once during the course of their game.

During the height of the golfing and growing season the greens are frequently cut on a daily basis, but prudent greenkeepers know the beneficial effects of skipping a cut on occasion! This can be compared to not shaving one's face for a day after routinely doing so every morning. The skin on one's jowls immediately improves after a day of rest. It feels softer and healthier. So it is with a green that has been given a rest from daily mowing.

Figure 1.4. Repetitive cutting of the cleanup pass often results in tire track damage. The resulting damage is referred to as the Triplex Ring Syndrome.

Although it is good for the health of all greens not to be cut for a day, there are some weak greens on almost every golf course that need special attention. Such greens may need to be cut with a walker, when all other greens are cut with riders, or perhaps the height of cut of these "weak greens" can be raised ever so slightly in order to enhance their chance of survival. Greens that are stressed-out do not respond well to a cutting. Superintendents should be aware that more grass is killed by machines than by all diseases put together!

Which days should superintendents select not to cut their greens? Usually a day is picked that is least busy on the course. It may also be a rainy morning, or a cloudy day with no dew on the grass. Other factors also enter into the decision. Intelligent superintendents who wish to survive the pitfalls of club politics should be aware of the playing schedules of their owners and club officials. That is only common sense, but forgetting this obvious fact of life can quickly shorten the career span of a dedicated but foolhardy professional.

DEW REMOVAL

On mornings when greens are not to be cut and there is dew on the turf, it should be removed for the benefit of the golfers as well as for the health of the grass. Wet turf provides an ideal breeding ground for fungus disease, and drying the grass early in the morning either by means of dew whipping or simply by cutting the green is an essential part of disease prevention. Many superintendents still whip their greens prior to cutting, and some still use the bamboo poles imported from China in bundles of 50. These dedicated grass growers ought to be commended! We know from experience that disease budgets on courses that religiously practice dew removal are less than for those that never remove dew.

THE TRIPLEX RING SYNDROME

When riding greens mowers cut the same swath day after day along the outer edge of the green, the tires of the mower are on the same track each time. If, in addition, the green is small or has been designed with many exotic curves, the weight of the mower and the wrenching action of the tight turn quickly kill the grass. Ugly dead or brown concentric rings, the dreaded Triplex Ring, will result. This is not some mysterious disease related to fairy ring, but pure and simple mechanical damage caused by the misuse of a mower.

TRS Prevention

What can be done to avoid the buildup or the appearance of the Triplex Ring? Most simply, superintendents, at the first sign of concentric damage, switch back to walk-behind greens mowers. This is not always possible, nor is it completely necessary. Many superintendents have successfully eliminated the Triplex Ring by the simple expedient of skipping the cleanup pass every other day. Even for one day on a weekend, the cleanup pass can be conveniently forgotten. It is amazing how quickly the stressed-out grass responds to, and recovers from, a rest from a regimen of daily shearing. It should also be noted that removing the Wiele rollers and the groomers from greens mowers will help eliminate Triplex Ring damage.

Golfers generally don't notice that the grass has not been cut for the first three to four feet near the edge of the green and if they do, they probably won't mind! Golf balls that are putted from this area are rarely deflected in the initial stages, when they are at their greatest velocity on their way to the hole.

It is possible that the green along the outer edge may look shabby from not having been cut. This is especially true during times of heavy dew on the grass. Carrying a whipping pole and brushing the greens along the outside perimeter will solve this shortcoming. Another method involves simply disengaging reels prior to turning, but not lifting the cutting units! This helps to stop the clippings from falling off the rollers and leaving a mess along the outside of the green.

Figure 1.5. Whipping the green to remove dew prior to mowing results in a better cut and is a beneficial means of preventing turfgrass diseases.

It is also a good practice to move the cleanup pass in from the edge of the green from time to time. This can be done to the extent of one or two feet. The method results in the tracks of the wheels being straddled and thus helps prevent the buildup of the Triplex Ring.

Other Methods of Preventing Triplex Ring Buildup

Longtime golf course superintendent Dudley Smith at the Silver Lake Club, a public facility near Chicago, uses riders and walkers on alternate days. On the days when the riders are used, no cleanup pass is done at all! Other superintendents use walkers for the cleanup pass consistently. In such cases, a single cleanup pass just won't do, and two or three passes may be necessary.

Architects wanting to break the monotony of round and oval greens continue to design fancy-shaped greens with many tight turns, much to the chagrin of the superintendent. The Supers, however, have a friend in Brent Wadsworth, owner of Wadsworth Construction, a company that has built more than 500 golf courses in North America and beyond. Wadsworth refuses to make curves on greens that have a radius of less than 30 feet, no matter what the drawings call for. That makes the birth of a Triplex Ring virtually impossible.

Repairing Damage Due to Triplex Ring Syndrome

In the initial stages, when the Triplex Ring is just starting to show, it is relatively easy to stop the damage from becoming serious. Simply using a walker on such greens will do the trick. Once the grass has become seriously injured, more drastic measures are needed. Aerating with minitines and overseeding (a process that will be described in detail in another chapter) are probably sufficient to promote the recovery of the turf. In really serious cases, the affected part may actually have to be resodded! In either case, sodding or seeding, the portion of the green that is being treated should be roped off and put out of play until recovery is complete.

HYDRAULIC SPILLS

A most unpleasant side effect of the riding triplex greens mower is the occasional hydraulic hose burst. This usually happens when least expected and often goes unnoticed by the operator until it is too late. The results can be disastrous! A careless operator may not notice a hydraulic leak until the machine actually stops functioning. A perfect pattern of brown lines may result on several successive greens. Most often the burn of the grass is limited to a single strip across a green and a turn on the apron.

There have been many miracle cures advocated by fast-talking salesmen to save the grass from hydraulic burns: activated charcoal, liquid soap, kitty litter, and strips of felt tissue, to name but a few. None of them work! They make the superintendent or the greenkeepers feel better for a little while, because at least they are doing something, but none of these magic cures can bring dead grass back to life. The hydraulic oil from the mower that is squirted onto the green because of a loose-fitting or a broken hose is very hot! It is so hot, in fact, that the grass immediately singes and dies upon contact with the oil. It may still look green, and a bit shiny at that, but as sure as God made little green apples, it will be brown in just a few days. Just the same, the damage can be mitigated if the area is washed off with a powerful spray of water during the initial stages. Adding a wetting agent at this point may also help, as long as it is also washed off.

Prevention

What can be done to prevent or at least minimize the occurrence of hydraulic burns on grass? It all starts at the Turf Care Center, the maintenance headquarters, and it starts with a good, well-qualified mechanic, the unsung hero in the golf course maintenance industry. A conscientious mechanic will regularly check and repair the hydraulic hoses on all machinery, but especially on the mowers. If a particular hose is worn or breaks, he will order not one, but two, to replace it. That way, a stock of spare hoses is built up in the parts room.

The mechanic and the assistant usually work together and put all machinery out from the storage area in the morning, starting the engines and warming up the machines before taking them out onto the course. In addition, trained operators look for telltale danger signs before taking mowers out. A small drip can be an indicator of a loose fitting. Fixing it, then and there, will prevent a disaster on the greens later.

Mixing a dye into the hydraulic oil makes it somewhat easier to see a leak, and this will help prevent running the hydraulic tank completely dry. Some superintendents and mechanics have installed elaborate alarm systems that will detect a drop in hydraulic pressure immediately, and alarm the operator. Such systems are very expensive but can be justified in terms of damage to a precious green, tee, or fairway that might be prevented.

As long as there are cars on our highways, there will be smashups. So it is on golf courses. As long as we use mowers equipped with numerous hydraulic lines, there will be mishaps and damaged turf. It is inevitable. Therefore, prudence dictates that we be prepared for the worst and be able to restore the damaged grass.

Repairing Burnt Grass Caused by Hydraulic Spills

Quick action and clear thinking are necessary to cope with unexpected hydraulic spills. Several key members on the greens staff should be familiar with one or all of the following steps.

1. Remove the excess oil by spreading Turface® or kitty litter over the affected area. This will soak up much of the oil and prevent the burn from becoming a much wider strip than it needs to be. Applying a solution containing a wetting agent will further dilute the remaining oil.
2. Use a narrow aerator with tines closely spaced, about 1" apart, and make a double pass. Hand-forking is an alternative method. Apply seed, making sure that some of it ends up in the tiny aerator holes. The seed that falls on the surface is mostly wasted, but the seed in the aerator holes has found a growth chamber! Below the surface, in a moist and warm environment it will quickly germinate and sprout up. The small tufts of grass, firmly rooted below the surface, will withstand golfer and mower traffic and rapidly join together to make an acceptable turf. In two to four weeks' time the ugly scar will disappear.
3. If you absolutely must, take a sod cutter and remove the affected area and replace it with new sod. This is a drastic measure that will affect the putting surface much longer than seeding. If there is no sod nursery from which to take the sod, consider taking the sod from the putting green, along the edge or from the back of a regular green. Make sure that the sod is cut thicker than normal, so that the sod won't shift under golfers' feet or the greens mower. After sodding, the strip must be topdressed and rubbed with the back of an aluminum rake or, better yet, with a Levelawn. This makes for a perfectly smooth surface that will quickly grow in and become part of the regular green. Instead of using a mechanized sod cutter, hand-pushed, narrow-bladed sod cutters are available and are ideally suited for this type of repair.

   The problem with sodding is that the sod needs regular watering until it becomes firmly rooted. That means someone has to be around, even on

Figure 1.6a. Repairing a hydraulic oil spill: Step 1: Remove the burned sod.

weekends and perhaps during late afternoons and evenings. If the sod were to die, it would be one mistake compounding another, and a crisis difficult to survive, especially for novice superintendents.

4. Repairing turf on damaged tees and fairways is slightly less cumbersome because these surfaces are not as critical as the green. In many cases, when the scar is narrow, the adjacent turf will grow in quickly. It may still be necessary to either seed or sod or even use a divot mix to help promote growth. In any case, it is always better to repair the damage than to let the visual effects of the dead turf linger. Golfers will lose their patience with superintendents who are indecisive and who procastinate.

CLIPPINGS

We have already discussed the importance of constantly checking the grass clippings in the basket of the mower when cutting greens. Important information can be

Figure 1.6b. Repairing a hydraulic oil spill: Step 2: Replace with sod from the back of the green, so it will blend into the green. Then use sod from the nursery to replace the sod taken from the back of green.

gleaned from uneven distribution inside the basket. The mower may be dull or out of adjustment, but there is more to be learned from the clippings!

Grass clippings have an odor all their own. It is very pungent and distinctive when the green is healthy, but when the green is sick, the clippings don't smell nearly as good. Early warnings of a pending fungus disease outbreak can often be detected by simply sticking one's nose into a handful of clippings. A foul-smelling odor is a sure giveaway that brown patch disease is trying to gain a foothold. Old-time greenkeepers knew of this secret long ago and could often be seen on all fours, sniffing a green and trying to learn about pending problems. In the baskets, among the clippings, look for adult insects of the hyperodes weevil or the aetanius bug. Keeping track of the number of bugs found in the clippings may help to determine the need for spraying an insecticide.

Clippings can also reveal the succulence of the turf. Over-fertilized greens produce an abundance of fat, juicy snippets of grass. Lean greens make for wiry, thin, stringy leaf blades. If there are fertilizer granules mixed in with the clippings, it probably means that the green should have been cut with the baskets off. It is always a good idea to cut without baskets after fertilizing with granular materials. Even the small-particle, homogenous fertilizers get caught in the reels and end up in the baskets, and that is definitely not the idea! It makes no sense to pick up the expensive nutrients from the greens and spread them in the roughs. Better to remove the baskets, and water in the fertilizer.

It is a common practice to empty the baskets after cutting a green. If the baskets need emptying before the green is finished, it probably means that the green is over-fertilized. If, on the other hand, the baskets still need not be emptied after four or five greens, it indicates that the turf is lean and thin and possibly did not need cutting at all. A light rolling with the high-speed greens roller might have been a better method of creating a perfect putting surface.

The greens rollers were first used on lawn bowling greens in Australia. The original models were six feet across, much too wide to cope with undulations of putting greens but ideal for flat bowling greens. Their purpose was to speed up the green without cutting it. Lawn bowling greens are frequently maintained at the very edge of survival in order to be hard and fast. Cutting greens under such stressed-out conditions would almost certainly mean instant death to the grass. A light rolling achieves the desired result without removing any of the grass growth.

Australian golf course superintendents, who often manage bowling greens as well, adopted the speed roller for putting greens, by the simple expedient of making it narrower. These rollers quickly became a hit in North America and are now widely accepted all over the world.

THE FIRST CUT OF THE SPRING

Northern superintendents look forward to the first cut of the spring. It is the harbinger of a new season full of hope and expectation, and many Supers insist on making the first cut themselves. The thrill of trying new mowers, combined with the fragrance of the freshly cut grass, bring memories of past seasons and lost youth. At the same time there is a wonderful opportunity to outline the greens.

During the previous season, greens may have lost their shape because cautious operators made the greens smaller with each successive cutting. In the process, curves and shapes were lost. Spring is the time to cut into the apron and reoutline the green to its original configuration. Small adjustments can be made without getting off the mower, but if the green will be substantially enlarged, it is best to outline the change with a paint gun. It may be necessary to mark the new outline several times before it becomes established.

Cutting the apron to greens height is a drastic measure that should only be performed during the spring when the grass plant has an inner drive to recreate and is able to recover from the severe scalping. At any other time of year such treatment will result in instant death of the grass plant, but in the spring the grass will manage to survive.

Many superintendents like to cut greens themselves from time to time during the season, even at large operations where there is plenty of staff. Peter Voykin at the 36-hole Twin Orchard Club near Chicago loves to cut a green or two. Not only for exercise, according to Voykin, but also to get a feel for the course. It is part of the mystique of being a golf course superintendent and having a love affair with one's golf course. Such a relationship needs constant nurturing on the part of the superintendent, and cutting greens from time to time is an important ingredient of that process.

Figure 1.7. Greens rollers make putting greens smoother and faster.

FAST GREENS

Television golf and the stimpmeter have combined to put pressure on superintendents to provide faster greens; greens so fast, according to some witty tour players, that a dime left as ball marker would slide off the green. An exaggeration, of course, but with an element of truth. Greens have been cut to the quick, rolled, and left to dry, all in a quest for speed. It is a miracle that the poor grass plant manages to survive, and frequently it does not.

The stimpmeter is a device to measure the speed of greens in feet and inches. A ball is rolled from a slotted steel bar at a predetermined height, and its progress is measured on the green. The direction is reversed and repeated two to four times. Several measurements are averaged and a value for a particular green is arrived at.

It is not uncommon for greens to reach speeds in excess of 11 ft and even 12 ft at times. The stage is set every spring at the time of the Augusta National, where lightning-fast greens are commonplace. Golfers all across the world watch, and demand that their superintendent emulate not only the conditions, but especially the speed of the greens. Those weak-willed souls who give in to their golfers and cut their greens to the root hairs, usually lose their grass and their jobs at the same time.

It is a fact that no grass, be it bermuda, bent, or *Poa annua* will survive being cut at 1/8th of an inch for any length of time! Yet rookie superintendents will keep on trying at their own peril. They will accommodate the club champion and the captain but completely forget about the needs of the grass. In the horribly hot and dry summer of 1995 when grass across the continent was dying by the acre on the golf courses, many greens could have been saved if they had just been cut a little higher.

Figure 1.8. Superintendents use the stimpmeter to check the speed of greens and to ensure that all greens are consistent.

No factor affects the speed of a green as much as the height of cut on the mower. Superintendents should select mower settings that will ensure the survival of the grass and produce a greens speed that is acceptable to the majority of the golfers.

For special events, such as club competitions and tournaments, the greens speed can be increased a trifle by the simple expedient of double cutting. This is an old trick that smart superintendents have known about for ages. The double cut results in a smoother and faster putting surface. It is not necessary to double cut the entire green, just three or four cuts on either side of the cup will do nicely. Remember, the ball is most likely to deviate from its true path as it slows near the cup. All the more reason that the turf should be perfect near the hole, so that more putts will drop and golfers will applaud the hardworking superintendent.

Recently a new machine was introduced to the golf course industry that helps speed up the greens without cutting the grass. The greens roller was first used on bowling greens in Australia and later adapted for more undulating golf greens. These fast-moving machines can roll a green in a jiffy, and appreciably increase the stimpmeter readings by as much as six to eight inches. After a rolling, the grass blades are still there, to breathe, and keep the plant alive. The greens roller is a useful tool and can be used occasionally instead of cutting.

SLOW GREENS

Amazingly, there are some golf clubs that don't want any part of fast greens! Such courses take pride in having slow greens. The question is, how slow is slow? Using the United States Golf Association scale, greens that stimp between 5 and 6 ft must be considered slow. In terms of height of cut this translates to one-fourth of an inch or six millimeters.

The problem with slow greens is that they tend to develop thatch and grain. Superintendents who cut their greens at the quarter-inch height should be vigilant about the potential formation of a heavy layer of mat or thatch. On such greens, the groomer attachments on the mowers must be used on a regular basis. Topdressing frequently becomes important as well, to prevent the buildup of thatch.

TEMPORARY GREENS

There are times when the regular green cannot or should not be played upon. On such occasions, the ingenuity of the superintendent is called on to create a temporary green. If the temporary green is to be in use for only a few hours or perhaps even a day, it is simply a matter of moving the pin of the regular green and cutting a hole in the fairway. A sign, explaining the reason for the temporary green is advisable, and it is best to place the sign on the tee of the hole that is under repair.

Golfers will accept a temporary green much more readily if they know the reason. Another little trick that will put a smile on a golfer's face is to use a larger-than-normal cup on a temporary green. Use an 8"-hole auger for the initial cut and then place the regular hole inside it. Even a square hole which can be made with the help of an Australian Turf Doctor, a handy turf repair tool invented by an Aussie greenkeeper, can be used to give an unusual twist to a temporary green.

When a temporary green is planned to be in use for an extended period, more care should be taken in its preparation because golfers deserve a decent putting surface at all times. Prepare the temporary green at least two months in advance of its intended use. Select a level portion of the fairway and mark out the green with a paint gun. It is very important that even this temporary green be of sufficient size, at least 3000 sq ft. Double cut the temporary green about one-eighth of an inch lower than the existing fairway. Now, verticut the new putting surface in two different directions. Fertilize moderately with a starter fertilizer, and topdress heavily. For such a relatively small green it is best to work the topdressing in with the backside of an aluminum rake or, better still, with a Levelawn, another marvelous Australian invention. If there are old divot marks in the green, these should be repaired with a hole cutter or similar tool. In northern climates the temporary green should also be seeded. In southern regions the bermuda turf will automatically adjust to the new cutting height.

At this time, it is important that the green be soaked thoroughly. This can best be done with a roller-base sprinkler connected to a fairway outlet. Finally, it is necessary that the temporary green be fenced off with stakes and ropes and be declared as "Ground Under Repair" or GUR for short. It is best to place a sign on the green explaining to the golfers what you are trying to do. The golfers will gladly take a free lift as long as they know its purpose.

Over the next 6–8 weeks institute a regular cutting regimen, lowering the height of cut by 1/16th of an inch every week until the normal cutting height is reached. In the meantime, topdress and verticut at least two more times and also consider aerating at least once prior to opening up the green for the golfers. Temporary greens

Figure 1.9. An alternate or temporary green can be used to save the regular green and give it a chance to recover.

have to be treated with tender loving care by the superintendent and greens staff. They should be inspected frequently to ensure their health and condition. If the reason for a temporary green is the rebuilding of an existing green, then it is all the more important that the temporary green is a near perfect putting surface. There will be less pressure on the superintendent to open the new green prematurely if birdie putts are frequent on the temporary green.

ALTERNATE GREENS

In addition to regular greens and temporary greens, there are alternate greens. Golf courses in moderate climates frequently use alternate greens for play in the off-season or when work is being done to the regular greens.

On occasion, an architect will specify an alternate green on a particular golf hole, to give the golfers an option. The 12th hole at the Fazio-designed Worldwoods Pine Barrens course near Brooksville, Florida, has two greens. In fact, it also has two fairways. There is no end to which imaginative architects will go to create golf holes that are different and unique, and in the process often adding to the burden of the superintendents who have to maintain such dream holes.

DOUBLE GREENS

Ever since St. Andrews was established along the shores of the North Sea, double greens have been part of golf. In recent years North American architects have specified double greens on our continent. Such greens can be of immense size, as much as an acre, and they take forever to cut, especially with walker mowers. Just the same, double greens are spectacular to look at and to play to, although much of that grass is frequently never used. The perceived saving in maintenance is frequently not realized.

SAND GREENS

There are places in this world where it is just too darn difficult or too expensive to grow grass greens. Arid areas and extreme locations fall among them. We have found that in the prairie states and provinces of the U.S. and Canada, sand greens were until recently quite common. We also discovered sand greens on the Royal Kathmandu Golf Course in Nepal, although these have since been converted to grass. In order to create a firm surface on sand greens, old engine oil is added and a local rule permits players to smooth the putting line to the hole by dragging a small mat over the intended line of play.

GREENS FOR HOMEOWNERS

Every superintendent is asked from time to time to build a putting green in someone's backyard. The temptation to accept the assignment is often irresistible. Ardent and enthusiastic golfers have a way of making otherwise stable-minded superintendents lose their heads. We have built several backyard greens during our long greenkeeping careers and every single one has been converted to flower beds, a swimming pool, or has just become part of the lawn, characterized by an overabundance of *Poa annua*. During their brief existence, such greens are the pride of their owner, but rarely do such greens last beyond a few years.

THE EXPENSE OF BUILDING A BACKYARD PUTTING GREEN

1. When homeowners dream of a putting green for their backyard, they think in terms of one of similar size to their living room or the master bedroom, and that is just too small. Minimum size for a backyard green is 1,500 sq ft. Twice that size would be better. Invariably the existing soil needs to be modified, which means importing several truckloads of sand and topsoil.
2. An automatic irrigation system is a must! Hopefully, the existing sprinklers can be modified, but undoubtedly several new irrigation heads, pipe, and a new controller may be needed.
3. Although it is initially less expensive to seed the new green rather than sodding, both operations require expertise and much can go wrong before a desired result is achieved.
4. Maintenance involves buying either a new or used mower and cutting the green 4–5 times a week. Perhaps it is best to use a push-type mower for a small backyard green. Using such a mower would provide an opportunity for

Figure 1.10. In arid climates, sand greens are an alternative to grass greens. The sand is made firm by adding oil.

regular exercise and eliminate the need for joining a health club. Maintenance also includes fertilizing, spraying pesticides, and topdressing the green on a regular basis. Spraying for disease should be postponed as long as possible. Once the green has been treated with a pesticide it quickly becomes dependent on regular chemical sprays.

5. Obtaining a cup and a flagstick are probably the easiest part of the assignment. Making sure that the maintenance work gets done on a regular basis is the toughest part of the equation.

Homeowners should analyze their reasons for wanting a backyard putting green. Is it to improve their putting and chipping skills, or is it because they want to live on a golf course? Most golf course superintendents discourage golfers from building backyard putting greens. But if the golfer has completely lost his senses and insists on proceeding, then as a last resort we advise our colleagues to charge double the normal rate for all the work. Hopefully, this will bring the irrational golfer back to his senses. If this does not occur, the client deserves to pay through the nose as a penalty for foolishness. Knowing beforehand that the backyard green will probably not last very long should make homeowners realize that it is best to build such greens modestly.

Recently, the manufacturers of artificial turf have improved the quality of their materials. There now are available ready-made contoured greens that are completely made from artificial materials. Such greens are used as target greens on driving ranges and are ideally suited for backyard use. Like artificial Christmas trees, they look just like the real thing and are much less expensive to boot.

BALL AND SPIKE MARKS

Perhaps the greatest detriments to a smooth putting surface are ball marks and spike marks. Ball marks, also often referred to as pitch marks, quickly become an ugly scar on the face of a perfect green. They are caused by negligent and forgetful golfers, and it is the responsibility of the superintendent to make sure they are repaired. On a daily basis, that task falls to the greens cutter and/or the hole changer. Some superintendents assign special staff to fix ball marks with seed and divot mix. Others find that periodic topdressing alleviates the problem. Spike marks are caused by metal spikes, scuffing, or just penetrating the turf mat and leaving blades of grass standing up above the surface. Spike marks, just like ball marks, deflect golf balls and slow the roll of the ball. Recently many golf courses have mandated that metal spikes no longer be permitted on their courses. Superintendents generally have applauded this move. Stressed-out greens during the heat of the summer seem to benefit from the much gentler soft or plastic spikes.

SUMMARY

We must assume that the great majority of golfers will want to continue putting on grass greens and that these greens must be smooth and reasonably fast. A superintendent's greatest accomplishment will be to provide such greens. In the process, the superintendent walks a fine line between ultimate success and abject failure in balancing the needs of the grass with those of the golfers.

Cutting Tees

Golfers receive their first impression of a course on the tee, usually the first tee, unless they are playing in a shotgun tournament or are starting on the back nine. Although all tees are important, none is more important than the first tee. We want our golfers to feel comfortable on the first tee. Everything possible should be done to allay fear and anxiety, so that the golfer will be relaxed and able to execute a near perfect drive from the first tee. Such a marvelous beginning sets the tone for the rest of the game.

Golf course superintendents contribute much to a golfer's happiness, or at times to their despair. What do golfers expect from the superintendent on the tees, particularly on the first tee, that will put them in a positive frame of mind?

1. The surface of the tee must be perfectly flat! The tee may tilt slightly forward, backward, or sideways, depending on the architect's specifications, but the tee itself must be flat and even. No bumps or hollows are permitted; no sudden grade changes allowed. The reason is obvious: the golfer needs a level stance to make a perfect shot.

    On elevated tees, the surface may tilt slightly forward, so that golfers can see more of the fairway when the blocks are at the back of the tee. On fairways that slope uphill, the tee should also have a built-in incline. The advice of an architect or a golf course builder should be sought before determining the incline of the teeing surface, but regardless, the tee itself should always be flat and remain that way.

2. The first tee must provide some degree of privacy. Most golfers are apprehensive about driving from the first tee. To have to hit one's drive in front of a critical gallery can be nerve-wracking. Without creating shady conditions that are detrimental to the growth of healthy grass, superintendents should work with architects to provide some privacy. Once away from the clubhouse, tees should be as open as possible and trees and shrubs should be kept away from the tees.

Figure 2.1. Cutting tees requires a keen eye to make straight lines that line up to the center of the fairway.

3. Tees should not be cramped, but spacious and sufficiently large enough to accommodate 200–300 golfers a day. Hopefully, some of that number will use the forward or ladies tees, and perhaps an equal number will play from the championship tees. The main tee, from which the majority of players will hit their drives, should be at least the same size as the corresponding green. On par 3 holes, the tee should be twice the size of the green. A rule of thumb dictates that 100 sq ft of teeing area is needed for every 1,000 rounds of golf on par 4 and par 5 holes. On par 3 holes, that area should be doubled for every 1,000 rounds. Others believe that the tees should be the same size as the green on par 4 and par 5 holes, and double the size of the green on par 3 holes. Whatever rule is applied, tees are rarely too big.

   The tee on the first hole should be larger than normal. Many golfers come to the first tee and need to warm up. Frequently they do so by hacking away at the turf on the first tee. Provide plenty of space, and the tee can be repaired on a regular basis and recover quickly.

4. The slopes surrounding the tees should be gentle, so that golfers can ascend to the deck without having to climb a steep grade and be out of breath when they must drive the ball. Although steps and stairs are objectionable around tees for a variety of reasons (expensive to maintain and aesthetically unappealing), in some cases the location of a particular tee makes it necessary that a means be found for a golfer to get up to the tee. It is then up to the superintendent to concoct something that is functional and not too ugly.

5. A tee should be firm, for better footing, but not so hard as to make it impossible to get a wooden tee into the ground. The tee should also be free of ugly divot scars, especially the first tee, for that all-important first impression. The grass on tees is usually cut somewhat longer than on greens, but it should be sufficiently short to ensure that there is never any grass between the clubhead and the ball at the time of address.

CUTTING TEES

Because most tees are elevated, they are inherently difficult to cut. Steep slopes make it hard for operators to keep control of their mowers as they make tight turns. Just the same, it is important to cut a tee perfectly; otherwise, its appearance will be destroyed by a shoddy job of mowing. Before beginning to cut, walk over the tee and be on the lookout for spikes that may have come loose from a golfer's shoes. Metal spikes will cause expensive damage to the reels and bedplates of the mowers. Also look for broken wooden tees and debris such as branches and twigs. Everything must be picked up and discarded before cutting the tee.

It is important to change the direction of cut on the tee just as on the green, in order to prevent the buildup of thatch and grain. Usually, on the day before the weekend, the tees are cut lengthwise. The striping that points to the center of the fairway assists the golfer subconsciously to drive the ball in that beneficial direction.

Many superintendents use riding greens mowers on the tees but on smaller tees, walk-behind mowers are preferred. Since tees are usually not cut on a daily basis, the Triplex Ring is not a serious problem. When it does develop, omitting the cleanup pass will quickly remedy the problem.

Tees are normally cut every second day, or three times per week at a minimum. It is a mistake to not cut tees over a long weekend. On the third day of the long weekend the grass on the tee will look quite shabby and by the time the tee is cut on the morning of the fourth day, the grass is much too long and will suffer from the shock of having so much of its growth removed. Tees that are growing actively and are not cut on a timely basis become spongy, an objectionable condition from a golfer's point of view.

We have already mentioned the slopes that make cutting tees a difficult operation. There are other obstacles on and around tees, such as benches, ball washers, garbage cans, and divot boxes that must be circumnavigated while cutting tees. Then there are tee blocks that have to be put aside while the tee is being cut, and returned precisely to their former places. For all those reasons, cutting tees requires not only great dexterity but also much savvy and experience. Cutting tees is a job for veteran golf course workers, and for rookies only as a last resort.

Ever since the U.S. Open was played at Pebble Beach in 1992 on rectangularly cut tees, golfers have been demanding that superintendents follow suit and cut the tees with right angles, so that they can be lined up perfectly with the fairways. This is not possible with banana-shaped tees or free-form tees that are shaped like an hourglass. To cut a tee rectangularly is very difficult and it can be done only with mowers that are equipped with On and Off devices for individual reels. Cutting tees in such a manner is a luxury that not every club can afford.

**Figure 2.2. Since Pebble Beach hosted the U.S. Open, rectangular tees
have come into vogue. The advantage is that tees always
line up to the center of the landing area.**

Golf courses with modest budgets may decide that cutting tees with greens mowers is too expensive for their liking, and choose less sophisticated mowers. Some will use utility reel type mowers or even rotary mowers to cut their tees. In either case the height of cut will be higher and golfers on such courses will need to use the longer wooden tees.

Many otherwise near perfect tees are spoiled because the surrounds have not been trimmed adequately. Long grass at the front of the tee may impede a low ball as it is driven from the tee. At the back of the tee, long grass may make it impossible for the club to be taken back at the time of address. Superintendents should be vigilant about such adverse conditions and make sure that the surrounds of tees are trimmed regularly, especially on tees in out-of-the-way places. The latter tend to be forgotten because they are not inspected with regularity.

When all is said and done, golfers of all calibers will agree on one thing only, and that is that tees need to be perfectly flat in order to execute a perfect shot. Golfers will accept divot-scarred tees, worn tees, hard tees, or soft tees but never tees with too many undulations. Superintendents must do everything in their power and employ all their skills as greenkeepers to make sure that tees are kept flat and firm and have an adequate cover of grass at all times.

Tees are rarely constructed with the same degree of diligence that is devoted to the creation of greens. Tees seldom have a network of tile or a bed of gravel in their base and as a result, the drainage on most tees is not nearly as good as it is on greens. In addition, the soil mix used for greens tends to be selected after much study, whereas for tees it is frequently just a matter of pushing the topsoil back on the finish grade. Tees therefore will lose their shape and their grade.

WHAT SUPERINTENDENTS CAN DO TO IMPROVE THEIR TEES

1. Improve the drainage. Not all tees are equal! Some drain well and others dry up very slowly. The latter must be tiled. This is routine maintenance and superintendents should not use the club's committee structure as a reason for inaction. When it has been determined that tiling a particular tee is necessary, prepare the plans and execute them during the shoulder or the off-season. In northern climates, improving the drainage will also reduce the deleterious effects of soil heaving as a result of deep ground freezing.

2. Regrade the tops of the tees so that they are perfectly level. It is best to remove all the sod before starting the grading operation. Chunks of sod will hamper the grading work. Use one of several new graders that are now employed by golf course construction companies. Some of these are laser operated and their use will guarantee a perfectly flat surface. It is vitally important to maintain the edge between the flat level top and the side slopes. If the edge is lost during excessive grading, the tee top will be rounded, a result that is most undesirable.

3. Once a perfectly flat top has been established, it is necessary to keep it that way! Applying topdressing improperly will distort the flat surface. We have also seen tee surfaces that have been ruined by the improper application of divot mixes. How is this possible? Applying divot mix by the shovelful and working it in haphazardly! Greenkeeping tools such as a drag mats, the backs of aluminum rakes and Levelawns should be used at all times on the surface and only carefully near the edge. Brushes will adequately work soil mixes into the grass mat but often leave waves and undulations, results that should be avoided on perfectly level tees.

4. The location of sprinkler heads can be a nuisance on tees. All sprinklers need repair and maintenance from time to time and this may involve digging a deep hole in the middle of a tee. God forbid it should happen during an important event! Therefore, if at all possible, sprinklers should be located off to the side of the tees. On large, wide tees this may not be possible, nor is it nearly as critical.

FORWARD TEES

Playing mixed golf makes one realize very soon that female golfers who use the forward tees are often getting a bum rap. Superintendents must take part of the blame! They have been as guilty as architects in constructing overly small, poorly directed tees. Such tees are frequently an eyesore on the horizon and they stick out like sore thumbs on the landscape. Because they are often an afterthought in the scheme of things, they are inadequately built and cannot be maintained properly.

Superintendents owe it to their profession and to all women golfers to provide adequate tee-off space of the same quality as is provided for the men.

1. Site selection is best left to the resident architect, who should be encouraged to make the ladies tees part of the overall master plan. Naturally, the superintendent may have some input on the decision since he is familiar with the property, the drainage, and irrigation lines.
2. Construction can be done either in-house or by a reputable golf course contractor. Brent Wadsworth maintains that no tee should be smaller than 20 by 40 ft. Anything smaller makes it difficult for the mowers to cut the tee and for sprayers and aerators to get around. The importance of good drainage and high quality topsoil has already been stated.
3. The tendency to built hedges or shrubs on the sides of the tees should be resisted. Inevitably, such growth reduces the amount of usable space on the tees. Similarly, stairs leading to the teeing deck, by their very nature, restrict traffic and cause ugly wear patterns. No amount of expert greenkeeping can avoid the development of bare areas near the top of the stairs. Besides, the stairs themselves are maintenance-intensive and are often neglected, thus detracting from the overall appearance of the golf course.

CONCLUSIONS

When superintendents understand the importance of the need for perfectly flat tees, and assume the responsibility for creating and maintaining such tees, they will also make some of these recommended procedures part of the maintenance regimen. Often superintendents are at the mercy of the architect who has created the course. Just the same, during the career span of an ambitious superintendent there are many opportunities to improve the architect's shortfalls or highlight the brilliant features of the design. Foremost among these should be work on the tees. A golf course with many tees that provide panoramic views from flat firm surfaces will always be a favorite with the golfers.

3 Fairways

Nowhere has the improvement in turf quality and playability been more pronounced than on the fairways. Just a few decades ago, fairways were cut with tractor-drawn gang mowers, much the same mowers that had once been pulled with leather-shod horses prior to World War II. Nothing changed for the longest time, until the '50s and '60s, when large tractors equipped with multiple hydraulic cutting units made their appearance. These behemoths struggled with our fairways, twisting and turning and many times tearing the tender turf in the process. Although these cumbersome mowers cut a wide swath in short order, their excessive weight caused serious compaction, and subsequent turf damage.

Golf itself was undergoing a change of sorts. No longer a game of wide open spaces, target areas were defined by well-placed bunkers, trees, and water hazards. Fairways became contoured and smaller in total area. Superintendents needed lightweight mowers, and some experimented with the riding greens mowers. At first these handy units were tried on aprons or collars as well as on tees. The riders were ideally suited for this new application. They proved to be fast, relatively maintenance-free, and above all, user-friendly! The next step was to extend the aprons on the par 3 holes. The results were spectacular: the closely cut grass with the clippings removed looked awesome and was a delight to play from. Golfers loved it!

It was not surprising then, that enterprising superintendents began cutting entire fairways with greens mowers. The gentle machines cut the grass beautifully and produced a playing surface of outstanding quality. Perhaps the intent was to remedy a difficult mowing problem on a single fairway, but quickly it became apparent that all fairways would benefit from the new practice. Outstanding displays of striping were created in the process—at times so breathtaking that country club golfers applauded the work of their superintendents and raved about the new fairways to their friends and relations. At first, the professionals on the Tour were reluctant to accept the newfangled cutting patterns, and for a while, the Tour prescribed "plain" fairways, without stripes. Eventually Tour officials relented, and with some prodding from television producers, superintendents were given a free hand to use their imaginations.

**Figure 3.1. Contouring fairways emphasizes the landing area
and the hazards, as at the Devil's Pulpit Golf Course
in Ontario, Canada.**

There was an unexpected and beneficial side effect of cutting fairways with riding triplex greens mowers and removing the clippings. Northern superintendents who had been struggling with *Poa annua* infestation in their bent grass turf noticed that the bent grass thrived, once the switch was made to lightweight mowers. After only a single season of regular cutting with the riding greens mowers, bent grass could be seen spreading and outgrowing the *Poa annua*. This was most remarkable, and a huge bonus for superintendents who wanted to promote bent grass at the expense of *Poa annua* without resorting to costly and unpredictable herbicides.

Little scientific research has been done at our colleges and universities to explain this phenomenon and we know of no good reason why the bent grass should be able to outcompete the *Poa annua* as a result of lightweight mowing. We suspect, however, that it is related to compaction in the surface layer of the soil. Bent grass grows best on loose soils and *Poa annua* is one of only a few grasses that will survive on tight soils. Lightweight mowers by their very nature cause less compaction than the heavy tractors of years past, and hence the bent grass has a better chance to prosper.

Superintendents who were in the vanguard during the early '80s and switched to the new cutting methods deserve a great deal of credit for their foresight and determination. At first, those individuals were ridiculed and berated by their colleagues for catering to the whims of finicky golfers. They received little support from college professors who really did not know what was going on and thought the new method was a passing fad. The industry was also slow to recognize the potential benefits.

Figure 3.2. The cutting pattern, created by triplex greens mowers,
contrasts sharply with the rough at the Board of Trade
Country Club near Toronto.

Eventually, the Lesco Company, a young upstart at the time, saw the light and manufactured a five gang mower which was a hit in the industry and made the company's
stock soar on Wall Street. Jacobsen and Toro soon followed suit. The rest is history.
Even nine-hole public courses now cut fairways with lightweight mowers and collect the clippings in the process. Bent grass fairways are commonplace on formerly
exclusively *Poa annua* stands. In many cases the transition was a natural one.

New courses that were seeded to bent grass have been able to maintain homogenous cultures with very little *Poa annua* invasion. With the much-improved cutting
units, fairways can now be cut in a very short time and satisfy the most discriminating golfers, but it was not always so! Much of the credit must go the superintendents
who made the switch initially. We owe them a debt and our admiration for their
foresight and persistence.

If it were possible, in an ideal world, golfers would want to putt on bent grass
greens and play from bermuda fairways. That would be like having caviar as an
appetizer and pheasant under glass as an entree. Neither our culinary nor our golfing experiences are very often perfect. Along the way we often learn to play from
crabgrass fairways and putt on spike-marked greens and finish the day with ham-
burgers and beer. Some of the most scenic golf courses are frequently poorly maintained and conversely, a boring layout may at times be exquisitely manicured. Such
is golf, and we must accept and enjoy it wherever we find it, from the sand greens on
the prairie plains to the emerald jewels sparkling along the California coast.

Figure 3.3. Industry responded to the golfers' demands for shorter cut fairways and manufactured fiveplex mowers capable of cutting large areas in short order.

CUTTING FAIRWAYS

The objective is to provide the golfers with a consistent playing surface, and consistency can only be provided when the grass is mowed regularly and expeditiously. The height of cut must be sufficiently low to ensure that there is no grass between the ball and the clubhead at the time of address. The ball should sit up nicely on closely groomed lies. Low handicap golfers and professionals prefer tight lies with very little grass between the ball and the earth. From such lies they make the golf ball spin when it lands on the green. Higher handicap golfers tend to be happier with more turf under the ball so that they may scoop the ball with a fairway wood or a low iron. To achieve these conditions for all golfers alike is of course impossible and we must compromise somewhat, also taking into account the needs of the grass.

The following factors should govern the decisions that prudent superintendents need to make when cutting fairways:

1. The height of cut on fairways should rarely be more than half an inch. Golfers the world over demand closely cropped turf on the fairways. They want tight lies and lots of roll! It is only when a certain species of grass does not tolerate such a short cut that the cutting height is actually raised. Such is the case on bluegrass fairways in the northern zone. Not every golf course

wants or needs close cut fairways. Various bluegrass mixes make an excellent turf that is quite playable for even the most discriminating golfers. The cool season fescues and ryes are also often cut at below an inch. Fairways that are overseeded with rye and *Poa trivialis* in the southern states during the winter season are also cut at the half-inch height. Superintendents who, for whatever reasons, wish to grow one-inch grass on their fairways, should expect to struggle with their bosses, their committee people, as well as their golfers.

We fondly recall playing on a golf course in Durban, South Africa, where the fairways were 100% Kikuyu grass, a very coarse species that was cut at least an inch high. The turf was so dense that it made the ball sit up very primly, and it was easy to make shots from such lies. Almost anywhere else in the world, Kikuyu would be considered a weed and superintendents would go to great lengths to eradicate it, but at this course in faraway Durban it was an acceptable playing surface.

At many golf courses fairways are cut at less than half an inch. Both bents and bermudas will tolerate this height without any trouble. Really short fairways approach a turf quality similar to greens. Whimsical superintendents have been known to stimp such fairways and obtained readings in excess of 6 ft.

2. The frequency of cut is mostly determined by the rate of growth of the turf. The faster the grass is growing, the more often it needs to be cut. When the grass is fertilized regularly and growing actively, it may need to be cut every other day. Many superintendents cut fairways Mondays, Wednesdays, and Fridays. At times, the grass is growing so prodigiously that three times per week is just not enough. Arrangements then have to be made to cut the fairways on weekend mornings or add an extra day to the weekly schedule. It is at such times that greenkeepers curse the Julian calendar and wish that astronomers of old could have invented weeks with just six days instead of seven.

3. Pattern cutting on fairways is a matter of personal choice, but if it is not practiced with some degree of imagination, television spoonfed golfers will soon find a superintendent who can provide picture-perfectly cut grass. Straight cutting lines on fairways are as important as they are on greens and tees. The age-old method of cutting toward a tree on the horizon works every time. Sure enough, there are courses without trees and in that case a feature, such as a promitory, will do just fine.

Instead of cutting a straight line, superintendents have been known to follow the contour of a water hazard. This makes for an interesting deviation of the more commonly used checkerboard pattern.

4. With target golf and lightweight mowing machines came contouring of the fairway edge. The contrast between the short, light green fairway and the much darker and longer rough was startling. Sometimes there is an intermediate cut, or step cut to make the shapes and the shading even more interesting and pronounced. Golfers like the intermediate cut, and tournaments often specify that it be implemented. It reduces the severity of the

**Figure 3.4. Two superintendents examine a sprig of Kikuyu grass,
a prolific grower and considered a weed at most courses.**

penalty between a heavenly lie on the fairway and an impossible shot from U.S. Open rough.

To create the long sweeping lines with capes and curves, it is best for superintendents to seek the help of a recognized golf course architect. It takes a special talent, as well as possession of specialized knowledge, to make the curves suit the needs of the game of golf. Architects are authorities on where fairways should be narrow or wide, where they should bell out or crimp in.

Golf course architect Arthur Hills, although he is a great walker, likes to use a golf cart for this purpose. He drives the cart at a steady pace and at the same time he pulls the trigger on a spray gun, thus marking the fairway with a narrow white line. Arthur finds that he can make more naturally sweeping lines when he drives, as opposed to walking.

Golf course superintendents should mark the line with stakes, or the white paint line will disappear before the new cut becomes established.

Figure 3.5. The intermediate cut reduces the degree of punishment for golfers whose shots have landed barely off the fairway.

Some will go to great length to retain the new curves, and cut a strip of sod along the intended line and replace it with bent grass, thus ensuring that the line will be clearly visible for many years to come.

5. Collars, aprons, and frogs' hair are all similar terms to describe the short turf that surrounds the greens. At some courses the collar may just be one cut around the outside of a green, usually at a height slightly higher than the green and somewhat lower than the fairway. At other courses the collar, which now becomes an apron, is extended somewhat, especially at the front where it is cut in such a fashion that it blends in with the fairways. Superintendents all have their own particular preferences and usually are assisted by their green committee in determining what's best for the membership.

6. Cutters should be wary of sprinkler heads that they are apt to encounter when cutting the grass. Rarely are the sprinklers ideally leveled so that the mowers can drive over the top without worrying about cutting the sprinkler instead of the grass. It is best to slow down on the throttle and ever so gently ride over the sprinkler. If it is obvious that the sprinkler head is higher than the grass, there is no choice but to cut around the obstacle.

When a mower swallows a sprinkler, all sorts of horrible things are apt to happen. At best, the mower will just take a bite from the collar of the sprinkler. No big deal, just an ugly scar. At worst, the sprinkler will be torn from its subterranean mountings, which is immediately followed by a geyser of water of Yellowstone proportions. Operators better be prepared for this sudden catastrophe, because it will draw all kinds of unwanted attention, not the least of which is the wrath of the superintendent.

Good greenkeeping calls for level sprinkler heads, not just on the fairways but also on the tees and on the collar around the greens. If the sprinklers have been pushed out of kilter by vehicles or because of frost, they should be readjusted on a regular basis. There is no excuse for this condition to be commonplace on any golf course.

7. When clippings are picked up as part of the fairway cutting process, they must be removed in some manner that is economical and expeditious. Some superintendents have arrangements that include a large dumpster to be emptied at a local waste disposal site. This method tends to be costly and can be malodorous during the warm summer months when the dumpster cannot be picked up as often as is needed. Another way involves composting the clippings and in the process mixing fresh soil with the grass snippets. A large area is required for this method but the resulting mixture of humus-rich topsoil can be put to good use on the golf course.

   If the rough is spacious, the clippings may be spread there without causing any adverse effect on the play of the game. Keep in mind that the clippings disposed of in the roughs get beat up by the mowers on a regular basis. Of all the ways to get rid of clippings, spreading them in the adjacent rough is probably the most economical and environmentally friendly. Care must be taken that the clippings are spread properly. Operators who just dump the grass will cause grief to the golfers whose balls roll into these piles and make for unplayable lies. When the clippings are left for any length of time, the grass underneath will smother and die and be an eyesore.

8. Dew removal is no longer a common practice, which is a pity because the benefits are so numerous and beneficial. When the dew is allowed to stay on the grass blades for several hours in the morning, a perfect environment for disease organisms is created. Removing the dew helps dry up the turf and stops the spread of the dreaded mycelium dead in its tracks. In the process, a dry playing surface is created for the golfers to play on.

How do smart superintendents remove the dew from fairways? It can be done by syringing the fairways early in the morning before the golfers tee off. One turn of the sprinkler will do the trick just nicely. This works, but it is not completely satisfactory. After syringing, the grass is still wet although not as wet as before. Instead, try dragging the fairways with a rubber hose. Two trucksters, one on each side of the fairway, pulling a rubber hose, can remove the dew, rub the grass, and make it stand up, especially when one starts at the green and moves toward the tee. Two experienced operators can clean the dew off tees, greens, and fairways on an 18-hole course in just over an hour. It is so quick that once caught onto, superintendents will want to it before cutting the grass. The biggest benefit, however, is disease prevention. Dew can also be removed with a drag mat, a piece of tennis netting drawn behind a tractor or a cart. This method is just as beneficial as dragging a hose, but not nearly as quick.

Another benefit of dew removal by dragging a hose or a net is that such action breaks up worm casts. The messy little piles of earth are objectionable from a golfing point of view. Shattering the casts with a hose or whatever means turns the earth into beneficial topdressing.

SUMMARY

Fairways are prime play landing areas, and as such ought to be in excellent condition at all times. Superintendents should remember that the smoothness of a fairway is proportional to the number of times it is cut. Fairways that are cut daily will become shiny sleek, and balls that land on such fairways will roll many extra yards. The importance of dew removal as a method of disease prevention cannot be overemphasized. Anyone who has witnessed the ugly mycelium on damp grass in the morning will know precisely what we mean, and be motivated to make dew removal part of the fairway maintenance program. A well-cut fairway, exquisitely striped, is a magnificent piece of turf that even the most discriminating golfers will find irresistible to play from.

4 The Rough

When North American superintendents speak of the rough, they mean the grassed areas immediately in front of the tee, adjacent to the fairways, and on both sides as well as behind the green. The rough in these areas is, as a rule, maintained at just under two inches, fertilized and watered regularly, and generally of superior quality to most home lawns. On golf courses anywhere else in the world, rough is like it ought to be: unkept grass, gorse, heather, shrubs, and even small trees.

The rough on our courses in North America is very much like the fairways of a half century ago. It is trimmed regularly, often twice a week during the growing season, and fertilized so that it will be thick. The weeds in the rough are sprayed when needed and occasionally the turf is treated for fungus disease. It is apparent that the rough gets lots of tender loving care, but let the rough grow just a bit longer than normal, and golfers scream blue murder, referring to the long rough as "U.S. Open Rough." They use that term as a confession of their inability to extricate their golf ball from ankle-deep grass.

Our golfers in America are the most pampered players in the world. They play on the slickest greens, the flattest tees, and the smoothest fairways, but nowhere are they more spoiled than in the rough! Golfers on our courses rarely lose a ball unless it is hit in the water or out-of-bounds. Anywhere else, golf balls can be found with ease.

TOTAL ROUGH AREA

In terms of the total area of the golf course, rough occupies the largest acreage. A typical 18-hole course is built on approximately 150 acres. Following is a breakdown of the land area devoted to each playing area:

Greens:	2–3 acres	2%		Water:	0–10 acres	0%–6.7%
Tees:	3–4 acres	3%		Trees:	10–20 acres	10%
Fairways:	30–40 acres	23%		Rough:	80–100 acres	60%
Sand:	1 acre	0.7%				

It quickly becomes apparent from these figures that maintaining the rough when it is growing actively is a mammoth job requiring more men and machines than any other activity in the maintenance department. When the rough cutters go out in the morning, they are like a swarm of locusts, devouring the long grass in front as they move and leaving behind a sward of neatly trimmed grass that pleases even the most picky golfer.

Rough needs to be cut regularly for the sake of the speed of the game. To cut all the rough, superintendents use a combination of some of the following equipment:

- several rotary type mowers of varying widths
- a set of tractor drawn gang mowers
- one or more riding triplex reel type mowers
- several hand rotary mowers as well as a number of string trimmers.

It is not unusual on an 18-hole course to have as many as a half dozen people cutting the rough, especially in the springtime when the grass is actively growing. To coordinate the efforts of all these workers takes the skill of a well-organized superintendent.

It stands to reason that the largest area should be cut by the largest machine: either a large rotary with multiple decks, or a set of tractor-drawn gang mowers. The smaller rotaries are used to cut around and between trees. The riding triplex, reel-type mowers are ideal for steep banks around tees and bunkers and, finally, the hand trimmers and rotaries pick up the grass that all the other mowers miss. It is obvious that cutting rough is a team effort and the results are best when all well-trained participants know their parts and work together. That way the work gets done quickly and the entire course is constantly kept trimmed on a regular basis.

The danger with the rough is that the greens crew falls behind and the grass grows faster than it is cut. It happens in the spring when there is a sudden surge of growth. The worst scenario imaginable is a warm rain on a Thursday in May followed by a long weekend. In just hours, the grass will burst from its roots and provide a thick, green carpet that grows faster than the mowers can cut. Such circumstances will cause the golfers to experience inconsistencies in the playing conditions: in some areas the rough will be freshly cut, and of perfect playing height; in other places the grass will be much too long and golfers will waste time looking for balls. Be prepared for long weekends, any weekends in the spring that coincide with periods of rapid growth. The greens crew should be prepared to work overtime, or the rough will get out of hand and the superintendent is likely to receive phone calls from angry golfers.

Riding mowers on steep slopes present a special problem. If such areas must be cut at all, it should only be attempted when the turf is dry, and then only by the most experienced and fearless operators. The machines need to be in the best of mechanical condition, equipped with rollover bars and a seat belt for the operator. Recently cutters have been manufactured with hydraulically adjustable seats, so that the operator is seated horizontally while the mower cuts a steep slope. We feel that such slopes are very dangerous, and if at all practical, are best naturalized.

Mower operators, who watch television golf on the weekends, will notice the beautiful striping in places such as Augusta National and they will try to imitate

Figure 4.1. Cutting the rough is a never-ending task. Welding a bucket
to the mower frame allows for trash and debris to be
collected instead of run over.

Figure 4.2. A rotary mower can shred a paper napkin into a thousand pieces.
Operators need to be trained to pick up trash.

Figure 4.3. Cutting the steep banks of tees requires dexterity and skill gained after several years of experience.

these works of art at their place of work. Such workers ought to be commended for the interest they take in their work and golfers will also be impressed with and appreciative of their creations. In this context, a new verb has developed in greenkeeping jargon: striping, and it refers to creating alternate light and green stripes. The original function of cutting the rough seems to have become secondary.

Superintendents at many courses now cut a strip the width of an upfront rotary from the tee to where the fairway starts. This path is for the golfers who walk, so they won't get their feet wet. From time to time this path may have to be moved sideways so that the turf will not wear out and die. The practice is a nice touch, and makes many friends among the golfers.

SMALL ROUGH MOWERS

No matter how diligent the large machine operators perform, there is always some long grass left behind that can only be cut with small rotary mowers or with string trimmers. If left unattended, the course takes on an unkempt appearance that is objectionable and often results in the superintendent being dismissed. At every golf course, there is a routine of trimming around trees and other hard-to-get-at places. Such work is best done immediately following the larger rough-cutting units. In that manner, the entire area looks uniformly maintained.

Steep, grassy banks are especially difficult to keep trimmed. The wheel-less "Flymo" performs admirably in such areas, but it is an arduous task to handle such a mower on a continuous basis. String trimmers also need expert handlers, otherwise the end result will be a series of scalps and misses which will continue to look ugly long after the work has been done.

A rotary crew of several persons needs a leader for best results. The leader will look after gassing the machines, making small repairs and adjustments, and most importantly, making decisions about what area needs to be cut next. Aspiring assistants often get their first experience at personnel management as rotary crew leader. We emphasize that such a leader should be a working leader and not someone who stands around idly while others sweat.

Small trees of 3" caliper or less can easily be debarked by careless rotary mower operators. The danger is even greater when string trimmers are used. Extra caution must be taken around such small trees. Many superintendents, in an effort to save time and labor as well the health of the small trees, spray around the base of trees with glyphosate or "Round-Up." This universally-used grass killer kills only the grass and not the bark of the tree nor the roots. One or two applications around the base of trees during the course of a season will eliminate the need for mowing.

NATURALIZED ROUGH AREAS

Recently fescue rough has come into vogue on golf courses, and several architects now specify seeding some of the secondary rough with homogenous strands of fescue grass. Such turf is rarely cut at all and can look quite spectacular, especially when the wind blows and moves the stems and seed heads like waves on water. This action brings an element of tranquillity to a golf course that was absent before.

Superintendents who think that fescue rough is maintenance-free are sadly mistaken. Very quickly the sparse turf is invaded by all manner of weeds which make the naturalized rough look unsightly. Such weeds must be removed, and since weed spraying in fescue rough is not always advisable, milkweeds, burdocks, goldenrod, and thistles are usually pulled out by hand, an arduous job, to say the least. Others have employed the age-old scythe of a bygone era to cut the objectionable weeds.

Robert Heron, superintendent at the Beacon Hall Golf Club north of Toronto, looks after acres and acres of fescue rough and knows from experience that it is no easy task. The fescue needs to be cut once a year according to Heron, and the clippings, more like hay, need to be removed, otherwise the buildup becomes objectionable and piles of clippings will surely kill the grass underneath. Players also object to quantities of hay in the fescue rough. The fescue can be trimmed with a tractor-driven rotary mower or a front-mounted rotary mower, but the hay must be removed. Some superintendents use a farm-type sickle bar mower, windrow the clippings, and bale the hay afterward.

Heron also sprays the fescue with a herbicide and sums up his program by stating that, "It's easier to look after 45 acres of blue grass rough than 15 acres of the fescue variety." It appears that beauty has a price. The Michael-Hurdzan-designed Devil's Pulpit Golf Club near Toronto features acre upon acre of fescue rough. Superintendent Ken Wright has identified areas that are in play and these are cut on a regular basis, but by no means resemble the short rough at a traditional course. Wright, like Heron, trims the remainder of the fescue at a 6" height and sprays for noxious weeds.

Figure 4.4. Superintendent Paul Voykin at Briarwood Country Club near Chicago, whose talk "Over Grooming is Over Spending" started the movement to naturalized rough and wildflower areas many years ago.

During the mid-'70s, Superintendent Paul Voykin, from the Briarwood Country Club north of Chicago, started preaching the gospel of: "Overgrooming is overspending." Paul was one of the first superintendents who recognized that large areas on his golf course that were out of play could be naturalized and planted with native wildflowers, thus saving time and labor that might otherwise have been devoted to cutting the grass on such areas. He planted large quantities of black-eyed Susans, columbines, cornflowers, coreopsis, and many others, much to the delight of his golfers. Paul's frequent talks at turf conferences on this topic rapidly won converts, and now there are few golf courses in North America that don't at least have some wildflowers growing on their course.

Not satisfied with his initial successes, Paul Voykin went one step further: he also planted beds of wildflowers near his tees, where golfers could enjoy a constant change of colors during the course of the seasons. At the same time, these many flowers produced fragrances hitherto not experienced at Briarwood. His experiments with wildflowers made Paul a hit with his members. Combining that talent with his greenkeeping skills ensured him job security at Briarwood for a lifetime. He has been at his club for more than 35 years, an enviable record in any occupation.

It is not necessary to overseed with fescue grass nor to plant wildflowers in order to create naturalized areas. When out-of-play areas are left to their own devices, and are no longer cut, they will automatically revert to their native state. We have seen this happen time and time again, but the superintendent must be patient when adopting this method. It may take several seasons for the desirable species to become

Figure 4.5. Wildflowers are an attractive addition to green grass, but their maintenance is by no means without experience, nor expense.

established and predominant, and during that time some selective trimming may be necessary to achieve the desired results.

Some superintendents have combined their naturalized areas with tree nurseries. This idea has some merits, as long as it is realized that small trees need encouragement in their initial stages, such as being protected from rodents and rabbits as well as having to compete for nutrients with the thick grass that surrounds them. In the end, only the healthiest trees will survive in this natural environment. As the trees get bigger, they can be transplanted for use on the course or near the clubhouse; others may eventually become part of a forest. There are times that superintendents have wonderful opportunities to leave living legacies. Letting the grass grow in out-of-play areas, planting trees and wildflowers are just some of them. Visiting such havens of tranquillity and observing birds making nests and rabbits scurrying about makes one realize that being a golf course superintendent has many more benefits than most other occupations.

UNUSUAL TREATMENTS IN NEW ZEALAND

While visiting New Zealand we found an unusual golf course off the beaten path, where sheep were used to cut the grass instead of mowers. The nine hole layout was very hilly and it would have been difficult for gang mowers to cut the fairways, let alone the rough. The day we played this unique course there were 471 sheep, a number which included the lambs, grazing on the lush green grass. These animals were unfazed by our errant shots and kept on chewing regardless of where our balls landed. They did an admirable job of keeping the grass short. We never lost a single ball during our round.

The sheep served a dual purpose: not only did they keep the grass cut, but they also produced wool and a new crop of lambs annually, both valuable commodities for the club's treasury.

Sheep are kept off the greens by a fencing arrangement that includes a gate. Although the maintenance operation at this unique golf course may have been primitive by North American standards, our golfing experience on this obscure golf course ranks high, and on a level with visits to St. Andrews, Shinnecock, and Cypress Point.

AND IN ENGLAND

The rough at Sunningdale Golf Club in England is mostly heather. While he was superintendent, Jack MacMillan did his utmost to keep it that way. Seedling pine trees tried valiantly to become established among the heather on his course, but MacMillan and his crew would not let that happen: "The trees are encroaching on the heath and if left unchallenged, will destroy the character of the course," he said when we visited his course. Many superintendents would give their eyeteeth for trees in the rough, but to MacMillan at Sunningdale, they were nothing but weeds and needed to be eradicated.

SUMMARY

Rough means different things to different people. Golfers and superintendents rarely agree on what the rough should be like. Rough is never static. It changes with the seasons, it changes over the years with natural growth encroaching, and it also changes as a result of man's interference with nature. Whatever form or shape rough takes, it usually provides character and contrast on a golf course. If rough provides challenge as well, then most players will be happy.

5 Sand Bunkers and Their Maintenance

Only a few shots are played from bunkers during a typical round of golf, but nowhere are golfers more critical of course conditioning than when it comes to the sand in the bunkers. When golfers fail to execute a perfect shot from a sand bunker, it is rarely the fault of the person swinging the club. The blame invariably lies with the sand in the bunker. It is either too soft or too fluffy, too hard or too dry, too coarse or too fine, or even more politically correct: the sand lacks consistency! Sand and bunkers are a very emotional issue and otherwise rational persons can become quite unreasonable when discussing sand and bunkers.

Bunkers are an essential part of golf for the following reasons:

1. They add challenge to the game.
2. They frame and define golf holes.
3. They provide contrast and accent.

Trees and water can take the place of bunkers most effectively, but when a property lacks either of those, then sand bunkers are often the only alternative. Golf course architects use their creative talents to shape mounds alongside fairways and then accentuate these features by including hollows and flashes filled with sand. In that manner, they try to duplicate what the sheep and the winds did naturally in Scotland many years ago.

It has been alleged that the location of fairway bunkers on golf courses in Great Britain was often determined by the abundance of divots in certain locations. Rather than repair the divots constantly, the greenkeepers would simply hollow out a bunker. So much for the principle of design that form always follows function.

Near the green, the bunkers are placed with much forethought in order to add difficulty and challenge for the golfers to reach the putting surface. For a golfer to be buried in a bunker is a scary thought and often leads to a poor score. Being able to escape from bunkers or to avoid them altogether is what makes golf such an interest-

Figure 5.1. Aerial view of a golf course exemplifies the contrast between white sand and the green turf on fairways and greens.

ing and addictive game. Meanwhile, golf course superintendents have to deal with the realities of maintaining sand bunkers, which is often a much more difficult task than growing grass.

BUNKER DRAINAGE

The very shape of bunkers ensures that they become collectors and recipients of water, and all too often no adequate provisions are made for the water to drain from the bunkers. Elaborate gridiron tiling systems under greens are commonplace, but many knowledgeable superintendents still have not accepted the necessity of equally extensive drainage systems for bunkers. One single tile line through the center of the bunker is insufficient under most circumstances. A herringbone system of four-inch diameter tile, with the lateral lines no less than 10 feet apart, is essential to take away storm- and rainwater. The header of the herringbone should empty into a catch basin just outside the bunker, and from there be connected to a drainage main or taken into the rough. The catch basin serves as a means of cleaning out the tile, because it is possible that the lines may fill up with sand. Using a hose with pressured water will enable the greens crew to flush out tiles.

Many knowledgeable superintendents have experimented with stockings made from filter cloth around the drainage tiles. It is thought that the stockings prevent the sand from entering the tile. Others are equally adamant that the stockings block the movement of water or at least slow it down. We believe that the tile should be embedded in pea gravel for best results. On new bunkers, the trench should be 5–6

Figure 5.2. The importance of proper bunker drainage is demonstrated by workers bailing out water on a golf course in Swaziland in Africa.

inches wide and partially filled with pea gravel. The top of the tile should be at least 8 inches below the bottom of the bunker. This helps prevent frost bringing the tile to the surface. All during the installation, levels should be taken so that there is adequate fall. The pea gravel in the bottom of the trench can be used to make small adjustments to ensure proper flow. When the base is satisfactory, install either perforated, flexible plastic tile or rigid construction-type tile with holes in the walls. Either type should be of 4-inch diameter. Cover the tile with more pea gravel, but make sure that both the tile and pea gravel are below the base of the bunker. It is important that the pea gravel does not get mixed up with the sand. Golfers become justifiably irate when their expensive sand wedges are scratched or dented by stones. There is understandable concern that no matter how careful, some of the pea gravel will get mixed up with the sand. For that reason alone, one should consider backfilling over the tile with a coarse sand.

FILTER CLOTHS

It is a common occurrence for the material in the subbase of the bunker to get mixed up with the sand up above. This is guaranteed to happen when the bunkers are characterized by steep flashes. Such flashes often look spectacular and make the bunkers visible from afar, but they are a maintenance headache for the greens crew. Any sudden downpour, a summer storm, or a prolonged rainfall is guaranteed to wash the sand from the steep faces. Once the sand starts to run, the base underneath also erodes and mixes with the sand. An ambitious greens crew may shovel the sand

Figure 5.3. Installation of bunker drainage in a flat-bottomed bunker.

back up, but by doing so, aggravate the situation. The sand and the base material become inevitably mixed, and if the base should happen to be mainly clay, the resulting mixture will be as hard as cement once it dries.

Some believe that successive rains and consequent puddling causes the clay particles in the base to float to the top and mix with the sand. This also will predictably lead to the sand becoming too hard for a player's liking. To prevent this from happening, some have experimented with filter cloth as an interface. The felt-like material is rolled out and cut to suit the outline of the bunker. It is held in place with staples and tucked in along the edges, under the sod. Although a 4-inch depth of sand is adequate for new bunkers, on top of filter cloth, extra sand is needed. When using filter cloth in the base of bunkers, superintendents need to be wary about golfers getting their sand wedges stuck in the material. This happens when the sand cover starts to shift and becomes inadequate. Motorized bunker rakes have a tendency to dig in along the sides of bunkers and have been known to tear into the filter cloth with disastrous results. For all these reasons, superintendents should be cautious about installing filter cloth in the base of bunkers in the first place.

In northern climates ground frost may cause severe heaving in the subbase. Such natural action may free stones from the subbase and pop them to the surface. This is an unwelcome surprise for northern superintendents in the spring. Stones must not be allowed to remain as part of the playing medium, since golfers under the rules of the game are not allowed to remove them. Superintendents have an obligation to keep the bunkers clean from objectionable materials. If such impediments cannot be removed manually, superintendents should make use of the mechanized sand sifters that are now available.

THE SAND

An acceptable bunker sand is hard to find and rarely available locally. White Ohio silica sand is the favorite with many superintendents and golfers alike. The material is shipped from Ohio all over the Northeast and the Midwest and beyond. The particle size is uniform and the sand does not become hard even after several years' use. Its brilliant white color makes the bunkers stand out on the golf course. Particularly when the sand is still new, it can be dazzling and almost blinding to the golfers who have the misfortune of finding themselves in such bunkers. Precisely for that reason, some architects and superintendents prefer a more subdued color that will blend in better with the existing hues of the surrounding landscape.

Before superintendents switch sand, they should analyze precisely the reasons why a change of sand is necessary. It may well be that the poor conditions of the bunkers is not the fault of the sand, but the lack of drainage or the design of the bunkers. Whatever the reason, the bunkers may need to be rebuilt before any new sand is ordered. New sand should be compacted with a mechanical tamper before it is put into play. Wetting the new sand also helps. Since it takes time for sand to settle, it is best not to tamper with the sand immediately before a tournament.

The particle size of sand is extremely important! Fine sand blows away in the wind. Coarse sand leaves scratch marks on golfers' clubs and dulls the greens mowers. Sand that is characterized by round-faced particles tends to roll underfoot and is difficult to play from. When the sand particles are angular they will compact more easily and provide stable footing. At the same time, such sand may easily become too hard. The perfect sand is not too fine and not too coarse, nor is it too round or slippery. The perfect sand is hard to find, but once a source has been discovered it is prudent to hang onto it. To express the perfect sand in terms of particle size diameter leaves many factors from the equation. A superintendent charged with recommending a particular sand for use on his or her golf course is best advised to check with his neighbors in a wide area and do a thorough study of the materials available.

We recall an interesting incident where the superintendent had obtained several samples of sand which were exhibited in unlabeled five-gallon containers. The green committee was asked to examine the different sands, among which was the sand from their own golf course. The committee members did their job thoroughly. They fondled the granules and let them slip through their fingers. They rubbed the sand in the palms of their hands and even stuck their noses into it. Then they graded all the different sands and marked their choices on a notepad. When they had finished their job and the ballots were counted, the sand that they unanimously agreed was the best was the very same sand that they already had in their bunkers.

The story illustrates that decisions on the golf course are best left to the experts, which in most cases is a capable superintendent. Such a professional will not hesitate to seek outside advice for the benefit of the golfers.

Golfers have confided that they prefer firmer sand in fairway bunkers than in greenside bunkers, the reason being that they may wish to play a wood club from fairway sand, but from greenside sand they will invariably prefer to play a wedge. It certainly is a challenge for the modern day superintendent to provide bunker conditioning of varying degrees at different locations.

RAKING THE BUNKER

The daily routine of golf course maintenance includes raking the bunkers. Prior to the invention of the mechanical bunker rake, caring for the bunkers could be a monotonous chore taking the efforts of several men for a whole day on an 18-hole course. A smart-thinking superintendent from Georgia was the first one to invent a motorized bunker rake. Never mind that the contraption looked like a moon buggy. It was a prototype and soon copied by all the major manufacturers. Raking bunkers was changed forever. Architects were no longer restricted by the workload of the greens crew, and immediately set out to create large and impressive fields of sand that accentuated the playing areas and made for target golf at its best.

Raking bunkers is a chore usually reserved for junior members of the greens crew. This does not mean that superintendents consider the job of trap-raking bunkers any less important than other assignments. To the contrary, raking bunkers must be done with the same degree of perfection that is applied to all other tasks. To rake bunkers quickly and efficiently requires a young, agile person who can get on and off the machine in a jiffy. He can do his work between foursomes and get out of the way quickly when he must. A "trapper" is alert to the surroundings. He sees golfers coming behind his back and gets the work done without being in the way.

STEPS TO RAKE A BUNKER PERFECTLY

1. Inspect the bunker and remove debris and place the hand rakes on the grass outside.
2. Rake the bunker slowly at half throttle through the center and make a gentle turn at the end.
3. Stay away from the bunker's edge by at least a foot. Touching the grass or the soil with the rake will contaminate the sand.
4. When the entire bunker has been raked, exit carefully, making sure not to drag any sand onto the surrounds.
5. Hand-rake the edges upward and make sure that any marks left at the exit are obliterated. Any ruts in the bunker should also be hand-raked out.
6. Replace the hand rakes inside the bunkers, but not before checking for broken handles and tines.

There has been an ongoing debate about placing the rakes either inside the bunkers on the sand or outside the bunkers on the grass. Rules officials have had a difficult time making up their minds where the rakes belong. Now it seems that the majority of courses place the rakes on the sand where they can easily be seen by golfers.

If golfers complied with the ethics of the game and raked the bunkers every time they played from the sand, maintenance costs could be reduced drastically, but we live in an imperfect world. Golfers are usually so absorbed in their game that they either forget to rake the sand or do a willy-nilly job of it. A perfectly raked bunker in the morning quickly starts to resemble a miniature battlefield after just a few golfers have played from it. Superintendents who know the shortfalls of their players should consider sending out staff in the afternoon to touch up the bunkers by hand-raking, after they have been machine-raked in the morning. At the same time, golfers should be encouraged to rake bunkers with two hands on the rake so as to achieve an acceptable result.

On older golf courses with traditional bunkers there may not be enough space for the bunker machines to maneuver, and in such cases hand-raking is the only alternative. The bunkers at Oakmont of USGA fame in Pittsburgh were hand-raked with hay rakes for many years. These antique instruments left characteristically deep grooves that many golfers despised and others thought lent charm to this famous course. We remember playing at the Vintage Club in Indian Wells, California, and noted at the time that all the grooves were hand-raked toward the center of the putting green. Such attention to detail is not unusual on the part of many dedicated superintendents who have only the best interests of their members at heart. It is manifested time and time again and leads to professional longevity that is rare in any other industry.

The bunker rakes at the Vintage Club are stored in a unique way: a cylinder is buried in the ground surrounding the trap and the bunker rake slides into this cylinder like a hand into a glove. The only part that remains visible is the part on which the tines are mounted. Superintendent Doug Anderson has gone to great lengths to obscure the rakes from view and he has been totally successful.

There can be a problem with trees near bunkers, especially fruit trees. When the fruit ripens it falls into the bunker and golfers, obeying the rules of the game, are not allowed to move the loose impediments in the hazard. No matter if the superintendent removes the fruit several times a day, it keeps on falling, and some golfers will be affected by this bit of unjust adversity. Leaves in the fall season can have the same effect, and committees and architects should consider keeping trees away from sand bunkers.

EDGING THE BUNKER

On finely manicured golf courses, the bunkers are characterized by a sharp, distinctive edge. That is no accident, but the result of meticulous work of knowledgeable greensmen. If left unattended, the grass surrounding the bunker would quickly grow into the sand and the bunker would lose its shape and definition. Golfers would have difficulty determining whether their ball was inside or out of the bunker, and since different rules apply, there could be problems with interpretations and with fellow players.

For the longest time, superintendents and their staff hand-edged bunkers several times during the golfing season. Then came power edgers with oscillating blades and more recently, power trimmers with reciprocating teeth. The work can be done quickly and a sharply-defined edge created with little effort. The problem is that the location of the bunker line cannot always be determined with certainty. Unless edging is done regularly, it is possible for the bunker's edge to be lost. Bunkers quickly lose their original shape, and the architect's design may be lost forever unless construction drawings are kept on file. Before any serious edging is contemplated, the superintendent should outline the bunker with a paint gun on the basis of the con-

Figure 5.4. Plywood is used to reestablish a bunker edge in a renovation project. Once the sod has made root and is firmly established, the plywood is removed.

struction drawings. If these drawings are not available, the superintendent should use his best judgment or, failing that, bring in outside help. After the bunker has been edged, the chunks of sod and strings of rhizomes must be removed from the bunkers and the sand should be raked back up to the grass level. If the sand is raked flat with the bottom of the bunker, a sharp edge in the form of a deep cut will result which may occasionally produce unplayable lies.

Bunkers do not need to be edged mechanically; there is another way! It is quicker and in many ways more efficient, but it does not leave a sharp edge. We are referring to a process that involves spraying the edge of a bunker with glyphosate or Round-Up, a grass killer that effectively stops the dead grass from growing into the sand. There is another important benefit: by eliminating the edger we are also eliminating the opportunity for surrounding soil to mix with the bunker sand. That is an important consideration because once the sand loses its purity, it loses its playability at the same time. The Round-Up must be applied carefully in a narrow band; otherwise, it looks unsightly. It has been suggested that this method of trimming bunkers produces a less artificial look and is thus more appealing from an aesthetic point of view.

POT BUNKERS

The most interesting bunkers on any golf course are without a doubt the pot bunkers. Is it their smallish size or their awesome ability to punish an unsuspecting golfer, or perhaps both, that fascinate an interested observer? Pot bunkers, when

Figure 5.5. Bunker edging with mechanical trimmer.

properly constructed, capture far more balls than their size would lead one to believe. They are just a few square yards of sand in area, but all the surrounding land slopes toward the crater and golf balls easily become entangled in its clutches and released only with reluctance. We have all seen and commiserated with golfers trying to extricate themselves from pot bunkers, only to fail time and time again. How agonizing it must be to fail so miserably and to finally just throw the ball onto the green in disgust! Greenkeepers are only too familiar with the anguish of golfers because they observe it so often and on occasion experience it themselves when they play the game with their friends or colleagues.

The face of pot bunkers is frequently constructed like a sod wall, with layers of sod piled on top of each other and held in place with metal bars and wires. Such sides are hand-trimmed with Weed Eaters and at times even with scissors. Unfortunate golfers who find their ball up against the face may have to play sideways or even backward, to get out of the bunker.

Pot bunkers are invariably so small that they cannot be maintained by mechanical rakes and need to be looked after manually. Because of their size, they quickly become foot marked and need constant care by the greens crew. Pot bunkers are very maintenance-intensive.

BUNKERS AT ST. ANDREWS

Walter Woods, the longtime Links Supervisor at St. Andrews, has this to say about bunkers in his native country:

**Figure 5.6. Possibly the smallest pot bunker in the world, on a
golf course in southern France.**

"No one knows when bunkers came into play, and like many things in the old days, just evolved by trial and error. We do know that golf originated on the East Coast of Scotland on the sandy windswept coast from Aberdeen right down to St. Andrews and round to Edinburgh. This is where golf as we know it began, and the golfers would play on roughly-mown fairways through hollows and mounds from tee to green. Most of this land supported nothing else but rabbits and sheep and the golfers soon discovered that some areas in the lee of the hollow protected the sheep from the wind, and soon the whole depression was so severely worn that it was better to turf the banks and make the sand uniform to make it a fair hazard for everyone. As the years passed, more bunkers came into play, particularly at the greenside, for it was discovered that they did create more interest and demand more accuracy.

"St. Andrews was the forerunner of bunker building and the easiest way was to copy the stonemasons on how they built walls; therefore, revetting turf upward until it reached the top of the mounds was created.

"Owing to the introduction of the rubber gutta percha golf ball, which made golf easier and predictable and most importantly, less expensive, golf soon became popular first of all in England, then Europe and Asia, followed by North America. Scottish professionals were in demand to become golf course architects, having a head start in golf course design. Bunkers provided one area where strategy could be provided and used to create interest into the concept of parkland golf courses.

"Architects all over the world soon realized that bunkers could improve the visual effect to what could be flat boring ground into mounded interesting land which was more appealing to the eye. American architects took advantage of this and were soon constructing large bold bunkers filled with white silica sand which provided a more modern approach to golf course design.

"Starting at the bottom, a solid foundation is made to the shape of the inside of the bunker. Then a layer of turf is laid onto the compacted sand. This is continued upward by laying the next layer slightly back from the previous layer, which dictates the angle and prevents the face from being vertical. The more one sets the next layer of turf back from the previous layer, the greater angles one makes. At all times one must backfill with sand and keep the turf and the sand compacted. Once the revetted turf is up to the desired height, it is topped with a collar of turf. At St. Andrews, because of the steepness of the mounds, revetting is important and necessary because of the feature, but mainly to keep the sand intact, particularly when the strong wind blows. Revetted faces last for about 3–4 years but can be made to last longer if good maintenance is applied with brushing and watering with a fine hose and adding a wetting agent. Apprentice greenkeepers are taught this skill at an early age and just like golf, this has been introduced all over the world.

"When part of the turf wall is worn, usually by golfers walking or climbing out, it can be patched by creating a foundation at the worn part and then building upward and fitting the side into the existing turf. Revetting bunker faces is labor-intensive and can only be of value where mounds can provide no alternative. Links land is one area where revetted faces can be beneficial, mainly to prevent sand from blowing away. If a large amount of revetted bunker faces are required, it will be necessary to have a large turf nursery. The thicker the turf, the quicker the face can be built and the thick, fibrous roots also look more attractive, providing the block effect.

"When the bunker is selected which has to be built, an awareness of the surrounding features and flow of slopes and landscape will be required so that the bunker face is set to blend into these surroundings. On many occasions, on fairway or greenside, the bunker face can be shown to provide strategy and balance to the golf hole. Sand selection is also important. The sand should be compatible with the rootzone material used to construct the greens. It should also be able to compact sufficiently and yet allow the top two inches to be slightly softer. When the bunker is raked it should appear to be saucer-shaped with the sand drawn to the edges. The steeper the face, the longer the slope of sand should be to allow the ball to roll backward, away from the face or edge.

Figure 5.7a. Repairs to a sod-walled bunker at St. Andrews. A sod-walled bunker in need of repair. The first step is to install a solid base.

Figure 5.7b. Next, the foundation is set away from the vertical to allow for a sloping bunker face.

Figure 5.7c. The sod is grown in the turf nursery at St. Andrews.

Figure 5.7d. The space behind the sod wall is filled as the work progresses, and the final step is to set the top collar.

Figure 5.7e. The completed job.

"The selection of rakes to maintain the bunker is important. Old-fashioned wooden hay rakes are often chosen due to the fact that the wooden teeth provide evenly spaced grooves and the width of the rake can achieve the work fast and efficiently. Some golf clubs provide small bunker repair rakes which are often thrown about with no regard for the play that follows. Where to place the rake is often discussed. Some say outside the bunker and others say inside. Logically speaking, it would be better to place the rake inside and away from the line of play, to prevent golf balls from being deflected."

GRASS BUNKERS

As the name implies, the sand in grass bunkers has given way to grass. Nevertheless, such bunkers are still very much a hazard because they present the golfers with a variety of up- and downhill lies, as well as frequently longer-than-normal rough-height grass. Just like regular bunkers, grass bunkers need to be well-drained, and invariably are constructed with a catch basin in the lowest spot.

WASTE BUNKERS

Recently, architects have introduced large areas of unraked sand intermixed with clumps of grass and even shrubbery and small trees. Such areas are at times used to define a dogleg, and their purposeful neglect is in sharp contrast with the neatly manicured adjacent fairway turf. Waste bunkers are not hazards as defined by the

Figure 5.8. A waste bunker at the Monterra Golf Course in Ontario, Canada. Such bunkers are a formidable hazard, but not without maintenance headaches.

rules of golf, and golfers are allowed to ground their golf club in a waste bunker. Nor are waste bunkers raked on a regular basis, and difficult lies are commonplace in such bunkers.

It is a fallacy to believe that waste bunkers are maintenance-free. The vegetation inside the waste bunkers needs to be maintained. Trees and bushes need to be trimmed. The ornamental grasses that are frequently planted in waste bunkers need to be tended and the sand does need to be smoothed at intervals. If weeds become a problem, they must be sprayed. Since waste bunkers are generally quite flat and often lower than the surrounding lands, drainage must be provided for. Tile line similar to regular bunkers should be installed at the time of construction.

Ron Heesen is the superintendent at the Monterra Golf Course near the ski hills north of Toronto and his golf club is well-known for its many waste bunkers. This is what Ron has to say about such bunkers:

"Waste bunkers are photogenic, add greatly to the aesthetics, and also emphasize how the hole should be played. They make the fairways and greens stand out and provide a wonderful definition. Maintenance can, however, be a problem. We usually rake these areas once per week. The major problem at our course has been the winds coming off nearby Georgian Bay. A lot of the sand has literally blown away and we have added sand on numerous occasions, but this too has blown away. Regular maintenance includes rock picking and spraying with Round-Up to keep out encroaching weeds."

SUMMARY

The measure of a greenkeepers' competency is often appraised by the way the bunkers are maintained. There lies an opportunity: rake and maintain the bunkers to perfection, and be a hero with the golfers!

A regular routine of raking and edging the bunkers, of trimming the surrounds and making sure that the hand rakes are in good repair and that there is a sufficient number in each bunker—all these factors help create a favorable impression of the golf course to regular golfers and visitors alike.

Water

INTRODUCTION

There will be no grass without water. In those few words lies a simple truth about greenkeeping: green grass and water are as closely entwined as love and marriage! Novice greenkeepers learn early in their careers that they must have water to grow grass and in the days of rubber hoses, that lesson was brought home through hard work and long hours. Anyone who has done a night shift on the watering crew knows of groping in the dark for pipe fittings, of lugging water-filled hoses, and of hankering in the pumphouse between sprinkler changes. Not only did it take a strong back, but a fearless mind as well. There were always frightening shadows in the dark and inexplicable sounds that sent shivers up the spine of the most stouthearted waterman. The first glow of dawn was a welcome sight, and the company of fellow greensmen arriving for the day shift was warmly appreciated.

It can readily be understood from the foregoing that the advent of automatic sprinklers was welcomed by those charged with the responsibility of maintaining fine turf. Suddenly the superintendent was back in charge of the watering operation and no longer at the mercy of watermen who performed their work under the cover of darkness. The advent of automatic sprinklers was accompanied by a whole new philosophy toward watering. Manual watering by necessity had encouraged drenching an area until it was thoroughly soaked, and then not watering it again until it had dried out. This method of watering was supposed to encourage root growth because plants had to extend their roots between waterings to obtain the precious liquid for their metabolism. Once watering became automated, it also became possible to water the entire course, tees, greens, and fairways, nightly! Only a bit, perhaps one single turn of the sprinkler, but water just the same. Inevitably, nightly watering led to overwatering, and sloppy wet turf was commonplace at some courses. Superintendents had to learn how to water all over again and how to manage their watering systems for the benefit of the grass and the golfers.

**Figure 6.1. No matter how it is delivered, the grass plant needs water
to survive. Location: Royal Kathmandu Golf Course in Nepal.**

WHEN WET IS TOO WET

A good example of wet turf occurs when a fairway sprinkler is left on all night because it would not shut off when it was supposed to. Imagine an irrigation head spewing 90 gpm of water over a circle with an 80 ft radius for six hours. That amounts to the equivalent of a two and one-half inch rainfall, and the mishap will result in a wet spot for at least a day. A greenside sprinkler, with much less output and smaller coverage can still cause excessive wetness on the green and will more than likely result in plugged balls or mucky ball marks.

When excessive wetness is caused by a malfunctioning sprinkler, the affected area can be roped off and taken out of play. When rain is the culprit, power cart traffic may have to be restricted or even worse, the golf course may need to be closed. Soil scientists will testify that supersaturated soils should not be walked or driven on. If that does happen, the soil structure will lose its natural composition and become quite squishy, much like a mud cake in a child's hand. Such soil, when it finally does dry, may have lost structure and be a detriment to healthy root growth for plants. Therefore the excess water must either be allowed to drain naturally or removed mechanically, so that oxygen can once again enter the root zone. The poor grass plant almost choked to death when it could not breathe, and was saved in the nick of time by a vigilant superintendent.

Freestanding water in the heat of summer can frequently become quite warm and actually scald the turf. Superintendents should be aware of this phenomenon and make every effort to empty puddles. Sometimes this can be done by opening existing drains; mostly it means pumping the water away.

WHEN DYING GRASS NEEDS WATER

Of all the skills that aspiring superintendents must learn, none is more difficult than recognizing the latter stages of dying turf. Otherwise competent assistants often draw a blank or go color-blind when it comes to ringing the alarm bells for wilting grass. It can all happen so quickly. The greens look perfect in the morning, freshly cut with a distinctive checkerboard appearance. The wind freshens as the morning progresses and by noon there is a stiff breeze. As the temperature rises the humidity is lowered, and by mid-afternoon the grass plants are losing more water through the leaves than they can take up through the roots. The plants quickly lose their turgidity and characteristically turn a purplish blue. Footprints from golfers on turf in this stage show as depressed grass that won't spring back up. A keen eye will recognize all the symptoms and be prepared. Inexperienced operators who fertilize, topdress, or God forbid, verticut, when such conditions prevail, will have sounded the death knell for the grass plants.

SYRINGING

Wilting grass can be brought back to health by the simple expedient of syringing, a very light application of water, administered either by hose and nozzle or by the syringe cycle of the automatic watering system. Either way, the idea is to apply a small amount of water to the hot grass plant. The water will evaporate and in the process cool the turf. It is a proven method that works every time. Applying too much water can be detrimental; it once again will result in a soggy upper layer of the root zone, with all the bad side effects mentioned before.

It is not only the greens that may require syringing. More often than not the collars or aprons start wilting even before the greens do, and these sensitive strips often have to be wetted during the course of a drying day. The reason that aprons show signs of wilt before the greens do is that the turf on aprons is often more thatchy or spongier than the grass on the greens. If aprons are lost repeatedly they should probably be replaced with superior turf. One should also keep in mind that aprons are subjected to mowers turning and sand blasts from nearby bunkers. The first factor leads to compaction and the second to drying out. In both cases, the apron or collar needs repair or extra maintenance.

High knolls on fairways may also require some cooling on hot days during the summer. Superintendents who know their course, after many years of experience, know the weak areas that will show stress the quickest. Such areas are singled out and often receive extra water early in the morning at the crack of dawn, in anticipation of a stressful day. That is smart greenkeeping and results in success where others fail.

WHEN TO WATER

Every golf course has certain indicator areas, such as the back of a green or a high tee, that are the first to show signs of drought stress. Another sure sign of the need to water occurs when the tops of the French drains start to turn blue. Experienced superintendents know these signs, and know where to look for them. Their appearance rings a bell and triggers a reaction: it is time to start an irrigation cycle. Our recommendation is to water just a little less than seems to be needed and then play catch-up in the morning with the help of daylight. This method prevents overwatering and, in fact, keeps the golf course as a whole on the dry side and very playable.

There is a lot of fancy instrumentation available that will help a superintendent decide when to water. We prefer to use our own judgment, based on years of experience and some tricks that have been passed down to us. Just the same, we both use a rain meter to determine how much precipitation has occurred during the night and we place a wet sponge on the windowsill of the office and watch over the course of the day how quickly it dries out. It is our primitive way to measure the rate of evaporation.

LOCALIZED DRY SPOTS

The trend to high sand content greens had its beginning in California where it was believed that a so-called "dirty sand" would make the ideal matrix for growing grass on putting greens. Dirty sand occurred naturally in many places and was an easy shortcut for the establishment of golf greens. When dirty sand was not available, superintendents used washed sand and added peat or similar organics to duplicate the dirty sand. Whereas initially sand had been one of three components of the ideal greens growing mix, it now quickly became the major, in some cases the only component of the growing medium.

Sand has several advantages as a soil:

- It drains well and rarely gets overly wet.
- Sand is difficult to compact and needs little aeration.
- Sand greens hold golf shots well, even when dry.

Some superintendents liked sand so well that they started using it as topdressing material. A light application of sand was easy to apply and even easier to work into the turf. But all that sand had one ugly side effect: localized dry spots. Over time, almost all greens that had been topdressed with sand, or built from a homogenous sand mix, developed brown areas of wilted grass ranging in size from grapefruits to umbrella tops. The soil under these dry spots was so dry that it could not absorb water, no matter how long the sprinklers were left on. This hydrophobic condition is thought to be caused by a fungus that lives in the sand, and its mycelium, or fungal root system, shuts off the pore spaces and prevents water from entering the soil.

The ugly brown dry spots mar the appearance of otherwise perfect putting greens. Superintendents whose greens are subjected to these objectionable conditions have been struggling with various means of combatting the problem. Complete success has been elusive.

Wetting agents were introduced to break down the viscosity of water. Wetting agents made water droplets smaller and actually made water wetter, so that the water could penetrate even into the smallest of pore spaces and provide relief to thirsty plant roots. Greens treated with wetting agents are characteristically without dew in the morning, at least for the first few days after application. Wetting agents have much the same effect on grass and soil as rinsing agents have in dishwashers. Both break down the water into a thinner liquid. In a dishwasher this results in no spots on the glasses, and in the soil it means that grass roots can drink more easily. In fact, rinsing agents and wetting agents are very similar compounds chemically.

Wetting agents proved a valuable tool in the management of turf grasses on greens, tees, and fairways. Superintendents who used this new tool quickly realized its value, and although the benefits of wetting agents are difficult to document scientifically, many superintendents swear by their use. One would think that such a wonder drug would be ideal for the control of localized dry spots, but such is not always the case. Lately the dry spots have become so persistent that in addition to frequent applications of wetting agents, more drastic action is required.

Tyning the dry spots with aerators or even specially constructed drenching forks seems to alleviate the problem for a while. Adding a fungicide to the drenching liquid also helps. Adding iron, liquid nitrogen, and even kelp extract, seems to have a beneficial effect on the dry spots. Rarely is the problem cured completely, except after a prolonged rain followed by a cool period.

Many, including the authors, are beginning to question the benefits of sand greens and sand topdressings. Even when the sand has an organic component of between 5% and 6%, we feel that the sand is still a sterile medium that does not exhibit the life that can be observed in more traditional soils. Perhaps we have gone overboard and placed too much emphasis on the sand content of greens and topdressings. Ask yourself this question: How would I build this green, or what topdressing material would I use, if this were my green and my livelihood depended on the green fees? Perhaps we would not quite so readily advocate the use of sand.

THE PERCHED WATER TABLE

The late Dr. Bill Daniel from Purdue University is thought to have been the inventor and certainly the promoter of the perched water table in putting green construction. Dr. Daniel visualized a top layer of sand atop a layer of gravel and a bed of tile. Water in the sand layer would reach field capacity and then flush through the gravel into the drainage tile. Greens built in that fashion could not be overwatered, and drained perfectly. In his lifetime, Dr. Daniel witnessed many greens and sports fields being built according to his specifications. By the time of his death, even some of these showed signs of localized dry spots.

THE WATERING SYSTEM

Once it is understood how critical water is for the survival of the grass, it is equally easy to comprehend that the watering system is the lifeline on any golf course. That intricate system of underground pipes, tubes, and conduits must be in perfect working order for water to be applied when and where needed, all the time. When the system fails for whatever reasons, its repair becomes a priority of the highest order. Fixing pipe leaks, repairing sprinklers and/or hydraulic and electrical lines, has become a highly specialized technical occupation. Most golf courses now employ someone in charge of the watering system, someone who is knowledgeable about the pumphouse, someone who has the combined skills of an electrician and a plumber, and most of all someone who does not mind working in mud and water, often in the line of fire of the golfers. Such persons are rare to find and once found, should be made to feel appreciated so that they will stick around for a while.

Leaks and Repairs

The first step in repairing a breakage in the watering system, is to determine the nature of the break. Is it the pipe, the swing joint, or the sprinkler that is leaking? Once the cause has been discovered, close the valve(s) that control the affected area. By opening a trash valve or removing the innards of a low-lying sprinkler, the residual water pressure can be lowered. The remainder of the water can then be pumped out.

Excavation

Place a piece of plywood near the area to be excavated. Cut the sod and remove it carefully with a long-handled sod knife. Dig a square or rectangular hole to the pipe, being careful not to cut the hydraulic tubes or the electrical wires. The square or rectangular hole is necessary to provide adequate room to maneuver while making the repair. The excavated material should be placed on the plywood.

Repairing the Leak

If the swing joint is at fault, it is most often a broken nipple. Replace it, using Teflon tape to seal the threaded connections, but only one thickness of the tape. Several layers of Teflon tape on a plastic pipe thread can lead to breaks. Galvanized fittings are the major cause of leaky swing joints. They should routinely be replaced by PVC (polyvinyl chloride) fittings.

At times, the leak may be caused by a cracked sprinkler body. This is often the case in northern climates after a harsh winter. If a sprinkler is to be replaced, releveling the new sprinkler is absolutely necessary. Tilted sprinkler heads cause uneven water precipitation patterns.

The most difficult repairs are broken pipe leaks because they usually involve a section of pipe that needs to be removed. Invariably, a longer excavating hole is required to make the repair and therefore pipe leaks are usually more time-consuming to complete. Use a sharp saw so as to make a clean, straight cut. Bevel the edges of the cut with a rasp or a file. Insert a new section of pipe using gasketed Harco repair couplings.

Figure 6.2. It is never a good idea to build a green on top of irrigation lines. Invariably there will be breaks, and it is difficult to match the existing grades when making repairs.

Backfilling

Once the repair has been completed and the water pressure tested, the excavation is backfilled slowly, all the while packing the soil with one's feet. This helps to prevent settling, later on. If the original soil is of poor quality, backfilling with sand is recommended. In the root zone area, the sand should be amended. Replace the sod as level as possible and tamp it down firmly and lastly, fill the cracks with topdressing materials.

Many different tools are used to make repairs to the irrigation system. The following is a list of all the tools and items that should be available to make repairs. Most of these should be carried on a small maintenance vehicle, such as a Cushman or a Yamaha cart:

a. shovels, both a standard and a trenching shovel
b. a long-handled sodding knife and/or an edger
c. saws, a fine-toothed general purpose saw, as well as a hacksaw
d. a carpenter's hammer, as well as a small 5-lb sledge
e. wrenches: two pipe wrenches plus a set of vise grips
f. a set of screwdrivers, as well as a large slotted one, and a medium Phillips 5/16" nut driver
g. pliers, two, general purpose type, medium channel lock, and one pair of snap ring pliers

h. valve insert tools of various types for various sprinkler heads

i. plywood to keep the job site clean, and caution tape to keep curiosity seekers out. GUR signs to keep the golfers happy.

Irrigation maintenance carts are usually equipped with a small vise, a workbench, a low horsepower water pump, a hand pump, and a bailing bucket. All repair technicians carry a two-way radio or a telephone so that they can respond to emergencies quickly.

The Pumphouse

If the irrigation system is the lifeline of the golf course, then surely the pumphouse can be compared to the heart of the system. Without a sound heart, a heart with a healthy beat, the system cannot function properly. If the heart flutters at times or suffers from acute angina, it cannot pump properly and the result is fluctuating pressures which in turn lead to water hammer in the pipes and malfunctioning sprinklers. A typical pumphouse on an 18-hole golf course may have several pumps with a total capacity of 1,000 gpm. Nowadays the pumps are usually fully automated and maintain a constant pressure in all the lines.

The importance of the pumphouse cannot be overemphasized. The initial cost of an adequate pumphouse is a sizeable expense. The necessity of maintaining the pumphouse in good operating order is equally obvious. Yet, many a pumphouse that we have visited in our travels has sadly lacked good housekeeping. That is deplorable, because a messy pumphouse inevitably leads to problems with the watering system on the golf course.

We remember the time many years ago when we were shown the pumphouse at Bob O'Link near Chicago by then-Superintendent Robert Williams. It was impeccable, as was the rest of the golf course, but in the pumphouse one could literally eat from the floor, which incidentally was mostly covered by a rug. The casings of the pumps were freshly painted and there were no leaky bearings squirting water on electrical motors. The condition of that pumphouse has remained freshly painted on our minds and all of Bob O'Link, including its superintendent, have been an inspiration for our greenkeeping careers ever since.

WINTERIZING THE SYSTEM

In climates where a deep freeze sets in at the beginning of winter and solidly freezes the soil to a depth of several feet, it is necessary to winterize the piping system, supply lines, and perhaps even the pumphouse. Most systems can be drained to some degree, but not all water can be removed in this manner. It is best to connect an air compressor to the main pipe and pressurize the system with air. Once a static pressure of about 100 psi has been attained, the sprinklers can be cycled, much as if one was syringing, and the remainder of the water will be blown out through the sprinklers. This is a tedious job but one must make sure that all water is indeed gone from the pipes. It may be necessary to move the air compres-

Figure 6.3. It may take two 750 CFM compressors operating in tandem to blow out the water lines and winterize the irrigation system.

sor around to the extremities of the system, thus making sure that all water lines are thoroughly blown out.

THE WATER SOURCE

Irrigation water may be drawn from many different sources, such as rivers, lakes, wells, and even municipal water mains. Wherever the water comes from is not really important as long as there is enough. Some courses need as much as a million gallons during the course of a 24-hour period in the heat of summer. Most use much less. Computer-controlled automatic irrigation systems have made watering much more efficient, and as a result we can achieve the same result with less water.

A water reservoir that is fed by a river or from deep wells should be deep, at least 10 ft, so that the water will remain cool and is less likely to evaporate. The sides of the reservoir should be steep, very steep, to prevent the establishment of weeds along the shore. Aerating the water by means of fountains will help retard the development of algae. If weeds do build up, they may need to be removed with floating, mechanical weed harvesters. Aquatic weed controls by means of approved pesticides is governed by state statutes and in many areas it is a tedious process to obtain the necessary permits.

The quality of the water is very important. Sprinklers, controllers, valves, etc., often have very small tolerances and will malfunction when the water contains silt or other impediments. If dirty water is a problem, filtration devices will need to be

Figure 6.4. An adequate source of water is essential. Circulate the water to keep it clean, or try using bales of straw to help reduce algae buildup.

installed to screen out the pollutants. At the same time, beneficial additives can be added to the water that will make the precious liquid even more important to the plants. Fertigation, applying fertilizer through the water system, is quite prevalent and so is adding wetting agents. Less common is introducing bacterial cultures through the water system to the grass plants as a means of disease prevention. In all cases, high water quality is essential to make these new systems work to their optimum intent.

SUMMARY

Applying water has become incredibly sophisticated in recent years, and the methodology will continue to advance since water is such a precious resource. Managing the water system is one of the most important criteria in a superintendent's job description. At the same time it is often least understood by golfers, because so much of it takes place underground. For the same reason, it is frequently difficult for superintendents to obtain the necessary capitalization to maintain and improve the watering system. A word of advice: when seeking employment, superintendents should be wary of accepting a position where the water system is in a poor state. It would be difficult to improve the turf on such a golf course.

7 Fertilizer

A foursome we knew played golf every Saturday and every Sunday from April until November, whenever the course was open. They were the best of friends for many years in a way that only golfers can understand. That means they greeted each other warmly over breakfast and were polite for at least two holes. Then they would fight and argue over gimmie putts and strokes given or taken. The relationship of the foursome was based on acrimonious golf and backslapping drinking bouts spiced with clubhouse humor.

So it lasted for many years until one of the foursome suddenly died after a brief illness. The widow decided on cremation as a means of disposing of the remains. The three remaining friends were asked to help spread the ashes in a suitable place. They decided to approach the superintendent and ask him about spreading the ashes on the golf course. Now the Super knew full well that if he took this matter to the committee, it would be bandied around the table, without a decision being made. Therefore, he suggested that the three friends bring the ashes to the course late one evening, when there were no other golfers around, so that the ashes could then be spread on a green of their choice. The three golfers picked the 11th green as their choice, since that was the green the dead golfer had 3-putted most often during his lifetime. On the designated evening the three friends brought an urn, the size of a one-gallon paint can, containing the ashes. They also brought a quart of single malt scotch whisky which was drunk in its entirety while the three golf companions made silly speeches commemorating their dead friend.

The superintendent stood nearby, enjoying the smooth amber liquid as it slit down his throat and warmed his stomach. Then the ashes were spread over the green, and it was at this time that the superintendent began having second thoughts about circumventing the powers of the green committee. The ashes were not ashes at all, as he had expected and as the name would imply, but instead consisted of a fine granular material mixed with bone chips of the skeletal remains of the cremated golfer. The bone chips were far too large to filter in between the grass blades and settle below the putting surface, and to make matters worse, the whole green was covered with the chips and had become completely unputtable. By now the whisky had done its work and both the golfers and the greenkeeper were regaling in the ambience of the evening and enjoyed carefree feelings of having done well with the remains of their friend, and they were satisfied that they had complied with the wishes of the widow. As darkness neared, they headed for the barn and their homes.

The following morning Rosy, the greens cutter, had no problem with her first ten greens. The machine operated smoothly, and the reels cut to perfection. It had not mattered that her boss was late for work and seemed grumpier than usual. Her work was routine and she did it to perfection, until she came to the 11th. The mower suddenly developed a peculiar sound that had its origin near the cutting units. She kept going for a while, hoping that it would go away, but it got worse instead and she had to stop. Rosy noticed then that the green was covered with small, light-colored chips, the origin of which puzzled her. She was about to return to the shop for assistance when the bleary-eyed Super caught up to her. "Rosy," he said, "just skip this one, it has been fertilized!"

DIFFERENT TYPES OF FERTILIZERS

The ashes of a cremated golfer would hardly make for a good fertilizer and they would have very little impact on the growth of the turf. Yet one of the best garden fertilizers is bonemeal, a ground-up material high in phosphorous. For best results, bonemeal is forked into the soil and that is why it is rarely used on golf greens. Bonemeal has been around since time immemorial, and in recent years has been replaced by a wide range of sophisticated products that require a college degree or a technician's diploma to understand and apply. The terminology of modern fertilizers is so complex that one must have a thorough knowledge of chemistry and be conversant with soil physics. But when all is said and done, there are basically only two types of fertilizers: Those that burn and those that don't. That may seem like an oversimplification, but in terms of basic greenkeeping it is best not to cloud the issue with jargon.

Fertilizers that Burn

The most dramatic burn can be achieved by an overdose of ammonium nitrate. Just a few pounds of this deadly material per thousand square feet will kill the grass. This is not surprising, since ammonium nitrate can be used to concoct explosives for warfare or industrial purposes. Once this is understood, it makes sense not to apply fertilizers like ammonium nitrate to putting greens. Yet farmers use this material on their crops and when applied, it falls into the cracks of the earth, dissolves into the soil water, and becomes available to the plant roots. Lush, rapid growth is the almost immediate result. Ammonium nitrate can be applied to putting greens with relative safety if it is watered in immediately after, but why take the chance when there are so many other safe products to choose from? Ammonium nitrate is a water soluble fertilizer. Put some of it in a jar of cold water, shake it up, and watch it disappear. To make matters worse, ammonium nitrate contains almost 33 % actual nitrogen! When the granules are applied to the grass surface, they attract moisture from the atmosphere and literally dissolve in their own sweat. That's why this powerful solution can so easily burn the grass. Similar compounds such as ammonium sulfate and urea act identically and should also be used with caution.

Experienced superintendents know how to handle water soluble fertilizers, but rookies in the trade should become acquainted with these products carefully. Many mixed fertilizer formulations contain at least some water soluble components. As a general rule, the less expensive the fertilizer, the more likely it is to be water soluble and the greater the chance that it will burn.

Mixed fertilizers contain all three major nutritional elements: N, P, and K; nitrogen, phosphorous, and potassium in various proportions. Nitrogen encourages growth and color, phosphorous is needed for the roots, and potassium gives strength to the plants. All three can burn the grass but nitrogen is the chief culprit, and it should always be handled with respect. As a general rule, mixed fertilizer should be watered in thoroughly after application. Even then, it is possible to see some marking around the cup and between the tee markers at the end of the day, when a mixed fertilizer has been applied in the morning. Applying mixed fertilizers during cool weather lessens the possibility of burning. A sensible program, then, should consist of a mixed fertilizer during the cool or shoulder seasons, and nonburning fertilizers during the heat of the summer.

Fertilizers that Don't Burn

The original nonburning fertilizers were mostly organics, and the most famous organic of all is Milorganite, a by-product of Milwaukee sewage sludge. Most organics are low in nitrogen, and Milorganite is no exception. It contains just 6 lbs of actual nitrogen per hundredweight, and none of it is water soluble. That is why Milorganite, and most products like it, can be applied with impunity. The least intelligent member of the greens crew can be entrusted to apply Milorganite without fear of burning a green or a tee. One can spill a bag of the product, sweep it up, and still not cause a burn. Amazing as that may seem, we know it is true, because we speak from experience. The success of Milorganite has led many other companies to copy the product. Most recently Sustane, a by-product of the poultry industry, has shown promise. Beside having all the fine qualities of Milorganite, Sustane also possesses some fungicidal preventative characteristics. We are convinced that organic fertilizers do much more than feed the plants with the basic elements. They contain sulfur, iron, and many trace elements that seem to have a positive effect on the plant's metabolism and its ability to resist diseases.

We have to acknowledge that there are some golfers with delicate noses who object to the smell of organic fertilizers on their grass and who prefer more sanitized materials. Superintendents may well take the sensibilities of their customers into account and schedule their fertilizer applications with the golfers in mind. To simply give up on organics because of the smell is to miss out on some great fertilizers whose many benefits far outweigh this one small drawback.

Synthetic Organics

Fertilizer chemists have had their fun producing urea formaldehyde and its many polymer cousins, all in an attempt to create a product that could be applied just once a year and feed the plant at an even pace from spring to fall during the growing season. These marvelous products have changed our industry, and in the process made life so much easier for the superintendent and the greens crew. Mixed fertilizers in the past often suffered from uneven granulation. The various elements were of different sizes and as result, difficult to apply evenly. Modern fertilizer are characterized by a uniform granule, where each particle contains the formulation that is written on the bag. Such materials can be applied with greater accuracy and at reduced rates and still ensure that every plant will receive the specified nutrients that it requires. Sulfur-coated urea is a pellet of urea nitrogen enshrouded in a skin of sulfur. The idea is that the sulfur skin will crack or dissolve and in the process the nitrogen will become available to the plant's root system.

Manufacturers maintain that all these synthetics can be applied without fear of burning, and that they don't need to be watered in. We believe that it is best to at least wash these materials off the grass blades. Subsequent irrigation cycles or natural rainfall will ensure that the fertilizer granules filter down into the soil, where they belong.

Liquid Fertilizers

Liquid concentrations of balanced fertilizers have been formulated that make it possible for superintendents to apply nutrients through the sprayer or even through the irrigation system. This sounds marvelous and works well up to a point. The fertilizer elements in the solution are applied to the plant as a mist, and some of the solution actually enters the plant's metabolism through the grass blades. The rest leaks down to the soil and the plant roots. The response is almost instantaneous: lush green grass!

The process can be likened to intravenously feeding a patient in a hospital. Through a tube, a patient receives all that is necessary to sustain life, but to restore health, the patient will eventually need a hearty meal. So it is with grass plants. A liquid diet may suffice during times of stress, but it needs to be augmented eventually by a well-balanced feeding of a granular material.

Iron

Most superintendents apply small amounts of iron to the turf. Some, only on the greens and fairways; others apply iron from fence to fence as part of the preparation for televised golf. Iron applied as a spray is absorbed through the leaf blades, enters the plant's juices, and turns it green within hours. The dark green color will last from a few days to a week. Iron is used instead of a nitrogen fertilizer; it provides color without a surge of growth of regular fertilizer. Iron is also beneficial because it assists photosynthesis inside the plant. Combine iron with a wetting agent and you have a magic mix that seems to do wonders for the plants. Add kelp extract, and add to the magic. Such concoctions should be experimented with in the nursery or on the number one green, before applying to problem greens. When we refer to the number one green, we don't mean the numerical first green, but the best-conditioned; the healthiest green among all 18. It invariably has a pure stand of bent grass and is as smooth as a baby's bottom. It putts to perfection and never causes problems. On such a green it is all right to experiment, especially at the back of the green. Chances are the number one green will survive.

Applying too much iron is a scary experience. Too much could be in excess of 3–4 ounces per 1,000 sq ft. A miscalculation on the sprayer resulting in 8 ounces per 1,000 sq ft application will turn the turf black. Watering at that time will not help; the iron is already inside the plant and the damage has been done. Fortunately, the black color of the turf is not deadly, it just looks that way. The turf will lose its dark color in stages and will be back to normal in a few days.

APPLYING FERTILIZERS

For small areas such as tees and greens, a walk-behind spreader is usually quite adequate. Before starting, check out the spreader and make sure that it operates the way it is supposed to. Many of the small cyclone spreaders are not as reliable as one would expect. Test the spreading pattern on a cement or an asphalt floor. Make sure it spreads evenly. Now is a good time to calibrate the rate of application. Measure the area that has been applied and sweep up and weigh the material that has been used. From these two figures the rate of application can be determined.

For example, if 20 lb of material has been applied to 1,500 sq ft, the rate of application per 1,000 sq ft is 20 divided by 1.5, or 13 lb per 1,000 sq ft. If the average green on the golf course measures 4,000 sq ft, the calibrated setting would require a 50-lb bag per green. Should the green be fertilized in two different directions, a practice we always recommend, it would take 100 lb of fertilizer. If the fertilizer in question should happen to be Milorganite (formulation 6-2-0), it would mean that 6 lb of actual nitrogen was applied per 4,000 sq ft, or 1.5 lb per 1,000 sq ft. That's too heavy for a summer feeding but not unusual for a dormant application.

For larger areas such as fairways and roughs, one may use a PTO-driven spreader with a large capacity hopper. These big machines are best calibrated in the rough, to avoid causing mishaps on the precious fairway turf. Again, measure out an area, fill the hopper, and pick out an appropriate tractor speed. After the measured area has been covered, deduct the remainder of the fertilizer from the amount at the start. Calculations similar to the one before should provide a rate of pounds of material per acre of turf.

As was mentioned before, it is best to apply fertilizer in two different directions in order to ensure complete coverage. Experienced operators can make use of the mower patterns on tees and greens and thus ensure sufficient overlap, thereby avoiding the need to cross-fertilize, and saving time. On greens, the aprons, collars, and approaches are generally fertilized at the same time as the green. On tees, one may just fertilize

**Figure 7.1. Keep a straight line when applying fertilizer.
Apply in two different directions to ensure overlap.**

the tee top and not the sides, since fertilizing the sides merely promotes excessive growth and the need for extra cutting. With tractor-driven spreaders it is best to spread from tee to green down the center of the fairway and then an extra pass along each side. Extra passes may be needed, depending on the width of the fairway. Most spreaders are now of the cyclone type, but occasionally one may observe a drop-type spreader. The hopper lets the material fall onto a baffle board, from where it slides onto the grass. It can readily be understood that drop-type spreaders, by their very nature and makeup, can easily lead to poor application patterns. We don't recommend their use for that reason. Spreader technology has not kept pace with the innovations that we have witnessed elsewhere in turfgrass management. The spreaders are still very much the same as they were a quarter century ago. We look forward to the day that spreaders will be computerized so as to make it easier to apply more precise amounts.

FERTILIZER BURNS

When a fertilizer spill does occur, instant action is required. Use a lightweight square-mouthed shovel to pick up as much of the spilled material as possible. Be ready with a hose, and use water pressure to wash off the remainder of the material. No matter how tempting, don't use a broom to sweep up the material. The bristles of the broom break open the leaves' blades and make it possible for the fertilizer to enter the plants' juices. Instant death results. Even after careful removal of the spilled fertilizer and washing the remainder off with water pressure, it is very likely that the grass will burn. There is little choice left but to repair the burn with a sod cutter and new turf. Bill Fach, superintendent at Rosedale GC, suggests cutting the sod on which the fertilizer has spilled, and shaking it out, so that all the fertilizer pellets are removed. Replace the sod, and water heavily. Using a vacuum cleaner to remove the spilled fertilizer is also a good idea.

SOIL SAMPLING

When starting a new job as a superintendent, one is well-advised to take a soil inventory. It is almost impossible to make nutritional decisions without at least knowing what is already present in the root zone. A private soils laboratory or a government agency will specify how samples should be taken, and their resulting report should be the basis for a fertilizer program. The laboratories tend to stress the importance of pH and, indeed, a range of between 6.5 and 7.0 is probably best for optimum growth. The authors have grown excellent golf turf at a pH as low as 4.5 and as high 8.1. Grass adapts quickly to a variety of circumstances and rarely is the pH the most critical one.

There are many soil testing kits on the market that allow a superintendent to determine the nutritional requirements of the grass. Testing the nutritional content of the leaf tissue is yet another means of finding out what the grass plant needs for sustenance. To have a small laboratory in the maintenance building is an envious possession which will help enhance the superintendent's professional image. Is it really necessary? Certainly not, if time spent in the lab is at the expense of more pertinent chores such as managing the crew and making sure that the work gets done.

Knowledgable superintendents can tell at a glance when turf needs feeding. They recognize when color is fading and when tillering is slowing. They know when turf will respond and what materials are needed. Such knowledge comes from experience and is the result of many seasons of long days spent on the course. Combine this experience with modern technology, and the result is invariably consistently superior conditions.

FERTILIZER PROGRAMS

A plan to feed the grass must be in place at the start of the season. Such a plan should be carefully prepared and be based on soil testing. The plan should specify the number of applications, the timing, the amounts and the kinds of fertilizer to be used. Based on the plan, the materials can be purchased all at once or when needed. The superintendent should preferably be familiar with the products that are to be used. Just like workers get to know new machinery, so the superintendent should become acquainted with the various fertilizers. This can be done through testing in the nursery or in the rough. Never, ever, take a new unknown material to the first, the second, or any one of the 18 greens without first knowing how it works. We sadly remember applying a coarse grade of organic fertilizer, supposedly idiot-proof, to the greens in the morning. Participants in an important tournament that after-noon had their putting ruined by this mistake and the Super's name was mud for many months thereafter. A new fertilizer should be checked and tried, just like a new machine.

At both of our courses, the fertilizer program starts in the fall with the most important application of all: a heavy dose of an organic fertilizer on dormant or semidormant turf. This virtually assures us good greens in the spring. In addition, it will not be necessary to spend precious time in April and May applying fertilizer to tees and greens when there are so many other chores that need to be taken care of. In June we follow with a mixed fertilizer, and then in July and August we switch back to the reliable organic that is guaranteed not to burn our precious greens during the heat of summer. We also probably save one fungicide application by applying the organic during the summer. During the latter part of August or early September we like to apply some potash, either as sulfate of potash or as a mix with a high third number. One more mixed application in late September or early October provides healthy greens throughout the fall. The cycle is repeated in November.

The total amount of actual nitrogen that is applied to our old established greens by means of this program does not exceed 5 lb per 1,000 sq ft. We believe that the tees take a much bigger beating than the greens, and as a result we tend to apply slightly more materials to the tees. If the tees are large and spacious, this may not be neces-sary. In fact, overfertilizing large tees could lead to thatch development.

New golf courses and new construction areas on existing golf courses require more fertilizer than is applied to established turf. New turf needs to build up a body mass and a root system, and in order to do this it needs to be fed intensively, almost excessively. Some superintendents have become experts at growing in new golf courses and they are aware that large quantities of special formulations must be applied to result in a thick stand of turf.

CONCLUSIONS

Turfgrass nutrition is a complex subject that requires a thorough understanding of soil chemistry and the materials available to feed the grass plant. Most superinten-dents are now college graduates from either two- or four-year programs. In both cases they are well prepared to understand fertilizers and their optimum regimen of application. Why, then, are so many ready and willing to abdicate their responsibil-ity to the first fertilizer salesman who comes calling? We suspect because it is easier to have some other person do the thinking.

Superintendents ought to take their responsibilities seriously and formulate their own programs. They are best qualified, and they owe their employer a degree of frugality that will result in the best program at the most economical price.

Topdressing

No other practice but topdressing has such an immediate and positive impact on the health of grass. Whether one topdresses with straight sand or with a mixture of sand, soil, and peat, the grass responds almost at once. As the topdressing particles filter down between the grass blades, the plants get a welcome reprieve from the pounding feet of golfers and the shearing action of the mowers. The tiny blades of grass breathe a sigh of relief, almost audibly.

Topdressing that is watered in increases the vigor of the turf and makes the grass look healthier. When such a sward is cut with a sharp mower, it looks smooth and putts to perfection. In fact, it is impossible to create a perfect putting surface without the benefit of timely topdressings. The purpose of topdressing is not only to restore health to weak turf, but also to smooth the surface, by filling in pitch marks and other scars and blemishes.

WHAT KIND OF MATERIAL?

Old-time greenkeepers used compost for a long time and many, especially in Great Britain, still do. Compost has an extra benefit: it is rich in humus and thus becomes a natural fertilizer. The practice may have had its origin in Holland, where farmers dressed their meadows with the dredgings of the canals. That slushy, foul-smelling material sure made the grass grow.

For putting greens, the topdressing material needs to be fine, so that it will sink in between the grass blades and not be an obstacle to putting. That is why compost is often screened prior to application. The coarser particles are removed and the remainder is suitable to work into grass of a putting green. Topdressing with straight manure is not a good idea because the material is so difficult to work into the turf. There is another drawback: the rich organic content of manure needs nitrogen to help break it down. This nitrogen is extracted from the soil but at the expense of the grass plants. As a result the grass will often look yellow and sick after a dressing with manure. Superintendents who applied manure as a dressing in late fall, before freeze-

Figure 8.1. The benefits of topdressing are manyfold!

up, have mostly given up on the practice because it had little value as a preventative measure for winter injury. On the contrary, a heavier than usual application of topdressing as part of a winter injury preventative program has proven to be very effective.

A heavy topdressing is a relative term: how heavy is too much? Smothering the grass in November or December will kill it even quicker than the ravages of winter. After a heavy topdressing, the grass blades should still be clearly visible so that the growth processes can continue and the plants will not suffocate.

The choice of material on newly established golf courses is easy: always use the same material that was used in the original construction of the greens or tees. Superintendents rightly fear the buildup of layers of differing topdressing materials in the soil profile. Successive regimes of different superintendents who all had their favorite mixture can be documented by analyzing the core sample of a green. Layers of different materials are detrimental to both root growth and water movement in the soil.

SAND VERSUS SOIL MIXES

Straight sand as a topdressing material has found favor with many turfgrass managers. There are some obvious advantages:

**Figure 8.2. When labor is plentiful, topdressing may become
a more intensive process (Durban, South Africa).**

1. Washed sand is clean and easy to apply.
2. Golfers can even–putt over a light application.
3. Sand can quickly be worked into the existing turf.
4. Sand smoothes the putting surface very well.
5. Watering sand in is a cinch! It washes down after only one or two turns of the sprinkler.
6. As a result, there is very little interruption to play when using straight sand as a topdressing.

Why, then, does sand topdressing have so many detractors? Repeated dressings of straight sand will build up as a layer on top of the greens profile. Since topdressing with sand is so easy and quick, superintendents tend to do it more often and as result the layer can become as thick as an inch or two, after only a few years. The layer of pure sand then plays havoc in the root zone. The grass roots have difficulty growing through it, and the sand impedes the vertical movement of water through the soil.

Greens topdressed with sand for any length of time frequently develop localized dry spots: small areas from a few inches to a foot or more, where the water won't penetrate and the grass can't survive. Sand topdressings may or may not be the direct cause of the localized dry spots, but continuous dressings of sand will certainly aggravate the situation.

There is another reason why superintendents do not like sand. By its very nature, sand is an abrasive material that easily damages the grass blades, especially when a heavy steel mat is dragged over a sand-covered green. If such a green was under

**Figure 8.3. Dragging a steel mat or a brush attachment is
ideal to work the sand topdressing into the turf.**

stress to start with, the combination of the sand, the steel mat, and the dragging action will be the death knell. We have seen it happen time and again and although the sand topdressing was not the cause of the dead grass, superintendents will steer away from the material and use something much safer, such as an old-fashioned sand and loam mix.

Mixing topdressing material was an art of greenkeeping, acquired through experience under the supervision of a professional. Various proportions of sand, soil, and peat were mixed and shoveled through a shredder or over a screen. The old-time greenkeeper would occasionally take a handful of the material and finger it lovingly in the palm of his hand and then squeeze it. If the ball of earth formed in his hand crumbled easily, he was satisfied and the magic mix was approved for application. During the mixing process many different materials could be added, such as various kinds of manure, bonemeal, and other fertilizers. Many guarded the secrets of their mixes carefully, unwilling to share this hard-earned knowledge with their colleagues.

With time, the mixing process became more sophisticated. Loaders and high capacity shredders were used instead of hand shoveling the material up a slanted screen. Now it is possible to purchase formulated blends from companies that specialize in topsoil and sands. A physical as well as a chemical analysis can be provided on which to base the selection of the topdressing material.

Topdressing with a mixture that contains at least some organic component gives one a sense of security. Sand by itself is a sterile, lifeless entity that does not look and feel like the kind of soil that grass plants will grow in. They undoubtedly do, but for how long and with how many unsavory side effects? Now, take a handful of topdressing that contains humus mixed with soil and sand, and like the old-time greenkeeper, one can feel the life that exists in this small sample of soil. It even smells like life! Grass plants will surely flourish on such a mix.

METHODS OF APPLICATION

For a long time topdressing was spread by shovel onto putting greens. It had to be done carefully to avoid lumping. Workmen used square-mouthed, aluminum or light-weight shovels that made it possible to take a sizeable amount from the back of a truck or from a wheelbarrow. With a long sweeping motion, an experienced worker could spread the dressing to perfection. It would feather out as it left the shovel and never leave lumps. This method was difficult to learn and very time-consuming. Modern topdressing machinery quickly replaced the old-time greenkeeper and his shovel. The topdressing was applied at an even thickness and uniformly over the entire green. The new machines resembled a small version farm manure spreader and were equipped with a rotating brush, the bristles of which propelled the top-dressing particles into the turf.

An offshoot of the fertilizer spreader involves a cone-shaped hopper with an oscil-lating applicator that propels the topdressing material onto the putting surface. This model makes it possible to apply sand as a very thin layer to an entire green in a matter of minutes. Topdressing all the greens on an 18-hole course could be com-pleted in just a few hours. Cutting the greens prior to topdressing is a good idea, since it means applying the sand or the topdressing material to a dry green, which in turn speeds up the drying process and reduces the inconvenience to golfers. Instead of cutting, consider whipping the greens to remove the dew or syringing the dew into the green.

How much is too much? Anything more than one-eighth of an inch (three millime-ters) can smother the grass. Most knowledgeable superintendents apply less. It is usu-ally best to apply small quantities more often rather than a large amount all at once.

Grain on greens can be controlled with repeated topdressings and brushing, but, if the control of grain is the primary purpose of topdressing, it is better to verticut first in several directions prior to topdressing. Topdressing to some degree controls thatch, but it is a fallacy to believe that one can bury thatch with heavy topdressings. More drastic action is required that will be dealt with in a later chapter.

Once applied, the sand is left to dry and then brushed into the turf with either a steel mat or a series of brushes. In both cases, a golf cart is used to drag the mat or the brushes. Since there is a tendency for the brushes to bounce, the topdressing mate-rial may form waves or ripples and result in an undesirable unevenness. Dragging a steel mat prevents this from happening, but at times the jagged edges of the steel mat may separate and tear the turf, which is unsightly and objectionable.

The topdressing material should be watered in either immediately after it has been applied, or during the nightly irrigation cycle. The final step in the process is to cut the green, preferably by using an old mower. Using a mower with smooth or solid rollers is preferred, since the Wiele rollers or the groomers on the regular equip-ment have a tendency to kick up the topdressing particles and make a messy surface, instead of pressing the particles down into the turf.

Figure 8.4. Applying sand topdressing.

Invariably the reels on the mower are dulled after cutting a topdressed green. The sand, particularly, rounds the edges on the mower blades and the bed knife. Mechanics complain bitterly about the damage being done to "their equipment," which is a small price to pay for all the positive benefits that are derived from a healthy topdressing application. As always when making decisions and planning operations, there are many reasons why a job should not be done such as:

- The golfers will complain.
- It is either too wet or too dry.
- It is too hot or too cold.
- It is too close to the weekend.
- There is not enough staff and there is too much other work.

Single-minded superintendents will weigh all factors and move ahead anyway. The bunkers will not remember having missed a raking and the rough will not miss a day's cutting. An application of topdressing will benefit all the greens and ultimately improve the putting for all golfers. Remember the prior need for a perfect green in the scheme of the overall maintenance program.

There is no need to topdress entire greens all the time. Parts of all greens are more heavily used and require extra attention. Fastidious greenkeepers will recognize this and isolate such areas and treat them separately. In such instances it is often best to omit the high-tech equipment and revert back to the methods of yesteryear and swing a square-mouthed shovel loaded with topdressing. Then take a Levelawn and rub the material in.

TOPDRESSING TEES

The need for topdressing tees can be even more pressing than for greens. Tees take a terrible beating from golfers who often use several practice swings of their woods and irons before actually hitting the ball. Tees on par-3 holes quickly become scarred with divot holes, and unless such tees are repaired regularly, they suffer permanent damage. Since tees tend to be cut somewhat higher than greens, thatch and grain also develop more readily. Regular topdressing of tees is a must for those two reasons: to repair the divot scars and prevent the buildup of thatch.

Topdressing tees should always be preceded by seeding with one's favorite grass species or variety. Do not miss such glorious opportunities to apply seed just prior to it being covered with a thin layer of soil. Such seed has a much better chance of germinating and growing into healthy plants than when applied alone. The rate of seeding should be at least 1 lb per thousand square feet, and a higher rate would not be wasteful.

There is a case for using less sand and more topsoil in the mix when topdressing tees. Seed establishment in an all-sand medium is much more difficult than in a mix that contains topsoil and organic matter. The sand dries out very quickly during the heat of the day, even when watered nightly. Seed in an all-sand dressing will germinate, but wither and die once the sand dries.

Care must be taken when topdressing tees to preserve the flat surface that golfers value highly on tees. There is a tendency, particularly on long skinny tees, to topdress only the center, where most of the damage is. This is a costly mistake, since repeated topdressings in this manner result in the tee becoming rounded. We have seen this time and again, and many tees that were built perfectly at one time have lost their shape from careless topdressings. A flat footing on such tees is difficult to find and golfers suffer as a result of inferior greenkeeping skills on the part of the superintendent.

Whereas topdressing greens must be done in advance of the golfers and the material worked in prior to putting, the timing of topdressing tees is not nearly as critical. It can be done while regular play carries on, between groups of players, as long as there is a space between the markers that has been cleaned. Topdressing tees can be scheduled in the afternoon for that reason. There is another advantage: the topdressing material dries up much quicker and can be worked in almost immediately after application.

TOPDRESSING FAIRWAYS

Applying topdressing to all the fairways of an 18-hole golf course is a giant undertaking. Modern machinery has made the job a whole lot easier, but the quantities of material involved are huge, since it may take more than one tandem load to complete just one fairway. That is why few superintendents regularly topdress fairways. There is a case for dressing parts of fairways, such as the landing areas that may be badly divot scarred. Superintendents should identify those areas on their fairways that need special attention and these should be slated for timely dressings with sand or soil mixes. Since fairways are usually established on native soils, adding sand does not lead to the establishment of localized dry spots that are prevalent on greens. We have not experienced hydrophobic conditions on fairways and do not object to straight sand applications for that reason. The positive smoothing effect of the topdressing outweighs the questionable disadvantage of using sand. Such decisions are based on judgment acquired after much practical experience.

Recent innovations in topdressing machinery have made it possible to apply minuscule amounts of material to fairways. One manufacturer claims that his machine can literally "dust" the fairways with a light coat of topdressing. Such applications have the same rejuvenating effect on the grass as regular dressings do on greens and tees. If fairways are rough due to improper grading, topdressing using modern machinery may well be the answer to level out the hills and valleys, but it will take repeated applications.

Home owners who shovel large quantities of black muck onto their lawns, in a misguided effort to imitate the practice that they see performed on golf courses, all too often end up with disastrous results. The attractive-looking material is of poor consistency and difficult to spread manually. As a result, it is applied in streaks and the turf is frequently smothered. In addition, the highly organic muck needs lots of nitrogen to break down, which is extracted from the soil at the expense of the grass. The grass blade must be able to breathe at all times and should not entirely be covered with topdressing material.

TOPDRESSING SOD

Rarely is a sodding job so perfect that it does not require some topdressing to fill in the cracks and possibly even some footprints. Some superintendents prefer to wait until the sod has taken root; others apply topdressing immediately after the laying and rolling of sod. Topdressing sod is always limited to small areas on the short-cut turf of tees, greens, and fairways. A steel drag mat cannot be used to work in the topdressing. It would tear up the edges of the sod. Instead it must be done with a Levelawn or the back of an aluminum rake; any rake for that matter. Watering the sod will wash the topdressing material still further into the cracks where it is most needed.

DIVOTING

In addition to regular topdressing applications to tees, there is often a need to fill divot scars on tees with what is known as "divot mix." This marvelous concoction of several different ingredients is the essence of growth and regeneration. A perfect divot mix contains at least several of the following ingredients:

SAND + SOIL + HUMUS + SEED + FERTILIZER = DIVOT MIX

The sand can be either topdressing sand, bunker sand, or even beach sand. A regular loamy topsoil will do just fine, but for good measure many superintendents

Figure 8.5. Mixing divot ingredients to suit the need for individual requirements.

add an organic component. For seed, use whatever species or variety that is presently growing on the tees. The seed can be pregerminated or primed, as is now often the case. For fertilizer, use floor sweepings or broken bags of fertilizer. Both are ideal for divot mix. Although many superintendents manufacture their own special brand of divot mix, in large metropolitan areas the material can be purchased in bulk. Of course the seed always needs to be added at the last. Colored sand as an ingredient of the divot mix is a recent invention. The effort on the part of the superintendent to make the divot mix blend in with the surrounding grass is much appreciated by most golfers. Others find the artificial color unnatural and objectionable.

On the par-3 tees, golfers like to see divot mix stored in containers and available for the players who take pride in their course and wish to take part in its preservation. Golfers will often question the presence of seed in divot mix, simply because they cannot see it with the naked eye in the case of bent grass seed. On the other hand, rye grass seed in the divot mixes on southern courses during the winter months is plainly visible. When the snowbirds return in the spring, they question the superintendent and wonder if seed has indeed been added. Such people of little faith!

Divots on fairways, especially in the landing areas, can similarly be prepared, mostly by the greens staff but often with some help from the golfers. Divot mix is also made available for containers that are attached to power carts; all of this in an effort to help keep the golf course pristine. On several courses in Australia we observed golfers attaching a pouch filled with divot mix to their trolleys. They filled their divots as they played and frequently repaired other peoples' divots as well.

Figure 8.6. Divoting is tedious and time-consuming work, but the benefits result in better teeing areas. (Top photo, in the Bahamas; Bottom photo, at the Board of Trade.)

Divoting has become a regular maintenance operation that is usually scheduled for the afternoon, except for the tees, where the person who changes the blocks also fills the divot scars and checks the supply in the divot boxes.

SUMMARY

Topdressing grassed playing areas is an important part of turfgrass management. Topdressing revitalizes and smooths grassed surfaces, particularly putting greens. A perfect putting green cannot be maintained without timely topdressings. Equally, too much topdressing material applied at one time can be detrimental to the health of grass.

Aerating

INTRODUCTION

The cause of compaction and the need for aeration is demonstrated every time a footpath becomes established through repeated use. It happens at a college campus when students find the shortest way from one building to the next. It also happens on the front lawn of most peoples' homes when the mailman takes the same route, day after day, to the next house. In both instances the soil is compacted, the roots can no longer breathe, and the grass blades wither and die. Repeated foot or vehicular traffic compresses the soil, closes up the pore spaces, and forms a crust that shuts off the movement of water and air. No plant life will survive under those conditions, but long before it happens, superintendents recognize the symptoms and take remedial action: they bring out the aerifier, that hateful machine universally despised by golfers all over the world. Why should a practice that is so beneficial for the grass be so thoroughly disliked by golfers? That is a question that needs to be understood before aeration of any kind is attempted.

AERATING GREENS

We learned the fundamentals of aeration at the back of a Westpoint GL 5, which was a bear of a machine, so cumbersome in fact that it would often lift the operator right off his feet when making a turn. The spring-loaded tines left gaping holes in the green surface, but a core was extracted just the same and compaction was relieved to some degree. The GL 5 was invented by Tom Mascoro shortly after World War II and it was seen as a great step forward, because it replaced the fork as an aerating device. For a long time it was the only available aerating machine. At present there is a wide choice of aerators on the market. All have their distinct advantages that make it possible to aerate in different ways to meet the specific needs of almost every superintendent.

**Figure 9.1. Once the dense concentration of roots in the aerator
holes has been demonstrated, the need for aerifying
will never again be questioned.**

When greens become compacted, the beneficial grasses such as bent are the first
to give up the ghost and make way for *Poa annua*. Take a look at the popular cupping
areas on most greens; chances are that they are infested with *Poa annua*. Compaction can be felt through the soles of one's feet, especially when wearing sneakers. An
experienced superintendent does not need to consult a compaction meter, a device
that will measure the hardness of the soil. Instead, the expert will walk across the
green, frequently with closed eyes as if in a seance, and feel the need for aeration.
There is a difference between a dry green being firm and a moist green being hard.
The first condition is desirable, both for golf and for the plants. The latter may hold
a ball, but the bent grass will be replaced by *Poa annua* which will die, if not during
the heat of summer, then probably under the ice of winter.

Not all greens are equal, and some need aerating more often than others. Small
greens become compacted quicker than large greens for obvious reasons. Whereas
average greens may need only one aeration annually; small greens may need to be
treated two or three times; and large, sprawling greens can be omitted from the
aeration program altogether at times. As with topdressing, there is no need to aerate
the entire green all the time. Seek out the popular cupping areas and reserve special
treatment for those portions of the green. Every possible measure must be taken to
prevent the encroachment of *Poa annua* and none is more important and effective
than timely aerations. This bears repeating: the only turf that will grow on a compacted soil is *Poa annua*. In fact, when *Poa annua* rears its ugly head, the most likely
cause is a compacted soil.

Figure 9.2. Aerating a green may be started along the perimeter, but eventually the circles become too small for turning and then the aerator needs to go back and forth.

Timing of Aeration

A thorough greens aeration is scheduled once during the season and a time is chosen that inconveniences the least number of golfers and is still optimal from an agronomic viewpoint. In Chicago, Michael has chosen the first week after the Labor Day weekend. The plants are still actively growing then and they recover quickly from the inflicted injury. The golfers at Inverness are given plenty of warning and many stay away during that time. In Toronto, Gordon has picked the first week of August as the time that will least inconvenience the majority of his golfers. Although it can be quite warm in August, the nights are already getting cooler and the turf can withstand the pounding of the aerator. The Board of Trade golfers are warned about aeration week via newsletters, bulletin boards, and even the club directory contains mention of the pending aeration. Yet, at both courses in Chicago and Toronto, some golfers still seem surprised and annoyed when they come to play golf and the greens are aerated. It is critical that the superintendent warn the golfers of the pending disruption in plenty of time so that there will be no surprises.

Aerating a green is like major surgery to the grass plants that make up the turf. It is a shock to its metabolic system since the grass is often torn loose from its roots. At times there will be a setback instead of an expected improvement to the turf. This happens especially when the turf was weak to start with. As a rule, therefore, it is best to aerate a green when the turf is strong and healthy. The aeration then is a measure to ensure its survival when stressful times arrive. Aerating a sick green of weak anaemic turf is only attempted as a last resort, when the cause of the trouble has definitely been established as compaction. Aeration should never be a cure-all for all manner of mishaps and maladies that befall grass during the course of a growing season.

To aerate late in the fall, just before freeze-up, is a mistake. Some superintendents have tried this in the mistaken belief that opening up the soil and leaving the cores on the surface is an excellent means of winter injury prevention. Such is not the case! The open holes will suffer from desiccation along the periphery, and the cores make an unholy mess on the putting surface that is difficult to clean up in the spring and has no benefits whatsoever.

Nature's way of aerating the soil occurs during the winter season on northern golf courses. The freezing and thawing of the soil profile loosens tight soils and makes room for air and oxygen to pass through the pore spaces once again. For that reason, aerating in the spring is rarely necessary, but sometimes aeration in the springtime can be beneficial, especially when winter injury has thinned the sward. In that case the cultivating action of the aerator tines stimulate growth by opening the crust. Applying seed and some fertilizer at this time further promotes growth. Superintendents should determine which greens need to be aerated, and how often, at the beginning of the season and schedule this operation as part of the overall maintenance program.

Hollow Tine Coring and Tine Sizing

The purpose of most methods of aeration is to extract a core of soil from the green. The core may vary in size from 1" diameter to 1/4" minitines, and in length and depth from half an inch to almost a foot. It all depends on what is required and what needs to be accomplished. For overseeding and minimum disruption, use the minitines. For serious hardpan and drainage problems it may be best to use the largest size tines of the vertidrain machine. In between lie the most common aerating applications: relieving compaction in the top half-inch of the soil profile. For that purpose, tine selection is usually half an inch, and spacings are at two-inch centers.

If the soil in the green that is being aerated is desirable, the cores should be pulverized by verticutting, and worked into the green as a topdressing. If the soil is less than desirable, the cores should be removed and hauled away. In both cases the aerator holes need to be refilled, preferably right to the top of the holes, although that may be difficult and nearly impossible. Several subsequent topdressings, combined with brushing and matting, will fill the hole and restore the putting surface to

Figure 9.3. (Top) PTO-driven aerators can be used on greens, provided the tractor is equipped with turf tires and the green is firm. The eyes of both the operator and the supervisor are on the aerator, showing concern for the fragile turf. (Bottom) An alternative: The vertidrain punches 10-inch deep holes to improve the soil profile.

Figure 9.4. Seed germinates quickly in the beneficial environment of the aerator holes. Tufts of grass will show in just a few weeks.

its former condition. Golfers have cause for annoyance when the aerating practices are not completed properly and putting becomes erratic.

Case History

A worn area on a green infested with *Poa annua*, measuring approximately 500 sq ft, has become a source of aggravation for the superintendent, and spoils the otherwise perfect appearance of the green. The area should be aerated with minitines at one-inch square spacings to a depth not exceeding one inch. The tiny cores of soil and vegetative material are brought to surface and left to dry for just a short while. Meanwhile, bring out a drop seeder and apply about 1 pound of one's favorite bent grass seed. Since the seed falls vertically, many of the seeds will fall into the tiny holes. Some will fall all the way to the bottom; others will get caught up in the wall of the hole. Now take our favorite greenkeeping tool, the Levelawn, and rub the cores, pulverizing every last one. The core mass will quickly disappear and be converted into topdressing. Some of the ground-up earth will find its way into the aerator holes where it becomes part of the growing medium. Complete the operation by cleaning the treated area by cutting with a greens mower. Keep the cup away from the aerated area for at least a week, until it has recovered.

Meanwhile down below, in its tiny compartment, the seed has been exposed to moisture, heat, and light and in just a few days the magical germination process has taken place. The seed has burst from its shell and sent a root down and grass blades upward. Since all of this takes place in its very own growth chamber, none of the

physiological processes are impeded by foot or mower traffic. The grass quickly becomes established as a small tuft and becomes part of the greensward. How do we
know this? Because we have seen it happen, by getting down on our hands and
knees, and with the help of a magnifying lens, watching the grass take root. We
strongly recommend this method as one of the best means of introducing new bent
grass cultivar into an existing turf.

Shatter Core Aeration

Instead of using hollow tines, some superintendents have substituted solid steel
tines. When such tines are forced into a green, they literally shatter the soil profile as
they enter the greens surface. Holes are created as the aerator advances, and these
need to be filled with topdressing. Many believe that repeated use of solid tines creates a hardpan layer just below the surface of the green, a layer that impedes the
movement of both air and water. For that reason, the popularity of this novel practice has never really taken off.

The Hydro Ject

At the beginning of the current decade, the Toro Company introduced the "hydro
ject," a self-propelled machine that spouts streams of pressurized water into the soil
without disturbing the surface. Obviously, the pressurized streams create channels
within the soil profile through which air and water can move. The result is remarkable on compacted greens: there is an immediate relief for the struggling grass plants,
which are magically provided the necessities of life. It was thought at first that the
hydro ject would replace core aeration, since it apparently had all the benefits of
regular core aeration without the disruptive surface agitation. Although many superintendents use the hydro ject regularly and have made it part of their aeration
program, it has not replaced standard core aeration.

The Vertidrain

The Dutch invented the vertidrain and used it for sports fields at first, to improve
vertical water movement through the soil. The humongous tines penetrate between
10 and 12 inches into the soil, rock back and forth at their greatest depth, and literally shake up the surrounding soil. The Dutch soon discovered that their new machine was ideally suited to break up the layers of compacted soil on the push-up
greens in The Netherlands. The merits of the PTO-mounted behemoth were quickly
recognized elsewhere in the developed world, and the machine is now being manufactured and copied in North America. It can be modified with several different tine
sizes and spacings. Many superintendents now use the vertidrain on fairways and in
the roughs as well as the greens.

Recently Floyd MacKay developed a novel contraption consisting of a series of
drills mounted on a metal frame, that can be raised and lowered. The drills, working

in unison, bore holes into the green or tee and extract material as they penetrate. Once the desired depth has been reached, which may be several inches to a foot, the hole is refilled with sand or another suitable material. This unique method of aeration is finding favor with superintendents who want to drastically modify and improve the growing medium on greens. It may appear to be a cumbersome method but it is quite effective.

AERATING TEES

We already know how quickly tees can become scarred during the playing season. No matter how often the markers are changed, the turf on tees takes a terrific beating, especially if the tees are of insufficient size. A regular aeration program for tees is a must. Once a season is rarely enough. Aeration of tees should be a preventative measure. By the time a smallish tee becomes completely worn out, aeration will not restore its cover; sodding will be the only alternative. Before that happens, aerate and reseed.

The wear patterns on tees become established very quickly and it is these worn areas that need special attention. Once superintendents began to understand that only small portions of the tees need to be aerated, the task to tackle the tees becomes much more manageable, and can often be done in a very short time.

It is important on tees not to go overboard on the tine size. It is best to use half-inch tines or even smaller. If a tee is regularly aerated with large tines, golfers will have difficulty finding solid soil to plant their tees. The larger tines should only be used if the soil needs to be modified, in which case the cores should be removed and the aerator holes filled with desirable topdressing.

CORE DISPOSAL

If cores are raked off tees and greens or harvested with a collecting device, they can be put to good use on most golf courses. Adding the cores to the compost pile is a marvelous idea. The core in most cases is a combination of some form of topsoil and organic matter. It is an ideal ingredient to mix with fallen leaves and other debris.

When the grass portion of the core is desirable, such as bent grass, the cores can be used to fill in low-lying areas on the fairways. When such areas are raised, they should be firmed and roped off. It will take a week or two for the mixture to grow and form a turf. In the fall, this method of repairing scars and scrapes and low-lying areas is particularly effective because the growing conditions are so much better than in the summer. A word of caution: if the turf portion of the core is *Poa annua*, it is best to just put it in the compost pile, for obvious reasons.

When the soil on an area that is being aerated is acceptable, there is no need to remove the cores. It is much better to pulverize the cores on the spot and use the resulting material as topdressing, thus killing two birds with the same stone. On small areas, the cores can be beaten up and worked into the existing turf with the reliable Levelawn. On larger areas it will be necessary to use other means, such as a verticut mower. Running over an aerated area with a verticut in two different directions is usually all it takes to make the cores go away. Follow this by dragging the steel mat behind a golf cart or a Cushman, and all that remains will be rolls of fluff. The fluff is the vegetative material that once was the roots, the rhizomes, and the grass blades which made up the grass plant. To get rid of the fluff, simply blow it into a heap and haul it away, down the beaten track to the compost pile.

Although a cleanup cut after aerating a tee is not a matter of great urgency, it finishes the job and makes the work look complete. When the tee and the aerated area are subsequently watered, the job is complete and the healthy growing processes can begin and will restore the damaged area to its prior perfect state.

AERATING FAIRWAYS

Fairways encompass a much larger area than both tees and greens, and thus present a bigger problem to the grounds manager. In order not to be discouraged by the magnitude of the undertaking, it is best to tackle the project bit by bit, one fairway at a time! Post the progress on a bulletin board and check off each fairway as it is completed. The process becomes a game, with everyone involved anxious to see the project completed.

Some fortunate superintendents are able to close off nine holes while they aerate the fairways. Others close the entire golf course during aerating week and put all resources to work in order to complete not only the greens, but the tees and fairways as well. The process can be sped up in various ways. Contemporary equipment tends to be speedier than the machinery of just a few years ago. Adding extra units, either by borrowing or renting, will make the operation go faster. Working longer hours without the interference of golfers will also get the work done much quicker. A thorough aeration with closely spaced tines penetrating to a depth of three inches will take longer than using a machine whose tines are spaced at six inch centers and penetrate the soil barely an inch. Choices have to be made based on experience, the availability of equipment, and the degree of perfection that is required.

Once a fairway has been completely aerated, it needs to be cleaned off. The cores can be removed, but usually they are pulverized with a verticutter or a steel drag mat and worked in as a topdressing. The residue can be swept off by a powerful tractor-mounted blower. Cutting the fairway, perhaps with the buckets removed, puts the finishing touches on a job well done.

Successfully completing the aerating operation depends a lot on the weather. It must be dry enough so that the cores don't clog the verticutter heads or bog down the steel mat. A sunny day with a bit of wind, and not too warm, provides the best conditions. A word of advice: don't wait for perfect conditions to start the job. They rarely happen. Rather, anticipate optimum conditions and get on with the job. Make it happen and get the work done.

Once fairways have been aerated, superintendents will note a quick improvement in the water absorption rate during an irrigation cycle. The multitude of aerator holes aids in quickly absorbing the water and transporting it to the roots. The plants show their appreciation by growing more vigorously.

Figure 9.5. Aerating fairways is a time-consuming job. It takes several hours to aerate a par-5 hole. The cleanup process also takes much time.

There are areas in the rough that will also benefit from aeration. Vigilant superintendents recognize such areas quickly during their daily tour of the golf course. They may be concentrated traffic areas near bunkers, caused by power carts. Near greens there are frequently congested spaces between traps and fringes that suffer from too much traffic. In such cases the traffic should be diverted and the compacted area aerated, fertilized, and treated with a wetting agent to restore life and improve playability.

Although aeration is a marvelous rejuvenating process that can be used to great advantage, it is not a cure-all. Sparse turf on fairways, turf under stress, and turf with minuscule root systems will probably be worse off after aeration. The weak turf just will not tolerate the severity of the aerating process and often dies instead of recovering. It is best to leave such areas alone and aerate them when conditions improve.

Another pitfall of aerating occurs when the holes are left open and the grass desiccates along the edges. This may happen during the winter, when aeration was done as the last process before freeze-up (a questionable practice at best), or during the summer when drying winds make the grass wilt.

Aerating cultivates the soil while barely disturbing the surface. As such, it encourages renewed vigor of the root system and accompanying top growth. Aerating does not improve the inherent fertility of the soil. One cannot just keep aerating ad infinitum, expecting continuous plant growth. Somewhere along the line the plant must be fed. Timely fertilizer applications combined with aeration will result in a healthy turf cover.

SUMMARY

When soil becomes compacted it must be aerated. There are no shortcuts or painless remedies. There is a price for postponing the inevitable. It may be summer stress or winter injury. Greens, tees, and fairways must be aerated on a regular basis according to a well-thought-out program. Healthy turf is the result of hard work based on a plan, and that plan always includes aeration.

Spraying

INTRODUCTION

Between eradicating the lowly dandelion and the application of a soil-enhancing microbial solution lies the gamut of all spraying methods; to destroy, to prevent, to cure, and control diseases, pests, and deficiencies. Whatever the activity, whatever the means, a sprayer of some sort is usually involved to achieve the desired results. It is difficult to be a superintendent and not know how to operate a sprayer, be it a backpack sprayer or a tractor-drawn, computer-controlled tank sprayer with a shrouded boom. Not only does one need to know one's medicines in order to be a turf doctor, one needs to know how to apply the medicines effectively and safely. The mist that is dispensed under pressure from a single nozzle contains the particles per million needed to make change. It is little and fine, and it falls gently on the tender leaf of a grass plant or a weed. How can it possibly make a difference? But amazingly, it does. At times the magic solution to achieve the optimum benefit eludes us, and the result is a devastating death through overdose, a horror that every self-respecting superintendent fears but inevitably faces during the course of a career. Equally, a spray may appear to have made no difference at all, and a superintendent may fear having wasted the cost of the application. One never knows for certain unless an area is left untreated as a check plot to compare the results.

Sprayer technology in all its complexities is a fascinating subject that we plan to bypass. Instead we will focus on the common sense approach to the application of pesticides and all other ministrations that promote healthy grass plants.

TESTING THE EQUIPMENT

Every golf course should have in its arsenal several backpack sprayers. They are handy for spot treatments, for applications around the base of trees and ball washer posts and along fence lines where weeds need to be treated or grass eradicated al-

Figure 10.1. Applying a grasskiller around the base of trees is an operation that often leads to mistakes....

together. Such sprayers must be in good state of repair, preferably nearly new, for as the equipment ages, it becomes unreliable. The backpack sprayer should be filled with water and tested on asphalt so that the dispersal pattern can be observed. Novice operators should be taught how to operate the backpack sprayer filled with water in this manner. The importance of learning to open and shut the stream cannot be overemphasized. An ugly trail of dead grass reveals evidence, for many weeks after the mistake, of not doing it properly. When the superintendent is satisfied that the new operator is sufficiently trained, he can be let loose on the links. But a diligent supervisor will continue to check on the new recruits on a timely basis.

Larger spray tanks, either mounted on a Cushman or tractor-drawn, should also be checked out to perfection. Again, with the sprayer filled with water, start up the motor that drives the pump and check the On/Off mechanism to make sure it works smoothly. Clean all filters and check the spray pattern of each individual nozzle, and

Figure 10.2. Which becomes quite visible after just a few days.

Figure 10.3. There was no fear of the harmful effects of pesticides
in the olden days. Applying PMAS by a bare-breasted and
barefoot operator in the mid-'60s.

ascertain the overlap. Then drive the spray rig over a paved area again and make the necessary adjustments until completely satisfied that the equipment is running as it is supposed to.

CALIBRATION

The object of calibrating a sprayer is to calculate the application rate. Once understood, it is a fairly simple procedure. Select a tractor speed that is comfortable: the machinery should run smoothly at a speed that will get the work done in a reasonable time. Not too slow, or it will take forever to treat even one fairway, nor too fast, or the tank will bounce, fittings will loosen, and leaks may occur. The best speed is probably a bit faster than a brisk walk.

If the boom is 20 ft wide, one needs to travel more than 2,000 ft to cover an area of just one acre. That is a bit much to be practical. In fact, it makes more sense to travel a distance of 500 ft four times. Plant two stakes in the rough, exactly 500 ft apart. Fill the sprayer with water to the brim and spray the area between the stakes four times. At completion, measure how much water is needed to refill the sprayer to its former level. If it takes 30 gallons, then we know that the sprayer will apply 30 gallons of liquid to each acre. If the sprayer is equipped with a 300 gallon tank, we also know that we can cover ten acres with one tank filled to the top at the speed that we previously specified.

Modern sprayers are equipped with computer controls that monitor the application rates at varying speeds. A sprayer that ascends an incline will slow down; the computer senses the slowdown, analyzes the information, and translates it into a reduced application rate. Computer-operated sprayers function best when they are programmed with the correct information. The rate of application, the boom width, and the speed of the vehicle must be fed into the controller. A computer-controlled sprayer applies exactly the same amount of liquid to every square foot of turf. Such a spray rig results in much greater accuracy in reaching the targeted pest and in addition, immediate savings are gained through greater efficiency. Computers greatly simplify the calibration process, but basic calculations should not be forgotten by modern-day superintendents.

RULES AND REGULATIONS

Virtually all pesticide applicators are state licensed or work under the direct supervision of someone who is. The licensing process trains applicators to follow the rules. Most of the rules and regulations involve a common sense approach to spraying operations. Since the rules have been written by people who rarely do the actual work, the language is often cumbersome and difficult to understand. We will repeat what we know in layman language:

1. Read the label! Much of it is legalese to protect the manufacturer from liability, but there are tidbits of information that are helpful and useful. The product may have certain exclusions for specific plants or there may

be some allergy information of interest to golfers. In addition to the information on the label of the container, many products are accompanied by a small booklet that can be a treasure source of know-how. It is generally best to read all the instructions the night before, so the work will not be delayed in the morning.

2. Be thoroughly familiar with the product that is being applied. One needs to get to know a new pesticide, a wetting agent, or a biostimulant formulation, much in the same manner as one gets to know a new piece of equipment. Try it on the nursery, on an abandoned fairway, or in the rough. Never, ever, apply a new product on a problem green. Invariably Murphy's Law will kick in and the problem green will get worse instead of improve.

3. Determine the recommended rate of application and consider applying half as much. It has been our experience that often half the recommended rate will work just fine. Frequently pests do not need the full dose in order to be exterminated. Think of the savings that can be realized by this simple expedient. Applying a pesticide that is no longer registered is illegal in most constituencies and may result in serious penalties for the operator.

4. Avoid mixing pesticides to save time and labor. Few would mix a weedkiller with an insecticide, but some would try adding a fungicide to an insecticide. Although some pesticides are compatible in tank mixes, most are not, and it is better to be safe than sorry.

5. By all means add a defoaming agent while the tank is being filled, so that it won't overflow with big gobs of bubbles. Adding a dye such as Blazon is also a good idea. It makes it easy for the spray rig operator to see where the pesticide has been applied and what still needs to be sprayed.

6. When filling the tank, it is best to first fill half the tank with water, then add the medicine while the agitator is running, and finally top off the tank. Empty pesticide containers should be triple-washed and the rinsate returned to the spray tank. The containers should be sliced or crushed before being discarded, although they make excellent buckets for the divot crew.

7. The best time to spray is at the crack of dawn. Wind is usually of little significance at that time, one can see one's tracks in the dew, and there are no golfers around. It is often possible to complete nine holes before anyone tees off. Consider partially filling the tank with water the night before to gain precious time in the morning.

8. There are many devices that leave a mark in the grass to help the operator decide what areas have been done. The simplest is perhaps a small piece of chain that is dragged at the end of the boom over the grass and leaves a tiny trail. There is a need for an electronic device that will help steer the spray rig in such a manner as to provide just the right amount of overlap. In fact, it ought to be possible for sprayers to be operated by remote control.

9. When the job is done and the tank is empty, it is cleanup time. Partially fill the tank with water and spray the rough. Check all nozzles and screens and put the equipment away in such a fashion that it will be ready to go, next time there is an emergency.

**Figure 10.4. A computer-operated boom sprayer applies a
fungicide mixed with a coloring agent.**

10. A written report documenting the spray application is absolutely essential. Such a report is one of the most important pieces of record keeping in the superintendent's journal. The report should include date and time, weather conditions, the name of the medicine, and the applicator and the sprayer settings should also be recorded. The pest that is being treated and the extent of the injury should be described. In fact, the more information included, the more value the document has for future reference.

DECISION TIME: WHEN TO SPRAY AND WHEN TO WAIT

It is an important part of a superintendent's duties to check the golf course in its entirety on a regular basis. Such an inspection includes the tees, fairways, and greens, and during the growing season one must constantly be on the lookout for signs and symptoms of disease. There are at every golf course certain indicator greens that because of location, lack of air movement, or shade invariably are the first places for a disease or a pest to show its presence. It need not be a green, but can be the back of a tee or a low-lying area on a fairway. Established superintendents know from experience where these areas are and they base their decisions of when to spray on what is happening in these indicator areas.

When the first signs of Dollar Spot show in their usual location, and the weather prognosis calls for favorable Dollar Spot conditions, a wise superintendent will apply a fungicide just before a three-day weekend. Similarly, if signs of Pythium are prevalent in a damp swail with a southern exposure, danger bells ring in the Super's head and he is unlikely to leave the premises, especially if hot days and warm nights are also in the forecast.

We are often asked by our assistants what makes us decide when to spray and when to hold off. They have observed that we usually make the right decision and they wonder what secrets we possess that allow us uncannily to call the shots. Our sixth sense that we often rely upon when making difficult decisions has been nurtured by years of experience, is peppered by many past mistakes, and topped by the sauce of success. As we have matured over the years, we often surprise ourselves with how smart we have become, or could it possibly just be luck? And then we remember that we are lucky because we work so hard!

There was a time when some of us sprayed from fence to fence at the first sign of any kind of problem. Those were the trigger-happy days when pesticides were plentiful and inexpensive and there was very little concern about the impact our actions may have had on the land and people that live and play on it. At the same time, there have always been frugal superintendents who use their pesticides sparingly and only as a last resort. They are constantly on the lookout for the first signs of a pending attack, and in the initial stages of a pest infestation they spray only the affected areas. Such superintendents know that healthy turf is far less likely to be infected and therefore they make it their business to grow strong grass that does not get sick very easily. They have noticed that the vigorous turf on their tees, greens, and fairways is rarely infested with weeds and hardly ever needs a herbicidal application. Superintendents who are observant in this manner and practice their grass-growing skills to the highest levels have now been tagged with a bit of New Age jargon. It is called IPM or Integrated Pest Management, and is supposed to assuage the clamoring environmental activists who want us to grow altogether pesticide-free turf. Those of us in the know have practiced IPM in all its complexities since Day One. We were careful spenders and did not want to waste money needlessly. In the process, we protected the environment unwittingly. We do not now mind having IPM thrust upon us by well-meaning public relations experts because it does not infringe on the development of the all-important sixth sense of timing and experience.

For Tim Hiers, Superintendent at Collier's Reserve in Naples, Florida, IPM has become a religion. Tim is so dedicated to conservation and preservation that he talks about it all the time and even his staff, including the secretary, are governed in their actions and their work by the principles of IPM. Except Tim does not call it INTERGRATED PEST MANAGEMENT, but INTEGRATED PLANT MANAGEMENT, and furthermore the word PLANT does not just refer to the grass plant, but to the entire golf course operation, as in a manufacturing plant. Following are some of the practices that Tim Hiers and his management teams adhere to with religious fervor:

- Verticutting increases effectiveness of pesticides by preventing binding with thatch, thus reducing their usage.
- High mowing frequency and sharp reels reduce mechanical damage to turf and thereby, susceptibility to pest damage.
- Cart paths alleviate turf damage by carts. Soil compaction caused by cart traffic results in thin, unhealthy grass.

- Soil testing allows us to apply only what the plant needs.
- Test the spray water for pH. It greatly affects product efficiency.
- Anticipate worst case scenario when applying a pesticide near a water body. Then play it safe!
- Use wildflowers and native vegetation for low maintenance and water requirements.
- Practice wildlife conservation by installing bird houses and leaving dead trees (snags).
- Promote energy-efficient building maintenance including fluorescent lights, thermal windows, and insulated hot water pipes.
- Waste management includes composting and recycling.
- Most importantly, initiate employee training to make staff aware of, understand, and employ the IPM concepts. Then make staff training a regular occurrence.

These are just a few of the rules that Tim Hiers and the greens staff at Collier's Reserve live by. Such dedication is remarkable but by no means uncommon among the rank and file of superintendents.

FATAL MISTAKES

In the process of pesticide applications there have been some horrendous mistakes that have resulted in not just one dead green but several, and at times even all the greens on a golf course have been killed by an overdose, the wrong pesticide, or a lethal combination of pesticides. Not so long ago it was common practice to mix Calo Clor with either sand or Milorganite for snow mold prevention. The rate of Calo Clor varied from 1 ounce per 1,000 square feet to as many as 8 ounces. The higher rate can be quite phytotoxic, but when it is applied to dormant turf (= frozen turf) as in the upper Midwest, it is usually quite safe and very effective. Sand, being inert, does not affect the mix. Milorganite, an organic, likewise does not harm the turf; on the contrary, it is beneficial to the growth process and actually speeds up growth and color in the spring. Now, substitute a urea formaldehyde fertilizer for the organic component and a potentially lethal potion has been created. When it is applied to dormant turf it will almost surely kill the grass. If a heavy rain after application should wash the mixture to a low-lying area, there is double trouble.

Another of our favorite pesticides that provides glorious opportunities to make spectacular mistakes is PMAS, phenyl mercuric acetate. It is one of the original fungicides, at first used almost exclusively on greens and tees. When Dollar Spot became prevalent on fairways it could be controlled with as little as a half an ounce per thousand square feet. But not for long; doses needed to be increased to banish the Dollar Spots, and the control period was shortened. PMAS is fairly safe on bent grass but quite toxic to bluegrasses. The higher the temperatures, the quicker the grass will turn a golden brown. This happens on *Poa annua* green, and it also happens in the intermediate or primary roughs which frequently contain a large amount of both annual and common bluegrass. The burn is particularly pronounced where the sprayer overlaps: brown streaks will decorate the roughs. PMAS is no longer available and has been replaced with more environmentally friendly products, and that may have been a blessing for golf.

Some insecticides such as Diazinon are quite safe to use alone but in conjunction with other chemicals become very phytotoxic. Superintendents who take shortcuts and want to treat for cutworms at the same time as they deal with fungus disease often find themselves in trouble. Turf that is probably under stress already for a variety of reasons should not be exposed to a double whammy mixture of possibly synergistic chemicals. It is much safer to apply these chemicals separately and a few days apart, if at all. In any case, check the hard-to-read and difficult-to-understand label for registered tank mixes and compatibility.

Problem greens and tees located in difficult microclimates are often under stress during the heat of summer. To remedy the situation, turf on such locations at times receives more than its fair share of pesticides, frequently aggravating the situation in the process. When this occurs it is often best to practice total abstinence! The grass population is so sparse that the chemical applications per plant are several times higher than the recommended rate. Stop the spraying, and let the grass recover through natural processes. More chemicals are definitely a bad decision in such situations.

Mysterious diseases often take the blame for dead grass, the most popular culprit being Pythium, a close second is Anthracnose. Research laboratories gladly cooperate and usually have no trouble finding evidence of Pythium organisms in a sample of dead turf sent to them for analysis. This common pest strikes unexpectedly and can kill wads of grass overnight. We find it strange that Pythium will kill grass in straight lines resembling mower patterns or concentric rings, much like faulty sprinkler distribution problems. Pythium used to strike during hot humid weather with the nighttime temperatures staying above 80 degrees Fahrenheit. Low and behold, now there is a cold-weather Pythium to take the blame for mistakes that are made during the shoulder season.

We believe that more grass is killed by mechanical accidents or misapplication than all plant pests and diseases combined. Time and again we have seen examples of maladjusted mowers scalping grass, mowers cutting grass that was under irrigation stress and killing it, or cart traffic on stressed-out turf leaving its marks. In all instances the damage is "pilot error" and could have been prevented if the superintendent had been on the job, directing properly trained staff in the art of greenkeeping.

The late Bill Smart, a popular greenkeeper in the Hudson Valley, advocated the "theory of 100 days" during his working life. The 100-day time frame encompasses the summer months characterized by long, hot and humid days and warm languid nights. Smart knew from experience how difficult this period was for grass survival and he cautioned his colleagues in his newsletter to do nothing drastic during the period of 100 days. Bill Smart harangued his colleagues not to lower the mowers, and to take it easy on the topdressing. Spray at low rates and be ready to syringe, he emphasized. Bill Smart survived many summers with his grass intact and never used feeble excuses to cover up an occasional mistake.

O.J. Noer, a long-time traveling agronomist for the Milwaukee Sewerage Commission pulled no punches, either, when it came to telling superintendents what they needed to know. O.J. maintained that more grass was lost on Sunday afternoon than any other day of the week. The message was implicit: greenkeeping was and is a seven-day-a-week job, and those who leave their courses uncared for while playing on a beach are shirking their responsibilities. Although O.J. Noer has been dead for many years, one occasionally still hears mention of the term "Sunday Afternoon Disease," referring to grass that "mysteriously" died on the Lord's Day. Grass does not take a holiday, nor long weekends off!

EDUCATION

The spectrum of plant diseases caused by fungi or insects is very complex and requires a continuing stream of information from colleges and research centers. Add to that weed infestations and nutritional deficiencies, and it quickly becomes apparent that superintendents, their assistants, and key personnel need to constantly update their knowledge of pesticides and their applications.

The winter season is ideally suited to go back to school to refresh one's knowledge and keep up with the latest. There is so much to learn.

SUMMARY

At the same time that turf grass diseases have become more prevalent, a number of important pesticides have been taken off the market. It is becoming increasingly difficult to control and prevent turfgrass pests with the few remaining medicines still available. Superintendents more than ever need to grow strong healthy grass that can withstand the ravishment of disease. In some parts of the world neither pesticides nor chemical fertilizers are allowed to be applied to golf course turf. It is a frightening thought that such doctrinaire philosophies might become commonplace in North America. We need to be prepared, and old-fashioned greenkeeping methods may very well lead the way.

Flagsticks and Tee Markers

When all the work has been done and the golfers come to play and walk up to the first tee, it is essential that the markers are pointed to the center of the fairway and the flagstick on the green is in just the right place. Nothing annoys the ardent player more than a course that has been set up in a thoughtless manner. Most golfers are fussy that way, and to be careless about their wants and needs is jeopardizing one's status as a professional golf course superintendent. To delegate the course setup to an inexperienced worker is poor management, and shows lack of concern for the needs of the golfers and the integrity of the game. How the game is enjoyed on a daily basis is not only a state of mind of individual golfers, but also how the superintendent and his crew sets up the course.

THE TEE COMPLEX

Most courses have several tees. The forward tees are for the ladies and the senior players. The center tees are for regular play, and the tees farthest back are for championship play. These rear tees are of particular importance since they are being used by low handicap golfers who, because of their golfing prowess, think of themselves as experts. Such players tend to find fault with the slightest imperfection and have no compunction about voicing their displeasure. Since the rear tees receive very little play, they are often small in size. Such tees should be trimmed properly; not only the actual tee deck, but also the surrounds, to an acceptable height, so that the length of the grass does not interfere with the swing of the club, nor is there a chance that the ball will be obstructed and deflected by high growth in front of the tee.

The center tee is the largest, since it receives most of the play. There should be plenty of room to move the tee markers. As a general rule, the tee deck on this most-often used tee should be of size equal to the green. On par 3 holes the center tee should be twice the size of the putting surface.

The forward tee is used mostly by female golfers or senior players. They can be just as demanding as the golfers who play from the championship deck. Accommo-

**Figure 11.1. A T-bar made from PVC pipe is used to line up
tee markers with the center of the fairway.**

dating their wants and needs is an education in itself, and a skill that must be acquired. Persons who set the course up on a regular basis use varying methods to
align the tee markers with the center of the landing area. Most often it is done by
standing between the markers with arms stretched wide, one hand pointed to each
marker. Now, bring the arms forward in a regular uninterrupted motion and, as
the hands meet, the fingers should be pointed to the center of the fairway. Another
method not as widely used involves the use of a T-square made from PVC pipe. It
does not need to be very long; 6 ft is plenty. Place the crossbar between the markers. The stem should be pointing toward the center of the hole. Problems often
arise on dogleg holes. The center of the fairway for long hitters is different than for
shorter drivers. In the case of doglegs, first determine where the pivot point is—
that is the point where the hole changes direction—and line the markers up with
the pivot point. Some players will need a driver to reach the pivot point; for others
it may be a long iron, but the center of the fairway at the pivot point will be the
same in both instances.

The location of the markers on the tee is very important. There is a school of
thought that believes the length of a hole should not vary from day to day. When the
markers are at the front, the flagstick on the green should be on the back. This
method ensures that the overall length of the course is always the same. There are
other means that create greater variation in the length of individual holes, yet the
overall length of the course remains the same. A diligent hole changer will keep
track of the total yardage as he proceeds from one hole to the next. One hole may be
set up a little shorter than indicated on the card and the next will be somewhat

Figure 11.2. A special touch on Ladies Day: potted flowers are used at the Inverness Golf Club near Chicago as tee markers.

longer, but at the end of 18 holes the total yardage will always be as stated on the card. From a greenkeeping point of view, the wear must be spread in the most efficient manner possible so that no areas develop that are void of grass. At times, this means spacing the tee markers across the entire width of the tee. At other times it may be necessary to force golfers to use a corner or a side of the tee in order to give other sections a chance to recover. Unless play is very light, tee markers should be changed daily. At some courses where play exceeds 300 rounds per day, it may be necessary to change the tee markers twice on the same day, except that markers cannot be changed during a golf tournament since the course must play the same for all contestants.

AN UNUSUAL TOUCH

At several golf courses in both the United States and Canada, superintendents have for years been replacing the tee markers with potted plants on Ladies Day. No doubt this special effort on the part of the greens superintendent to please the ladies is much appreciated. At the Inverness Club north of Chicago, Superintendent Mike Bavier has been following this practice for more than 25 years. It all started with four-inch potted geraniums, but both the size of the pots and the plants have steadily increased with the years. Ladies Day at Inverness has become quite a floral display. The ladies like it that way. Yet another example of the efforts superintendents will make to please and charm their golfers.

OTHER FURNITURE

In addition to the tee markers, there are on most tees several other pieces of furniture that are standard items on many golf courses:

1. Benches are for comfort and for golfers to rest on while they are waiting to make their shots. Amazingly, some golfers use benches to climb onto so that they can get a better view of the hole. In the process, the benches are damaged by the metal spikes on golfers' shoes. Benches should be positioned just right: in shade to keep golfers cool while they are resting and out of the way of errant shots from backward tees. Benches should be lightweight so they can easily be moved, but not too light, or someone will take them away or they'll blow over in a hard wind. Benches should be durable because they are out in the open and exposed to wind and rain. They must be cleaned, scrubbed, and repainted from time to time so they'll continue to look attractive. The worst sight on a tee is to see grass growing through the seat of a bench. Keep the grass trimmed around benches and move the benches often, so there is no worn grass where golfers place their feet.

2. Ball washers are an important ingredient of any tee complex. We remember during our first year as a full-fledged golf course superintendent, receiving a call on a Sunday afternoon from an irate golfer reporting that there was no water in the ball washer. At the time, the complaint seemed frivolous: four years of college and a degree in agronomy to fill empty ball washers? Was that what we had studied so hard for all those years? Again and again during our formative years as greenkeepers the lessons were hammered home: ours is a service industry, which means looking after people and all their needs at all times, even Sunday afternoons.

   Ball washers can be a source of irritation to regular golfers. Most often they lack soap and water. At times the mechanism is broken and the brushes worn. Ball washers need to be checked on a regular basis, at least once a week. They should be cleaned thoroughly by removing them from the post or stand, and swished in soap and water. Some superintendents use a portable power washer to remove all the grime. Others add bleach to the cleaning solution as a disinfectant. The bleach certainly helps to reduce the smell that emanates from dirty ball washers. Too much bleach in the water may splash onto a golfer's shirt and pants and cause discoloration, however. After the inside of the ball washer has been cleaned, don't forget to scrub the top with a scouring pad and wipe the sides so that the paint looks fresh.

   Adding soap to the water in ball washers is requested by most golfers. Soap certainly helps to make the golf balls sparkle, but too much soap adds to a buildup of grime and the accompanying foul odor. Try adding a small quantity of wetting agent to the mix, or omit soap altogether. Well-known superintendent Robert Williams at Bob O'Link in Chicago did just that for many years, and kept the ball washers sparkling clean to the satisfaction of his exclusive membership.

Figure 11.3. It is a mark of distinction to have ball washers spotlessly clean (Bob O'Link Golf Club, Chicago).

There is a golf course in Canada that sports no ball washers at all on any of its tees. When we queried Superintendent Ken Wright at the Devil's Paint Brush north of Toronto about the absence of ball washers, he responded by asking us the following question with a devilish smile on his face: "Would you putt with a dirty ball?" The answer is self-evident, and since putting is the last action prior to teeing the ball up again, Wright believed there was no need for ball washers, and has never installed any to this day. All knowledgeable golfers carry a towel to clean their clubs after use. Why not use the same towel to clean the ball before putting?

Ball washers are frequently equipped with brushes at the base for golfers to clean their cleats. Such spike brushes must also be cleaned on a regular basis. Finally, the ball washer must be situated out of the way of play. Topflight players have been known to play errant shots from the championship tees, and if they ricochet from the ball washers, the greenkeeper will be to blame.

3. Permanent markers are made from granite, cement, or some other durable material and are embedded into the tee just a smidgen below the surface so that the mowers won't catch them. Permanent markers are placed precisely at the point from which the hole is measured, usually off to the side of the tee deck but clearly visible. The yardage of the golf hole as well as the number are part of the permanent marker. The permanent marker should be located halfway between the front and the back of the teeing deck, since just as much play should take place from in front of the permanent marker as from behind. If it becomes evident that there is more wear in front of all the permanent markers, it means that the course habitually plays shorter than indicated on the score card. This translates in golfers' handicaps or indexes being out of whack.

4. Trash containers on or near the tee are a must. Golfers are forever unwrapping packages of golf balls, candy bars, and using tissues to clean their noses. All this garbage needs to be put somewhere and unless a receptacle is available it will end up on the grass and despoil the golf course.

   Such containers should, as a rule, be small and unobtrusive so that they do not dominate the landscape around a tee. Occasionally a trash container is needed on a fairway, strategically located where golfers finish the soft drinks and coffees that they purchased at the canteen. Wherever trash cans are placed, they should be emptied on a daily basis, usually by the person who goes around, changing holes and markers.

5. Signs are found on most tees indicating the number of the hole, the par, the handicap, and the length. At times, quite elaborate signs are manufactured, providing a pictorial early marker. Such information is valuable to first-time players and guests. Members who play the same course day after day have less need for such detailed information. In addition to tee signs, many courses exhibit signs reminding golfers to fix divots, ball markers, and to erase the footprints in the sand. While all of this information is important, there is a tendency to clutter tees with so much furniture that the entire complex becomes cluttered and resembles a garage sale in suburbia. It has been our experience that some of fanciest golf tee furniture can be found on the poorest-maintained golf courses. The money spent on multicolored signs, fancy ball washers, and benches could be put to better use buying fertilizer and topsoil to create superior turf.

THE GREEN

Moving the hole on the green contributes greatly to the overall quality of the turf. On a large green this is not nearly so critical because the wear can be spread around so easily, but on a small green, moving the hole and maintaining quality turf is a difficult, and at times an almost impossible assignment. The problem is often exacerbated by undulations in the putting surface that limit the number of hole locations.

Choices have to be made: preserve the prime locations for weekends and the prime days; during the rest of the time golfers must accept difficult and at times "unfair" hole placements. The superintendent will have to learn to grin and bear the wrath of irate golfers for the sake of preserving a quality green. There is no other way.

All the systems that have been invented and instituted to organize a regular movement of hole placements from the front to the center and to the back, work fine on large, sprawling greens. The hole can be placed almost anywhere with impunity as long as the surface nearby is reasonably level and the location is away from the edges and the hazards. The next day the hole can be moved 30–40 ft to a similar location, and so on. Meanwhile the turf does not suffer because it receives plenty of rest between periods of play. On small greens, 5,000 sq ft or less, the moves are more likely to measure 15–20 ft. The hole often needs to be closer to the edge of the green, sometimes within the 15 ft limit. Incidentally, the 15 ft limit is not a Rule of Golf, contrary to what many golfers believe, but a recommendation for greens management that is adhered to by most superintendents on average size greens. On small greens the 15 ft limit does not apply because it is not practical.

As a rule, superintendents will set up the course with six hole placements in the front third of the green, six in the center, and six in the back. There are some deviations from this simple, straightforward method. These involve dividing the putting surface into several sections or quadrants. The sections are numbered to coincide with the days of the week, but in the process there is always a balance between locations at the front, in the center, and at the back. In other words, the overall length of the golf course does not change on the green.

To help golfers determine where the hole is located on the green, several systems have been devised:

a. Colored flags. Blue flags when the hole is at the back, white for the center, and red for the front. This method requires that the hole changer carry along extra flags or flagsticks with flags attached.

b. Pindicator flags are attached to the flagstick and slide freely except that their downward movement is impeded by a tight rubber ring. Golfers have been known to play tricks on their fellow competitors by moving the pindicator flags either up or down, and thereby confusing their opponents. An often-used variation of the flags is a round ball that also slides up and down the flagstick, but its movement is restricted by a cauter key in the pin.

c. The high tech method of lasering the distance to the pin exactly with an electronic device. A receiver is attached to the pin and a beam from the handheld gun measures the distance instantaneously and prints out the exact yardage. This method is precise and quick and takes all the guesswork out of club selection. It is also illegal, since the United States Golf Association has not approved it. It is worth remembering that 150-yard marker trees were also illegal for a long time.

Under the influence of tournament golf, superintendents have been spoiling their customers with "pin sheets" which show the exact location of the flagstick on the green measured in either yards, paces, or feet. Pin sheets are prepared for important

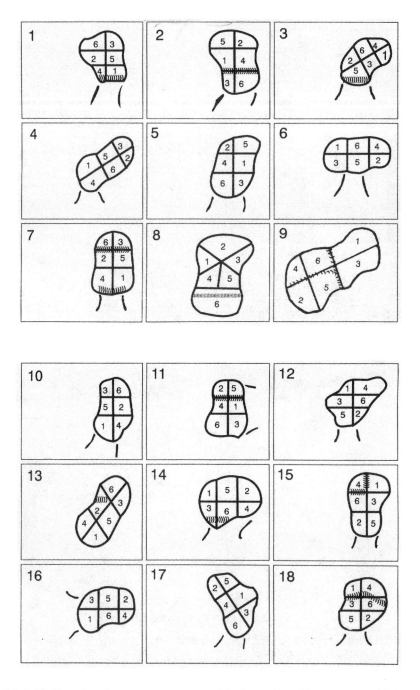

Figure 11.4. Daily pin placements are provided to all golfers as an addition to the scorecards at the Beacon Hall Country Club in Aurora, Ontario.

events such as club championship matches and member guest days. It should be noted that the number of such events is steadily increasing and golfers now desire to be pampered on a regular basis. At some courses the hole locations are made available on a daily basis to all golfers, and frequently displayed on the windshield of power carts.

CUTTING A HOLE PERFECTLY

Nowhere are the skills of a competent golf course worker displayed more prominently than when a fresh hole is cut into the green and the old hole filled and repaired. It is simple, yet so many things can and do go wrong. The hole may be mistakenly cut on a slant, which makes the hole slightly oblong instead of circular. The hole liner itself may be too far below the surface of the green, or worse, too close to the surface. When the lip of the hole liner is less than an inch below the grass surface, golf balls that were destined to drop to the bottom may be deflected and stay out. If it happens to the tee shot on a par 3 hole, it may mean the thrill of an ace spoiled. Replacing the plug in the old hole is often done either too deep or not deep enough. Either instance is objectionable. Following are seven steps that should be strictly followed when changing a hole:

1. The hole cutter should be in a good state of repair. The blade must be super sharp, and in order to keep it that way, it should be filed regularly. If the hole changer has been used on a daily basis for more than five seasons, it is time to pass it on to an unsuspecting neighbor or faraway friend.
2. In addition to the all-important hole changer, there are several other items that are part of the paraphernalia that is carried along. These are:

   a. a cup puller and a cup setter
   b. a sponge to clean the hole liner
   c. a water bottle to water the plugs under stress
   d. a knife or a flat screwdriver.

   All of the above are carried in a five-gallon pail or, better yet, in a "soft bucket," a canvas satchel made by an enterprising superintendent in Thayne, Wyoming (Jett Enterprises). This husband and wife team, besides acting as superintendent and assistant at the local golf club, manufacture soft buckets to make life easier for the fellow supers.
3. Select the place on the green where the new hole is to be. In many instances, this location has been predetermined or its selection is on a scheduled arrangement. In any case, it should always be level within its immediate vicinity. Now, plunge the hole cutter vertically into the green. Twist it down a few inches farther and carefully extract the plug. Remove it from the hole cutter and place it in the soft bucket. Make the next cut with the hole changer to the desirable depth. For inexperienced or novice hole changers, a white mark is often painted on the cutter blade for this purpose.
4. Remove the hole liner from the old hole and use a moist sponge to clean the inside of the cup thoroughly. Place the new clean cup into the new hole and press it down firmly to the desired depth, using the cup setter. Brush away

Figure 11.5. The hole changer carries along all the necessary tools in a handy satchel. Note the impact hole cutter, developed in Sweden, that permits taking the entire plug in one operation, hence the name: HOLE-IN-ONE.

any bits of soil from around the new hole. Super-fastidious greenkeepers will use a pair of scissors to snip off any misplaced blades of grass hanging over the lip of the hole. If the cutter blade was sharp in the first place, this should not be necessary. It is a good practice to keep an extra set of new cups on hand to change the cups at least once during the season. For having clean cups all the time, you'll be a winner with the golfers all the time.

5. Repairing the old hole is now the final step in completing a job well done. The hole must be filled to just the right level: too little earth and the grass plug will sink; too much, and the plug will be scalped by the greens mower. Use a knife or a screwdriver to break the earth between the lower and the upper plug. It helps the roots to find their way downward. The top plug should be broken at the edges so that it fits snugly, pressed down level with the surrounding grass. Squirt some water from the bottle onto the plug, thus

making sure that it will survive the heat of day. Clean up any spilled topsoil, making sure that any evidence of a hole ever having been there is removed.

6. Placing the pindicator flag or ball to the desired level completes the job of changing the cup on the green, but not completely. It is a good idea to check how the pin fits into the hole of the cup. If the fitting is loose, it probably means that either the pin or the cup should be replaced. A loose-fitting pin is easily whipped out by a brisk wind and at times may lean inside the cup in such a way as to prevent golf balls from entering the hole.

7. Finally, when the hole has been changed perfectly, check one more time, from a distance, to make sure that the flagpole is straight on the green.

In addition to changing the hole, the person charged with that responsibility should be aware of additional functions that can be performed in the round of their duties. Small scars to a green can be repaired with a hole cutter by taking healthy plugs from the back edge of the green. Similarly, old plugs that have not taken and have turned brown can be replaced in that manner. The hole changer should repair the most obvious ball marks and be always vigilant for the first signs of disease.

The hole changer, better than anyone else, knows from firsthand experience the need for water on any green. The need for water on the greens or tees should be communicated to the superintendent or the person in charge of irrigation. The hole on the green should be changed after about 250 players have passed through. In most instances, this means a day's play. In fact, changing holes is a daily chore except in the shoulder season, when some days can be skipped. Changing the hole on some greens and not on others is a dangerous practice that leads to inconsistencies. If the edge of the hole has been damaged, it should be changed, regardless of how many people have passed through.

SUMMARY

Golfers come to play with their friends and they value the comradeship of their companions even more than the condition of the golf course. Their games are memorable occasions long remembered afterward. The shape of the course is soon to be forgotten. All the more reason, then, that we should try to make their visits happy ones: May they sink many long putts, and may low scores adorn their cards. Nowhere have superintendents a better opportunity to directly affect the state of mind of their golfers than when changing holes and placing tee markers. Let's make sure to make the most of it.

Drainage

INTRODUCTION

If there were a choice, most would prefer to play their golf on high land rather than low land. High land is equated with dry land: rolling hills from where the water runs into the valleys, rivers, and creeks. Low land invariably means wet land, unless it is drained! There rarely is a choice, and golf course superintendents are mostly presented with the task of making wet land dry. Golf is meant to be played on firm fairways and greens, and on low land this can only be achieved by the installation of a network of tiles, culverts, and catch basins that facilitate the rapid removal of excess water. Good drainage extends the golfing season at either end, and can reduce or eliminate the need for course closures and no-power-cart days.

SURFACE DRAINAGE

When water runs unimpeded from grass-covered land the natural surface drainage is adequate because there is a fall between the high areas and the low areas. A 1% slope (1 ft vertical in 100 ft horizontal) is the minimum for the free movement of surface water. Somewhat steeper grades are more desirable.

Surface drainage often is hindered by faulty construction methods of long ago. Plow furrows may not have been graded adequately. Hollows have not been filled to blend with the surrounding terrain. Low-lying areas invariably result in dead grass. In addition, a bumpy surface is difficult to maintain, let alone to play from. Cutting heights at half an inch and less may cause severe scalping, and golfers expect smooth fairways. Superintendents are expected to take remedial action. Fairways with severe undulations should be regraded. If the turf is of acceptable quality, such as a pure stand of bent grass, it can be lifted, the soil smoothed with a landscaping device, and the sod relaid. On larger areas the process becomes more cumbersome, perhaps involving a golf course architect and an experienced contractor. In either case the

Figure 12.1. The problem: a low area on a green.

end result should be a smooth fairway that permits adequate runoff and is compatible with contemporary conditions.

On greens and tees, settling of the soil may take place many years after construction has been completed. Such low-lying areas must be repaired and the best time is in the fall at the tail end of the golfing season. By that time the daily number of golfers is drastically reduced and so are regular maintenance operations on the greens. The work can be completed in short order, probably in just a day, without much interference to play.

Step 1

Identify the area and mark it with a paint gun. Place a surveyor's level off to the side and take readings to determine the amount of fill required to facilitate perfect surface drainage with adequate fall. Outline the working area, making sure that it is 2–3 times the size of the actual low-lying area.

Step 2

The large working area is needed to make sure that the finish grade blends in well with the rest of the green. Remove the sod very carefully and store it off to the side. Discard sod of poor quality, such as *Poa annua* infested turf.

Figure 12.2. Step 1: shooting levels.

Step 3

Build up the working area with a suitable greens mix similar to the existing mix. This should be a gradual process. A few inches of material at a time is just fine and in order to compact it, workers should be encouraged to dance on the loose material. Rake the surface smoothly and compact it still further with a water-filled roller. Measure the progress by taking readings with the level as the work progresses. Add more top mix if necessary.

Step 4

When the desired level has been attained, apply a starter fertilizer at the recommended rate. Then continue rolling and raking, preferably with a wide aluminum

Figure 12.3. Step 2: cutting the sod.

Figure 12.4. Step 3: raising the grade.

rake, occasionally turning the rake and using the backside with the straight edge. Using a Levelawn is an excellent alternative.

Figure 12.5. Step 4: firming the base.

Step 5

When one is completely satisfied that the desired grade has been achieved, it is time to replace the sod. The greatest care should be taken that the sod is placed just perfectly. It is recommended that the best quality rolls of sod are used for the prime areas in the center of the green. Sod of lesser quality can be used along the fringe of the green. If there is insufficient sod, take some from the nursery or a strip at the back of a green. After sodding, roll in two directions. Check one more time with the surveyor's level to be absolutely sure that water will now run off.

Step 6

The final step involves applying a thick coat of topdressing and working it into the grooves between the sod with a Levelawn or the backside of the aluminum rake. Well-known Chicago superintendent Oscar Miles insists that topdressing be placed in the crack between the sod. This method is much more finicky, but well worth the extra effort when one thinks of creating a perfect putting surface. Water, if necessary, and keep moist but not soggy until the sod is well rooted. For good measure, fence the work area with stakes and rope, and place a GUR (Ground Under Repair) or explanatory sign in the middle. The sod will root before winter sets in and may need additional topdressings. It will probably survive the winter better than the adjacent turf and will be ready for the first cut in the spring. A few weeks later it can be played on.

Figure 12.6. Step 5: rechecking the grades.

Repair work of this nature exemplifies the essence of green-keeping: restoring poor turf to better health and improving the golfing environment. Many important skills are included in the process and unless one is experienced in these skills one should probably not attempt such a repair, certainly not on the 18th green in front of the clubhouse.

NORTHERN PERILS

Superintendents in northern climates should be aware that snow and ice can hinder the normal runoff on golf course turf. When banks of snow freeze and form obstructions in the path of water, the submerged turf will invariably die. This can be prevented by the simple expedient of regularly patrolling the golf course during the winter months and removing any obstructions that exist. Dedicated superintendents

Figure 12.7. Step 6: relaying the sod.

have been known to remove snow and ice from all greens and tees to ensure the survival of the grass. Such attention is to be commended.

SUBSURFACE DRAINAGE

Water that accumulates in the soil and builds up above field capacity must find a way to get away, or the soil and the turf above will stay soggy and sloppy, unfit for golf and golfer-related traffic. The answer lies in drainage and the installation of a complicated system of tile lines and catch basins connected to still-large pipes or culverts that ultimately drain into rivers and lakes. Such an elaborate system resembles an irrigation system in complexity, except that no electric power or fancy controllers are required. If the system is installed in accordance with accepted methods, the force of gravity will make the water find its way, always downhill, to the lowest part of the golf course.

Figure 12.8. Northern superintendents will go to great lengths to ensure survival of the grass, including removal of snow and ice in midwinter (Inverness Golf Club, Palatine, Illinois).

To install a drainage system, it is essential that one becomes thoroughly familiar with the lay of the land. An important step is to identify the areas that repeatedly stay wet the longest, and to mark these on an aerial photograph. All too often an aerial photo becomes a pretty picture on the wall in an office or the clubhouse. That is a waste. Several copies should be available and at least one should be used to record the location of the drainage system. In addition to an aerial photo, a topographical map should also be on hand. The graduated contour lines show the exact course that the natural flow of the surface water will follow.

Plans can now be made as to how the golf course needs to be drained. If it appears that it will be a large-scale project, it is probably best to bring in an outside contractor who has golf course experience. This latter criteria is important and it should be noted that being able to drain a farm field does not qualify one to drain a fairway. Projects of smaller proportion can be done in-house, even if it involves renting a trencher and a level.

DRAINING GREENS

Unless a green is built on top of a gravel pit, a bed of tiles should always be included in the construction of putting greens. Depending on the contours of a green, the tile drainage bed in the base is usually in the form of a herringbone system: one main drain with several laterals arranged to resemble the backbone of a fish. The tiles are imbedded in gravel and the outlet is connected either to existing drains in

Figure 12.9. Step 7: rolling the sod.

the fairway or rough or to a sump off to the side. The tile lines under a green should be 10–15 ft apart. In greens built according to USGA specifications, a "smile drain," or inceptor drain is often added across the front of the green and connected to the main drain. Such a drain promotes water movement in this potentially wet area at the front of the green. This is precisely the area subject to most golfer and equipment traffic, and thus prone to wear and tear. Having the approach well-drained will ensure good turf. A drainage system installed in this matter will function well for years and years without the need for repairs or maintenance.

Unfortunately, not all greens are built with perfect drainage. In fact, on many older greens a tiling system of any kind has been omitted. The result is that superintendents are faced with the problem of either improving the drainage or living with an at-times wet green. Installing tiles into an existing green is tricky, but by no means impossible.

Figure 12.10. Step 8: topdressing the sod.

Figure 12.11. Marking the work area as "Ground Under Repair."

Step 1

Lay out the drainage pattern that best suits the green. Spray paint the lines and remove the sod.

Step 2

Spread heavy duty plywood on either side of the proposed trench and excavate the trench to a depth of approximately 18".

Step 3

Remove the excavated material, clean the trench, and check for the necessary fall with the help of a level.

Step 4

Place a 1–2" layer of pea gravel in the bottom of the trench as a bed for the tile. Install the tile and cover with gravel to 12" below grade.

Step 5

Backfill above the pea gravel with greens-mix soil, and compact with a tamper. Add water to the fill to assist with the settling.

Step 6

Replace the sod and roll it well. Apply topdressing material over the sod and rub with a Levelawn.

Since tiling work of this nature is usually done during the fall, watering the sod is not so critical, except that the sod should not be allowed to dry out. Several topdressings will blend the tile line into the existing green. Only an experienced eye will ever be able to tell the location of the repair. After several months, putts will no longer bounce and the green will dry out nicely after a heavy rain.

There are other methods which involve slit trenching, and are thus less painful, that will improve drainage. Some enterprising superintendents have even used chain saws and filled the groove with sand or kitty litter. All these methods work somewhat, but none are as effective as installing a tile bed.

THE VERTIDRAIN

This unique aerator, invented in The Netherlands, punches holes into the soil to a depth of more than 12" and extracts a one-inch core. At six-inch centers, a tremendous amount of earth is removed from a playing surface. In the case of a green, these holes can be refilled with an approved sand to the top of the putting surface. In the process, whatever layers may have existed in the greens profile will have been punctured in innumerable places and the drainage, at least in the vertical plain, will have improved. The water still needs to be removed from the bottom of the green, and only a tile bed can do that.

DRAINING TEES

Tees, by their very nature, are usually elevated and drain exceptionally well for that reason alone. Elevated tees therefore rarely require tile drainage. Low-lying tees, however, are another matter. It is advisable in such instances to install a main drain with several laterals, also known as a gridiron arrangement, and drain the subsurface water away from the playing surface. Large flat tees, as well as driving range tees, should be treated as greens and drained accordingly.

Tees that are built into side hills often require an interceptor drain: a 12" wide trench, at least 24" deep with a 6" tile in the bottom and completely covered with gravel to the top. Such a drain will intercept the water that seeps from the hillside and prevent it from causing wetness on the tee. Interceptor tiles should also be used behind greens that are built in similar locations, as well as along steep banks that border fairways.

DRAINING BUNKERS

Modern bunkers are frequently flat in the bottom, which makes such bunkers particularly easy to drain. A tiling system similar to that used under greens is installed, and as under the greens, the tiles are covered with pea gravel. It is best to keep the gravel 2 inches below grade, so that it will not mix with the sand and damage golfers' wedges. The outlet of the tile empties into a catch basin, for easy clean-out, and is then connected to the main drain. It is important to remember that bunkers require just as many tiles as greens to guarantee good drainage.

Repairing poor drainage in an existing bunker is best accomplished by removing all the existing sand, shaping the bottom into a desirable form and firmness, and then trenching the lines and installing the tiles. Should one use stockings around the tiles to prevent the sand from entering the system? Our experience has been very negative in this regard. The stockings quickly become clogged themselves and prevent all drainage. Yet we know of other superintendents who swear by the use of stockings and would not install drains without them. Before deciding, it is best to check with a neighboring colleague for an outside opinion.

We feel the same way about filter cloth liners as we do about stockings. The liners are installed in the base of the bunker and tucked into the side under the sod. The purpose is to stop stones from popping up from the base and mixing with the sand. By necessity, the liners have to be covered with more than the usual amount of sand, as much as 5–8", whereas the normal coverage of sand in a bunker is rarely more than 4". Even under a thick cover of sand, the liner will eventually make its way to the surface, which precludes the use of mechanical trap rakes. Such bunkers are then destined to be hand-raked for the rest of their days. Golfers, whose misfortune has brought them a lie in a lined bunker, will not be happy when a ferocious swing of the wedge is abruptly shortened in the web of a bunker liner. It is a painful experience for the wrists and often accompanied by many expletives that make the pure golf course air turn blue. Superintendents beware!

DRAINAGE ON FAIRWAYS AND ROUGHS

Persistent wet areas on fairways and in the roughs need to be drained to make turf healthier and golf more enjoyable. A surveyor's line level is needed to prepare the plan and stake the lines. Use either a gridiron or a herringbone pattern. Employing a trencher equipped with a laser depth measuring device, will ensure that the trench has the necessary fall.

It is always a good idea to place a small amount of gravel in the bottom of the trench. Dragging a narrow trenching shovel across the gravel ensures a smooth bed for the tile. Covering the tile with gravel promotes the movement of water. At times the gravel can be taken right to the level of the sod, further ensuring that the surface water can enter the drainage system unobstructed. For a while the gravel will be visible, and may possibly interfere with play temporarily. Soon the grass on the sides of the trench will grow in and cover the gravel. Do not yield to the temptation to cover the gravel with topsoil; it quickly seals the surface and prevents water from entering the system.

There are some justifiable objections to having pea gravel flush with the surface of the turf. The stones in all likelihood will get caught in the mowers and dull the blades. Golfers often object to loose gravel interfering with the lie of the ball or the swing of the club. We encountered a novel way of coping with the problem at Beacon Hall Golf Club in Ontario. Superintendent Robert Heron covered the gravel with a strip of chicken wire which was tucked in under the sod. The chicken wire stabilized the gravel and minimized interference for both golfers and mowers. For good measure, Heron painted both the gravel and chicken wire green. In due time the surrounding grass will obscure both the gravel and the wire mesh.

When the grass completely covers the tile lines and forms a dense mat, it may become impervious to the movement of water. When, after heavy rains, puddles appear over the tile lines, the thatch layer needs to be punctured. A hole cutter is an ideal tool for such an operation. This tip was passed onto us by Superintendent Bill Fach from the immaculately manicured Rosedale Golf Club in Toronto.

All tiling systems should include plenty of catch basins. The grate on the catch basin provides an opportunity for more surface water to enter the system. Catch basins also permit a visual check on the performance of the tiling system. Long runs of tile, in excess of 200 ft, should be interrupted frequently by a catch basin to act as a clean-out. Large pipes and culverts require bigger catch basins or drains. During or shortly after heavy rains, superintendents should check how the system performs by lifting the grate and observing the flow of the water. The gush of the running water is like special music to the ear of the superintendent. It is a tune that tells a tale of a job well done.

FRENCH DRAINS

A French drain is a narrow trench filled from top to bottom with gravel but with no tile in the bottom. Such drains are connected to the tiling system or the outlet is taken into the rough. French drains are effective and aid in the removal of water, but it makes more sense to install a tile in the bottom of the trench rather than just gravel. French drains date back to the era of the baked clay tile, which was expensive and difficult to install.

MATERIALS

Tiles

There are still one or two factories that manufacture clay tiles for drainage. Such tiles permit water to seep through its wall into the cavity of the tile. Few people go to the expense of buying and installing clay tiles. Most use plastic tile, either with or without holes in the walls. Plastic tiles come in rolls, are easy to handle and to install. Drainage tile made from a bituminous material can also be obtained in straight lengths. Tiles in excess of 6" diameter, besides being available in plastic, can also be found in galvanized iron. All small-sized tile are available with fittings that make connecting the tiles easy.

Gravel

By far the best gravel for drainage purposes is pea gravel. The characteristic smooth, round surface of the individual stones makes pea gravel ideal for the passage of water. The pea stones allow the water to slide off its surface and pass freely into the tiles. Clear limestone can be used as an alternative, but only as a last resort. The angular surface of the limestone tends to become clogged with foreign materials such as grass clippings and soil. Granite stone chips are yet another alternative, but have the same drawbacks as limestone. The extra cost of pea gravel is well worth it in the long run.

Catch Basins

Plastic catch basins come in all shapes and sizes. They are easy to install and easy to clean. The grate lifts out to permit watching the flow of the water. Plastic catch basins are inherently light, whereas cement catch basins are very heavy and can only be installed with the help of a heavy-duty lifting device. Cement catch basins are used in conjunction with larger sized pipes: 12" and up.

Trenchers

There are two important criteria to consider when buying or renting a trencher: how deep will it dig and how wide will the trench be. In most cases a depth of 2–3 ft is sufficient, and the best width for a four-inch tile is 5–6". Making the trench any wider than it needs to be only creates extra work.

There are trenchers especially designed to make narrow slit grooves that permit the installation of flat tiles encased in pea gravel. Such tiles are generally joined into larger, main pipes.

Miscellaneous Tools

A saw to cut the tile is a must. So is a narrow trenching shovel to clean the trench. A pick to dig out rocks or stones is also essential.

SUMMARY

There are many jobs on the golf course that require committee involvement and approval. Drainage is not one of them! Golfers expect their superintendent to take charge and drain low-lying areas, just as they expect the grass to be cut and fertilized. Drains and catch basins should be installed as a routine matter. To drain a full-sized course may take a lifetime, but it should be started and once begun, little by little it will be completed. There can never be too many drains and catch basins on any golf course.

There is a strange phenomenon that can occasionally be observed on a golf course. It involves a superintendent bending down on hands and knees over a catch basin with his ear to the grate, listening to the water flowing through the pipes. It is a peculiar sense of satisfaction that comes only to those who have satisfactorily installed a perfect drainage system. The result is dry land that can be cut without leaving ruts, and turf that can be played from, without casual water.

13 Seeding and Sodding

INTRODUCTION

Golf is meant to be played on grass and the quality of the grass determines the reputation of the superintendent. Bare earth is almost always unacceptable. Every self-respecting superintendent strives to cover every part of the fairways, the tees, the greens, and even the rough with high quality turf. It is never an easy task. To establish a turf by means of either sodding or seeding requires both skill and knowledge. Once the turf has taken root, we find that grass rarely grows without encouragement. It is a never-ending job but it has to start somewhere, either through seeding or sodding, because that's where it all begins.

SEEDING

Seeds need warmth and moisture to germinate and once the skin of the seed hulk is broken, the tiny root must make contact with the soil for nourishment almost immediately in order to survive. That is why it is so critical that seeds must be surrounded by damp, warm earth. Unless the earth is warm, nothing much takes place inside the seed and this is precisely why late summer and early fall are the best time for seeding. The heat of the summer is still stored in the soil, and the heavy dews so characteristic of the latter part of the growing season help provide the most favorable growing conditions for the grass plants. Since weeds are not nearly as active in the late season, the lack of competition from weeds is yet another factor that makes the time slot from late July till late September the best opportunity for seeding.

Minimum Soil Temperature Requirements for Seed Germination
Perennial rye grass   50°F
Bent grass   59°F
Bluegrasses   55–60°F

Figure 13.1. Sodding a fairway near Durban, South Africa.

Seed can be applied in early spring in the cold soil, but it will just sit there waiting for the temperature to rise. Covering seeded areas with a thermal blanket, such as a geo textile membrane, will speed up the germination process. In fact, it is a good idea to cover the seed bed overnight when the air temperatures are low, and remove the covers during the day when the sun is shining. Judicious manipulation of the growing medium by alternately covering and uncovering the seed bed will speed up turf establishment by several days. To achieve success it is necessary to practically babysit the tiny grass plants. Constant attention is required. The covers need to be removed when the heat under the blanket builds up, and rolled back on with the cool of the night. All the time one must be vigilant about the nutritional needs of the grass and aware that excessively lush growth may spawn fungus diseases.

Seed Sizes and Germination

The smallest seeds are those of the various bent grasses. Their minuscule size makes them almost invisible individually and even a handful of bent grass feels light as a feather, but under favorable growing conditions invariably all of the millions of seeds will produce a grass plant. Bent grass will germinate in 5–10 days. Under ideal conditions a haze of green can be detected early in the morning of the fifth day when the grass blades are covered with dew. Not all seeds germinate at once; over a period of several days more and more seeds will raise their heads from under the earth and collectively form a cover of grass.

The seeds of bluegrasses and fescues are very much the same in size. The various cultivars of Kentucky bluegrass take at least 14 days to germinate and twice that long to form an appreciable grass mat. The fescues are a little quicker, but the really fast grass is perennial rye. It has been known to sprout a blade after just three days, and inside a week a green sward is clearly visible. Coincidentally, ryegrass is the biggest in size of all the common lawn grass seeds. It is just as well that it grows so quickly; birds would surely eat all the seed before it had a chance to take root.

Seeding Rates

The following seeding rates are for the application of seed to bare earth only. Overseeding on top of established turf is a totally different matter that requires judgment and experience, and is not bound by hard and fast rules.

Bent grasses: 1–2 lb/1,000 sq ft or 40–80 lb/acre
Bluegrasses: 3–5 lb/1,000 sq ft or 100–150 lb/acre
Fescue grasses same as bluegrasses
Ryegrasses: 5–8 lb per 1,000/sq ft or 150–250 lb/acre

It is obvious that seed size and seeding rates are related. The smaller the seed, the greater the number of seeds per pound. The number of individual seeds per square foot of soil needs to be adequate to achieve complete and thorough coverage of the area to be seeded. There is a danger, particularly with the fine seeded bent grasses, when applying too much seed. An overly thick stand can easily lead to disease, such as "damping-off" caused by Pythium and Rhizoctonia fungus species. The mycelium of this fungus will quickly wipe out a large stand of newly germinated grass seed. As soon as it has been identified, it should be treated with an appropriate fungicide.

Preparing the Seedbed

In order for seed to germinate, the seeds must make contact with the soil so that the sprouting root can embed itself among the soil particles for anchorage and to extract sustenance from the growing medium. It is therefore obvious that the seedbed must consist of a layer of fine soil particles. This can be attained by rototilling the area to be seeded and firming and leveling it with a landscaping device that includes a roller of some sort that breaks up the large clods and leaves in its path a bed of fine topsoil. Landscaping tools such as the Gill and the Viking can be attached to the three-point hitch system found on most tractors and do an admirable job of fine grading the area to be seeded or sodded. Other methods include dragging a steel I-beam, a piece of chain link fence, a steel mat, or even just the power rake used for sand bunkers. All of these methods work well, except there is a danger that they work so well that contours carefully designed by architects may be obliterated. On smaller areas such as greens, where prescribed contours are absolutely essential, hand raking may be the only alternative.

Debris, rocks, and stones must be removed from the area to be seeded. Usually such items are hand raked into piles and carted away. When the quantities are too large, mechanical stone pickers are needed. Nothing must be left to interfere with the growth of the grass and the ultimate maintenance practices.

Fertilizing the Seedbed

Ideally, a starter fertilizer should be applied prior to rototilling, so that the fertilizer granules can be mixed into the growing medium. Since this is not always possible, applying the fertilizer to the finished grade is perfectly all right. There may be a justifiable fear that too much fertilizer will burn the root hairs as the grass germinates. We have never seen this happen. On the contrary, we have observed a lot of retarded new grass that suffered from lack of nutrients rather than too much. In fact, grass in its infancy needs to be fed generously, just like little babies on their mother's knee. Rates of 500–800 lb of a 10-10-10 type fertilizer or similar material per acre are not excessive.

Seed Application Methods

For the smaller bent grass seeds it is best to use a drop-type spreader. The larger seeds may be applied by means of a cyclone spreader. On steep and uneven terrain, consider using a seeder that is strapped over the shoulder and disperses seed via a cyclone mechanism propelled by a hand crank.

Spreading of the small bent grass seeds can be made easier by using a carrier such as sand or even Milorganite. This method increases the bulk of the material and makes achieving uniform coverage much easier. Whatever method of seeding is used, it is best to apply the seed in two different directions to ensure overlap. Wind is an important factor! A brisk breeze can easily blow the seed away from where it is wanted. It is best to seed on still days with little or no wind. After the seed has been applied, the soil should be lightly raked and rolled to create optimum growing conditions and a smooth surface.

For larger areas use a tractor-drawn "Brillion" seeder which consists of a hopper and a drum-like packer that causes the seed to be covered with a fine layer of soil. The weight of the cast iron packer draws the moisture of the soil to the surface, thus assisting the germination process.

Mulching

Covering seed with straw is an excellent method of promoting germination. The straw helps provide a damp environment which reduces the need for constant watering. In addition, a cover of straw is an excellent means of preventing erosion. The old-fashioned method of spreading bales of straw with a pitch fork has given way to rolls of straw interwoven with plastic strands that keep the straw in place. Such blankets are particularly effective on steep hills. Attached to the soil with biodegradable metal staples, these straw blankets provide a wonderful cover and speed germination immensely. They also extend the time frame for successful seeding. Add at least a month in the fall when using straw blankets. The soil moisture and heat are preserved under these cozy covers and the seed germinates quickly, raising its leaves through the straw mesh. The resulting growth forms a thick stand of turf, ready for use in the spring.

Watering

Newly seeded areas need to be watered on a regular basis, but ever so gently. Too much water at a time causes runoff, and once erosion gains a foothold it is difficult to stop. Automatic underground sprinklers can be set with precision accuracy, thus making watering an easy exercise. The objective is to keep the soil damp while the tiny grass plants are sprouting their roots. Once the grass plant is established it must be kept moist to grow actively and form a mat of dense grass. Once again, overwatering of the young seedlings will lead to Pythium infestation.

Establishing bent grass on high sand content greens can be tricky. The sand dries out so quickly that it needs to be watered frequently, often as much as once an hour, especially during the heat of the day. Even after the seed has germinated it needs constant attention or the grass plants will wither and die. At such time, the vigilant eye of the professional superintendent must be ever present to ensure success and prevent disasters.

The First Cut

Once the grass is growing actively and has formed a thick mat it is ready for its first trimming. Prior to cutting, it is often a good idea to roll the new turf lightly. This action presses the plants into the soil and promotes firm root contact that will prevent death from the tearing action of the mower. A day or so after the rolling, the grass plants, having at first been pressed down, will once again rise up and be ready for a cutting.

It is vitally important that whatever mower is used be exceedingly sharp. The tops of the grass blades must be sheared off with ease and not torn, which happens when the mower is dull. On a new green or tee, the first cut can be made with a rotary mower set at a very low height. A regular greens mower may be also be used but conversely, it should be raised to its upper limit. In either case, the clippings should be removed. Gobs of grass left unattended will kill the grass underneath and cause unsightly dead spots. Amazingly, after the first cut, the rate of growth of the new stand increases rapidly, and with successive trimmings a healthy sward soon becomes established.

If the cover of grass is imperfect because of washouts or poor germination, remedial action is required. Spot seeding for small areas may be necessary. In such cases the seed can be mixed with soil, much like a divot mix. If the washed-out areas are deeper, sodding may be the only means of rectifying the problem and preventing it from becoming more serious. Don't wait and waste time. The need for action should be clear very quickly. Repairs must be made so that the success of the project is not impeded by indecision.

New seedings are prolific growers and, subsequently, big users of nutrients in the soil. These nutrients must be replenished, and a follow-up fertilizer program is essential. During its infancy the grass plants will quickly turn yellow or purple, depending on whether it needs nitrogen or potash. Regular applications of balanced fertilizer are essential to overcome these deficiencies. It must be understood that the nutritional requirements of new turf are at least twice as high as those of established stands. Growing in new turf to maturity has now become a recognized art and a small group of elite superintendents make their living traveling from new course to new course, growing in the young turf to maturity, until it is ready for play.

Hydro Seeding

A novel method of establishing seed, especially on steep slopes, involves a process called "Hydro Seeding." As the name implies, the method involves water. In fact, a mixture of seed and fertilizer combined with a fibrous material, such as chopped up straw, is added to water. As can well be imagined, the ingredients form a slurry that is sprayed under pressure to bare hillsides or other areas to be seeded. Sometimes a dye is added which makes it easier to see what parts have been treated. The slurry tends to form a crust over the soil which helps prevent erosion and speeds up germination.

Not only are steep slopes ideal for hydro seeding, greens and tees have also been established in this manner. In fact, entire golf courses can be hydro seeded. It is much less expensive than sodding and almost as quick in achieving a grass cover.

SODDING

Preparing the soil for sod is very similar to the methods used for seeding, except that at times one need not be quite as finicky. A roll of sod quickly covers a lot of sins, which may come back to haunt a person too much in a hurry to get the job done. Stones and rocks will find their way to the surface and eventually pop up through the sod, hurting the mowers as well as the golfers' clubs.

The surface of tees and greens that are to be sodded must be perfectly smooth and firm, almost a bit hard, so that there is no footprinting when the sod is laid. Fertilizer should have been tilled into the soil mix, but it is not too late to spread fertilizer on the finished grade. Planks or sheets of plywood are often used when sodding a green. The workers can now walk on the wood instead of the grass or the soil and prevent footprinting. The first row of sod is laid straight down the middle in a perfect line and the next row butts up against it tightly, making sure that the ends are staggered just like the bricks on a wall. The outline of the green can be painted with a gun, but to obtain a perfectly smooth naturally flowing line, use a heavy water hose. Place the hose in the approximately correct position, then snap and whip the end. The result will be a contour that is cuttable and looks pleasing to the eye. Use a sharp edger to cut the sod. If the apron is to be sodded as well, sod can now be rolled around and around to the desired width.

Helpful Hint #1

When sodding during the heat of summer, consider syringing the dry earth just prior to sodding. That little bit of moisture at the interface of sod and soil will speed root formation and prevent the sod from drying out.

Rolling sod after it has been laid is essential. The weight of the roller draws moisture to the surface and makes sure that the sod comes into firm contact with the soil. Air pockets will be eliminated by repeated rolling.

Sodding slopes, bunker faces, or surrounds of tees requires special care. On steep slopes, lay the sod across the fall line; that is, the most direct path from top to bottom. The sods should be attached to the soil with biodegradable metal staples. On severe slopes consider using wooden pegs, and hammer these into the soil to a depth of 6–10 inches. Once the sod has rooted, the wooden stakes can be removed. The metal staples will disappear with time.

Around bunkers it is best to lay a strip of sod along the edge of the sand and work out from there. It is much the same with tees: lay a strip of sod perfectly around the perimeter of the teeing area and butt the rest of the sods up against this strip, using staples wherever the grade exceeds 10%.

Recently, sod producers have started to lift turf in giant rolls, as much as two feet wide and almost a hundred feet long. Special attachments for tractors are needed to lay the heavy rolls. The obvious advantages of large rolls are that it is quicker to cover a given area and there will be fewer seams to knit.

Washed sod is also a recent innovation. As the name implies, the soil has been washed away from the roots, and the mass of roots topped with green grass is simply laid on its destined surface, rolled, and presto: it begins to grow immediately. The obvious advantage is that no foreign soil is imported into the soil mix. The lightness of the washed sod makes it possible to ship it by air from coast to coast.

Watering Sod

During the first week or so, newly laid sod requires more water than new seeding. Not only must the grass mat be kept alive, but it must be encouraged to grow roots. It is best to water until the moisture has just passed through the grass mat. Apply too much and you will have created a messy quagmire; too little water and the sod will wilt and die. Dead sod with the edges curled up looks ugly and is one of the deadly sins against the principles of good greenkeeping. Strangely, the dead sod is often just dormant and will turn green after a rain. Rather than experiment, it is best to keep the new sod moist by daily watering. Check often for the development of white root

Figure 13.2. Sodding a bunker face. Staples are used
to keep sod from sliding.

Figure 13.3. Using a strip of bent grass sod to outline a fairway
at the Board of Trade Country Club.

Figure 13.4. Sod, delivered on pallets, is ready to be laid.

hairs. Once they appear, they will quickly find their way into the soil and provide anchorage for the new turf.

Whether sod arrives on pallets, skids, or in rolls, it should be laid immediately, especially in the summer. The rolls of sod, tightly packed together, provide anaerobic conditions that produce heat which in turn will kill the grass in just a few days. In the spring or fall, sod can be stored somewhat longer, but the absence of light will also turn the grass yellow.

Sod may temporarily be stored on plastic, laid out in full. It must be watered regularly. A mass of roots will develop where the soil meets the plastic. The sod can be left in this manner for as many as ten days and used to complete a construction project. The roots of sod that have been stored on plastic will be particularly anxious to renew their contact with the soil. Such sod, when watered, becomes firmly attached to the soil in just a few days.

Helpful Hint #2

There are times when a sodding job just has not turned out well. The surface is bumpy and the grade uneven, not fit to putt on or to hit drives from. Before ripping it up and starting again, consider using a vibratory roller. Place several sheets of plywood on the ugly sodding job and run the vibratory roller several times back and forth. This drastic measure often results in a smooth surface. Some aeration may be necessary at a later time.

Figure 13.5. Sod can be stored for short periods on plastic sheets to prevent rooting.

Figure 13.6. Repairing a poor sodding job with a vibratory roller.

The First Cut

Be gentle on the first cut. Don't wait too long or the grass will be too high and the shock of the cutting will set the grass back. On a green, use a walk-behind mower. In the rough, use a rotary mower at a high setting. It is very important to be gentle with new turf.

Deciding When New Turf is Ready for Use

With each successive cutting, the grass will thicken and form a dense mat. On greens and tees the establishment of the turf is greatly assisted by frequent topdressings. On the larger fairways, topdressing may be more cumbersome, although equipment is now available to topdress widespread areas quickly. With each successive cutting, the height can be lowered a bit, but during the first growing season it is best not to lower the height to the eventual setting. This is certainly the case on greens, and perhaps on tees. Fairway turf should be taken down fairly quickly to prevent the development of thatch.

There comes a time when the new grass looks just perfect and the temptation will be irresistible to permit play. Wait a while! The new shoots are still very tender and the onslaught of hundreds of golfers' feet can cause severe damage that may necessitate closing the golf course again.

A new green on an established course, having been rebuilt and seeded, is subject to the pressures of impatient golfers to be put into play prematurely. This is a situation where the mettle of a superintendent will be put to the test. Such new greens will look and feel perfect, but we have seen them destroyed in a matter of just a few weeks or even days. The turf needs to mature before it can withstand the hardship of golfers' feet and the regimen of regular maintenance. In such situations, new golf courses have an advantage. The number of players on new courses is generally low at first and gradually builds up over a period of months or even years, thus giving a turf a chance to mature. On an existing golf course, with 200–300 golfers per day, when a rebuilt green is put into play there is a sudden shock from no play at all to constant foot traffic all day long.

If at all possible, a new green should not be opened till fall, when there is a natural decline in the number of players. To open a new green during the hottest weekend in July is sheer folly. The sudden shock on stressed-out turf will be a sorry sight in short order. The ability to say "NO" to the clamoring hordes in such situations is very difficult, and the assistance and support of the greens chairman will be much appreciated.

A new green among 17 established greens presents special problems. For a long time the new green will putt and play differently. Pitch shots don't hold and the putting speed, whether real or imaginary, seems at odds with the rest of the greens. This is not surprising. In all likelihood the soil underneath is different. It will take time for the roots to find their way, and it will take many waterings, topdressings, and fertilizings for the new green to resemble and play like the existing greens. A new green has to mature! Not just the turf on top but the soil underneath needs to adjust to regular maintenance. At the same time, superintendents should be aware that the new green may need to be treated differently for quite a while. Almost certainly, the new green will require extra fertilizer and topdressing. Don't be surprised if the turf around the cup wears out more quickly on the new green than it does on all the others. On busy days be prepared to change the cup more than once. New greens should be inspected frequently and all little imperfections should be remedied immediately. Such greens should be babied until they grow up. The old Dutch saying that the eye of the master will fatten the cow applies equally to new greens.

SUMMARY

The magic of new grass covering bare earth is a phenomenon both satisfying and inspiring. It is satisfying for those who do the work and reap the rewards of seeing a landscape develop. It is inspiring because birth and growth signify renewal and the perpetuity of life.

Both sodding and seeding present opportunities to demonstrate skill and knowledge of basic greenkeeping. The actual ability to make things grow is a unique and special gift. Hard work and dedication are translated into an almost instant green sward. To a layman it is wondrous, even awesome. To the initiated it is the sweet fruit of one's labor.

14 Golfer Traffic and Paths

INTRODUCTION

When a golf course gains in popularity, the wear and tear of the golfers tramping over the grounds leads to the development of traffic patterns. It happens near the greens and tees at first, later along the hazards, and eventually even on the fairways. Since worn areas make for poor lies and bad bounces, such conditions are unacceptable to discriminating golfers. Superintendents are expected to repair the worn areas or try to prevent the development of paths by spreading the traffic. There are certain threshold values beyond which the damage caused by golfer traffic can no longer be alleviated by the simple expedient of spreading the wear. Then, plans need to be made to construct foot and cart paths. Forcing golfers to walk or drive where they don't want to go is at best difficult, if not impossible. Superintendents need to be quite inventive if not ingenious to devise ways and means to control the golfer traffic and to develop a system of functional paths.

FOOT PATHS

Foot traffic is most severe near tees. By their very nature, tees are elevated and require firm foot pressure to ascend the tee deck to prevent slipping. The extra pressure wears out the turf that much quicker. A knee-jerk reaction is to install a set of stairs, but rarely are stairs the best solution. Almost immediately after installation the grass near where the steps begin will start to show signs of wear. At the top of the stairs, on the tee deck, the grass will also quickly die. The problem with stairs is that they concentrate the traffic instead of spreading it. In addition, stairs are costly to maintain. Their location invariably interferes with mowing patterns. Adding a railing to a set of stairs may give golfers a sense of security, but it adds to the unnatural appearance of the contraption.

Figure 14.1. A removable footbridge over a wide stream helps get golfers around.

On shallow grades, paths can be made from a variety of materials, many of which provide good footing. Railroad ties cut to a uniform width of four feet and laid on a gravel bed, side by side, provide sure footing, blend in well with the surrounding terrain, and are no obstacle to mowers. A path of interlocking stones can be both appealing and functional. The texture of the stones provides a firm grip for both metal spikes and spikeless golf shoes. Rubberized tiles can be used in the same manner and with the same effect. Keep in mind that used conveyor belting is extremely slippery when wet and should only be used with great hesitancy. There are nonslip rubber mats available, and these can be used to prevent wooden decks from wearing prematurely.

To avoid the need for paths and steps or stairs altogether, architects should be encouraged to build tees that are surrounded by slopes which are easy to ascend and which make it possible for superintendents to spread the wear through their management practices. Unfortunately, championship tees or gold or back tees tend to be constructed far back and way up, often making the construction of a goat path, combined with steps, a necessity. The best place to learn about the maintenance and construction of foot paths is on the many hiking trails that crisscross most countries. We have walked the trails in England, Italy, Spain, New Zealand, and South Africa as well as our respective homelands, and come away with many excellent ideas to provide comfort for our golfers.

After striking the ball, golfers leave the tee in an undefined pattern. Some slice, some hook, and a few drive the ball down the middle. Yet, amazingly, paths often develop quite naturally off the tee, especially if there is an obstruction such as a water course or a gorge in the way. A curving goat path through a stand of long

Figure 14.2. Railroad ties are used to create a solid footpath for the golfers at the Devil's Paint Brush in Caledon, Ontario.

fescue can be quite appealing to the eye. Its presence lends aesthetics to a golf hole and often tranquillity to a golfers' turbulent mind. There is always the small chance that a dubbed tee shot might find its way mysteriously to the middle of the path. Such luck befalls those that are at peace with nature and appreciate their hardworking superintendent.

In some instances, grass is cut short at rough height off the tee, and the foot traffic is spread sufficiently to prevent the development of any kind of paths. Superintendents who are concerned about golfers keeping their feet dry will cut a swath several feet wide from the tee to the fairway at a low height of cut. Early in the morning, with the dew heavy on the grass, golfers can walk down this strip and keep their feet from becoming soaked.

On the fairway, much of the wear happens near the hazards. Wherever there is a concentration of traffic such as between closely placed bunkers, near streams or ponds, foot traffic will pound the grass to death. This is especially true near bridges.

**Figure 14.3. Wire hoops are used to direct traffic at Mount Juliet
Golf Course in Southern Ireland.**

On small stream crossings the use of bridges can be avoided by using culverts. The latter are much wider and spread the wear. On very small bridges, the plank structure can be moved at regular intervals.

Near the green, wear patterns inevitably develop between the edge of the green and the bunker face. If the bunker is located in a direct line of traffic it will be necessary from time to time to stop all foot traffic by means of a temporary obstruction device such as stakes and ropes. A thin metal bar, partially bent like a hoop, can also be quite effective. On occasion, steep slopes near the green necessitate the installation of stairs. Such stairs, just like those near tees, are a maintenance headache. They should be avoided if at all possible or eliminated with the help of well-known and sympathetic golf course architects.

It is important to recognize all worn areas early in their development and take preventative action. Early in the morning thin turf or turf under stress is characterized by the absence of dew. This is an early warning sign of turf needing help. Immediate action is required! Not only must the foot traffic be diverted, but the compaction in the soil must be remedied. Get the aerator out, remove the cores, and overseed. If at all possible, use some of the marvelous new varieties of perennial ryegrass. Once established, ryegrass wears like iron and takes traffic much better than any other turf.

We have always encouraged our golfers to walk. We believe that golf is a healthy sport that can best be enjoyed on foot. Therefore, we want to avoid as much as possible placing obstacles in the way of walkers. Golfers who carry their own clubs are the masters of the links. They can go wherever they please and there are few rules that obstruct their movements. Those who pull a trolley or are pulled by one of the battery-operated caddy carts unfortunately must face some obstructions. The total weight of their carts and clubs is much heavier than the bags that golfers carry. It is for this reason that trolleys must be kept off tees and away from restricted areas such as between traps and greens.

POWER CARTS

Most of the damage to golf course turf is done by the hateful power carts. Much as we may privately detest power carts, golf as we know it today could not exist without motorized carts. We have learned long ago to live with power carts. We have also learned to control the use of power carts and to repair the damage that they inevitably cause to turf.

As soon as more than 10 power carts are regularly used on an 18-hole golf course, wear will start to appear; at first, only near the tees, but signs of wear will quickly begin to show near the greens and near the bunkers. At first the damage can be controlled by changing the traffic and by keeping the grass strong, but as the number of cart users increases, the need for a partial system of paths becomes apparent. When a threshold level of 50 power carts is reached, tee to green paths on par 3 holes become a necessity. Between 80–100 carts on an 18-hole course requires a continuous path from the first tee to the 18th green.

DIRECTING THE TRAFFIC

There is much to be said for keeping power carts off the fairways, especially bent grass fairways. Bent grass is a very fine-leaved turf that is subject to stress and disease. At the first sign of root zone compaction, bent grass gives in to *Poa annua* and loses its foothold as the dominant grass. Bent grass does best on loose, moist soils. Years ago, when we cut fairways with heavy tractors and gang mowers, we noticed that *Poa annua* quickly became the foremost species in the mixture. When we switched to lightweight greens mowers, compaction was reduced and bent grass once again took over as the number one species.

It is the same with power carts. No matter how many times we have been assured by the manufacturers of power carts that the wheel pressure on the turf is negligible, we all know that cart traffic on fairways causes compaction, and compaction means *Poa annua* will make inroads. Do we allow power carts to drive on our greens? Of course not. The greens are much too small and the carts would cause compaction very quickly and the grass would die. Then why should we allow carts on fairways, especially, since the turf on our fairways is comparable to the greens of yesteryear? Bent grass fairways during July and August with temperatures ranging from 90–100° are very fragile. It is precisely during those dog days of summer that the golfers who normally walk, insist on taking carts and driving on the fairways.

Many superintendents have withstood the pressures of their golfers and insisted on keeping the carts in the roughs. At such courses golfers follow the 90-degree rule, which means that carts can drive across the fairway at a 90-degree angle to their ball.

This is the shortest distance and minimizes power cart traffic on the fairways. A serious drawback of forcing carts into the rough is that many golfers follow the rule precisely and drive in the rough along the very edge of the fairways. A path quickly becomes apparent and the resulting bad lies are used as arguments to persuade the superintendent to give free rein to the carts, everywhere. Superintendents who give in to such brainless logic have only themselves to blame when fairway turf deteriorates.

There are well-known methods that involve the use of unobtrusive barricades to direct cart traffic in the roughs in an acceptable manner to spread the wear. Turf in the roughs, consisting of a mixture of fescue, rye, and bluegrasses and cut to a height of 1.25 to 1.5 inches, can comfortably withstand the beating of the golf cart tires. If such turf is regularly aerated, overseeded, and fertilized, it can be almost as strong as asphalt. The fragile bent grass on the fairways, although providing beautiful lies, is as temperamental as a race horse: one day it wins the race, the next it suffers from gout and is unable to compete.

Golf courses that do not require the tightly mown bent grass turf and instead select various mixtures of rye, fescue, and bluegrasses, either alone or as a mixture, escape the difficult decision of where to let the carts drive. Similarly, bermuda fairways in the southern states provide a strong turf that takes traffic very well. We played a course in Durban, South Africa, where the fairways consisted of a pure stand of Kikuyu grass. A herd of elephants could not have destroyed that turf and it provided fine lies with the ball sitting up perfectly. Zoysia is another turf that provides good playing conditions and withstands traffic very well. It is only the race horse bent grass that must be treated with kindness, and therefore power carts should be kept off it, as much as possible.

TRAFFIC-DIVERTING METHODS

1. Exit stakes, uniformly painted either brown or green, can be placed in the rough a short distance from the green on either one or both sides of the fairway. Such stakes serve notice to golfers that they are no longer permitted on the fairways beyond that point. In fact, if paths are nearby, golfers are expected to head for them. The stakes range in height from 1–2 ft and are equipped with a spike at the bottom, so that they can be moved with ease.
2. On some golf courses, a white line is painted across the fairway to act as a reminder that carts cannot proceed, but must head for the roughs. The line must be repainted regularly to remain visible, and if left in the same place the grass will eventually die.
3. Ropes suspended on stakes are also used as a physical barrier to stop carts from getting near the green. They are effective but visually unattractive. In addition, they do at times deflect golf balls. Some superintendents have removed the stakes and stapled the ropes to the grass.
4. Signs reminding golfers not to proceed seem to work for a little while but quickly lose their effectiveness. A series of small stakes, placed in a row just far enough apart for pull carts to pass through, form an effective barricade to divert power carts.

5. Near the green, when there are no paths for carts to drive on, the 30-foot rules should be observed. This rule dictates that no power carts should ever be parked or driven closer than 30 feet or ten paces to the green. The aim is to protect the turf and to provide acceptable lies for golfers.

Whatever devices are used, all need timely attention. They must be moved, replaced, and put back again for the mowers that pass and the golfers that forget to replace them. Controlling the flow of traffic is a difficult assignment that should be attended to on a daily basis. The person assigned this responsibility should have a thorough understanding of the need to balance the demands of the golfers with what is best for the grass.

NO CARTS TODAY!

There comes a time when superintendents must make an unpopular decision. It happens after a heavy rain, a sudden downpour, or a violent storm. The sodden ground is soft and not suitable for power cart traffic. The weight of the cart loaded with golfers and bags would compact the soil and affect grass growth adversely. The carts may even leave ruts that are costly to repair. On wet slopes the carts would lose traction and could easily spin out. The superintendent has the responsibility to bring the unhappy news—that there will be no carts today—to the golf shop and the clubhouse. The message should be delivered in a professional manner. Notices should be posted, including the anticipated time that the ban will be lifted. Irate members with important guests can bring to bear lots of pressure to persuade the superintendent to change his mind. At such times it is best to be visible and stand one's ground. Reasonable people will as a rule understand sound explanations. Unreasonable golfers probably just need to vent their anger, and an understanding superintendent can make a good listening board. To hide in the office at such occasions is poor policy and a professional cop-out.

Who should have the ultimate authority to decide the fate of carts on wet days? It should be the person who is best trained to measure the agronomic impact of the potential damage that cart traffic can do to rain-soaked soil and turf. It should be the person who is on the job to assess the potential danger that may occur to golfers when carts slip and slide. It should be the person who derives no direct financial benefits from cart revenue. In all cases that person is invariably the superintendent, the only person who has no axe to grind, who has no vested interest in the outcome of the decision, and who is committed to do what is best for the grass and for the golfers. It behooves the golf professional, the manager, the club's president, and most of all, the green chairman, to back up the superintendent. To make unpopular decisions takes a strong backbone, and the total support of the management team makes life a lot less stressful.

On "no cart days" there are a number of things that a superintendent can do to improve the professional image. Grass mowing equipment should be restricted to dry areas only or kept off the course completely. Golf course workers should limit their excursions in maintenance vehicles that resemble golf carts. It is a good idea for the superintendent to walk and set an example during course inspections. Golfers will respect a superintendent who adheres to the rules that are good for everyone.

ANECDOTAL INTERLUDE: TWO OF A PAIR

A few years ago I went shopping with a friend at a wholesale shoe store in Boston and bought two pairs of sneakers; one pair was light brown and the other dark. Sneakers are convenient footwear on the golf course. They make one feel young and athletic when one walks across a green; vibes enter the body and are translated into the needs of the grass. My sneakers had worn unevenly and I ended up with just one pair, one shoe dark brown and the other light brown. I used them on my early morning inspection trips. For the first few hours one's feet always get wet and it makes sense to wear old shoes. No one ever noticed until...

It was a cloudy Monday morning. A dull day after a duller weekend. Three consecutive rainy days had forced me to cancel golf carts and the Annual Allied Shoeman's Golf Tournament was on. Two hundred and fifty golfers were anxious to play golf and most were angry with me for forcing them to walk. The golf pro was also very unhappy with my decision. He had brought in extra carts. What should have been a little bonanza had turned into a write-off.

My popularity was at a low ebb, but I smiled bravely as I approached the clubhouse to pick up my mail. One of the tournament players spotted me from the putting green. He looked at me attentively and headed toward me. "Oh-oh, here it comes," I thought as I prepared myself for the forthcoming blast.

"Young man," he said as he walked alongside me, "you remind me of Stephen Leacock." My spirits were lifted immediately. To be compared to the great Canadian humorist, the Canadian Mark Twain, was a wonderful compliment. Finally someone had recognized my wit and wisdom. Needless to say, I was very flattered! Anxious to make the good feeling last, I asked my new friend what characteristic in me had reminded him so much of the great humorist. He replied without hesitation that just like Stephen Leacock frequently did, I was wearing two different shoes.

CART PATHS

Cart paths are first needed near tees, followed soon after by greens. Par 3 holes which inherently are characterized by spectacular changes in elevation, water hazards, and plentiful sand bunkers demonstrate the need for paths the quickest. Such holes quickly add a strip of macadamized pavement to help move the riding golfers. Once a few paths are in place in strategic locations and the number of cart rounds increases, the need for a continuous path system quickly becomes apparent. A wet week of no power carts on the course and the subsequent loss of revenue speeds up the process of installing tee to green paths on all golf holes.

Cart Path Location

Golfers rarely agree on where cart paths should be located on the course. Walkers, who prefer not to have any paths all, will reluctantly agree to put the paths as far away from the playing areas as possible. Riders, on the contrary, want cart paths in the roughs but close to the fairway, so their walks to where their ball landed is not too painful. A compromise seems almost impossible. The loudest voice at committee meetings is liable to carry the most weight and the result may be paths located where no one will use them. A better solution is to hire a golf course architect. Their experience and knowledge of the game makes them best qualified to make the final decision. Every golf hole is different and only an architect who sees many, many golf courses and golf holes day after day is capable of clearly visualizing where the paths should go. After careful study, an architect will lay out a routing plan for the paths that will become the basis for a construction program. Such a plan should seldom be deviated from.

The Width of Cart Paths

Whereas at first, cart paths were narrow, just wide enough for a single cart to drive on, it is now generally agreed that the minimum width for paths should be 8 ft, and many feel that 10 ft is better. Narrow paths crumble at the edges and the turf wears along its sides. Narrow paths cannot accommodate the need of golf course maintenance equipment. On wider paths, carts can pass each other, and mowers and tractors feel comfortable about not driving over the edge.

Drainage on cart paths is important. Puddles after a rain on a path are unacceptable. Paths should be slanted slightly so that water will run off. The use of catch basins near cart paths is to be encouraged. It is best to slant paths in such a manner that golf balls which land on the path will bounce toward the fairway, instead of into the rough. An added feature of cart paths is including distance markers at regular intervals. Such markers help golfers decide what clubs to use for their shot from the fairway, or more often, the opposite rough.

Cart Path Construction

Ideally, the routing plan prepared by the architect provides details not only about the location of the paths, but also specifics about cut and fill and adjacent mounding. Architects will try to hide the paths so that they are invisible from the tee and do not detract from the natural beauty of the golf hole. This is not always possible, but much can be done by curving the path and placing mounds in strategic places. Nothing is more boring and visually unattractive than a straight line of asphalt or cement along either or both sides of a fairway. A good architect with an artistic flair will avoid creating such an ugly scene. Trees in strategic places can assist in hiding and directing paths in an attractive manner. Besides, the canopy of the trees over a path will filter golf shots and prevent or at least reduce bad bounces.

Paths should be excavated to a depth of 6–8 inches. The excavated material can be used to help create the mounding or hauled away for other projects. No matter what topping is used, it is always best to use a solid foundation of gravel. Most granular materials are satisfactory as long as they are not too coarse. Ground-up asphalt forms a solid base and can be used as an intermediary path until funds are available to put

Figure 14.4. Construction of an asphalt pathway with a cement curb.

on a topping. As opposed to screenings or fine limestone, ground asphalt does not kick up dust during dry periods. In fact, the heat of summer will solidify the asphalt, and what may have started as a temporary plan may become a permanent solution.

What Makes the Best Top for a Cart Path?

Like the highways that span the width and length of a country, cart paths use very much the same materials, but on a much smaller scale.

CEMENT

No matter how carefully a base is prepared for a cement path, freezing and thawing in cold climates tends to crack the surface. So do heavy trucks and tractors. Once a crack appears in cement, it quickly becomes at least a small bump and the path loses its visual appeal. Cement should be poured to a thickness of 4–6 inches, a steel mesh should be included for strength and expansion joints, and cuts provided at regular intervals. No wonder that a cement path looks expensive. It also provides a smooth ride and seems to last almost forever.

ASPHALT

The base requirements for asphalt are the same as for cement, but there is where the similarity ends. Asphalt by its very nature is more flexible and moldable. It can be placed around curbs and over humps, and it requires no forms to keep it in places while it solidifies. More than one coat of asphalt may be needed where the road is to be used by vehicles heavier than golf carts.

PAVING STONES

The use of paving stones for cart paths is a relatively recent development. The stones are expensive to install, requiring hand labor exclusively. Once in place, such paths look attractive and provide excellent traction for both carts and walkers. When the stones move for whatever reason, they can easily be replaced and repaired by trained greens staff.

OTHER MATERIALS

We have often seen a bed of wood chips as a cart path. Invariably such paths are terribly dusty when dry and provide a potholed surface when wet. We feel that wood chips are better suited for bridle paths. The use of gravel is at best a temporary measure. Frequent washouts require constant repair and in the long run, paths made with gravel as a permanent top are expensive to maintain.

The Need for Curbing

There is an unexplained tendency on the part of golfers who drive power carts to drive ever closer to tees and greens. Only the installation of curbing will stop carts from going where they are not supposed to. Curbs are an effective barrier when the ridge is high enough, at least 4–5 inches. Both cement and asphalt paths permit the installation of curbing as part of the initial construction process. Curbs can also be installed at a later date. Some superintendents use pressure-treated timbers or railroad ties; the latter rarely last more than 7–8 years. Others resort to prefabricated cement curbs. The first tend to wear out quickly and the latter are more durable. Whatever type of curbing is used, provision must be made for golfers with pull carts to cross the curb. A simple, narrow cut is usually sufficient.

OTHER DIVERSIONARY TACTICS

1. When a paved path comes to a sudden end, the inevitable result is for the grass to thin and die. The bouncing of first, the front tires, and then, the rear tires, onto the turf wears out the grass very quickly. Such damage can be

prevented simply by flaring the path to either the right or left, thus randomizing where the carts will exit.

2. Others use a bubble pattern to end the cart path. In effect, this widens the path and spreads the wear. Using barricades such as wooden bumpers or plastic pylons is yet another means of spreading the exit points from the path.

PATH MAINTENANCE

Both foot paths and cart paths need to be maintained on a regular basis. Asphalt needs to be patched before potholes develop. Cracks need to be sealed to prolong the life of the paths. Paths need to be swept and the edges need to be trimmed on a regular basis. Poorly maintained paths are a blemish on the face of a golf course and inevitably lead to slovenliness elsewhere.

SUMMARY

Golfer traffic will find its way across the golf course in the most economical way. Scars, scrapes, and worn areas will develop until the installation of designated paths. Unless a qualified architect is engaged to determine the best location for the paths, a committee design, wrought in compromises, will prevail, to the detriment of the golfers. Whatever topping is used, the path must be maintained just like the rest of the golf course. In some ways the paths on a golf course are like the frame around a picture: a poor quality frame may easily spoil a fine painting.

Rules of Golf that Affect Maintenance

Every superintendent should be familiar with the rules of the game, and since most superintendents play golf, many make it their business to know the rules thoroughly and to play by them. In addition to playing by the rules, superintendents are called upon to assist with setting up the course so it can be played comfortably within the rules. The superintendent should be prepared to accurately define the course and the out-of-bounds, the margins of water hazards and lateral water hazards, ground under repair, obstructions, and other integral parts of the course. It is imperative that the staking and the marking is done in such a manner that even the most pernicious interpreters of the rules will be satisfied.

WATER HAZARDS

Golf is played either alongside the water or across it. Different rules apply and different colored stakes or lines should be used to define the margins of the hazard. Water to the side of a hole is generally a lateral water hazard and should be marked with red stakes or red lines. When play crosses a body of water, the hazard is generally marked with yellow stakes or lines. Stakes defining the margin of the hazard should be placed in the grass as nearly as possible along the natural limits of the hazard. The distance between stakes is important. At all times, an imaginary line between two adjacent stakes must be on dry land. Such a line of sight must be clearly visible when one lines up behind one stake and looks toward the other. The stakes cannot be too far apart or else the margin of the hazard may be hard to define. Our experience has been that it is seldom advisable for stakes to be more than 30 yards apart. Stakes should be closer together when play is around an irregularly shaped pond or river bank.

When a golfer is playing a hole and his ball is in or lost in a water hazard or lateral water hazard, the player needs to able to determine where the ball last crossed the margin of the hazard, to apply the rules. If hazard stakes are placed on sloping ground, it may be difficult to drop the ball and have it stop, thus complicating the procedure. It is far better to place hazard stakes on somewhat flat ground, so that a ball can be dropped without complications.

Hazard stakes have a tendency to be moved by both golfers and maintenance personnel. It can be difficult to replace the stake in its original place because the hole cannot be found in the long grass. Both golfers and greenkeepers have been known to just drop the stake somewhere and let someone else worry about it. This causes confusion and irritation to the golfers who follow behind.

To avoid this problem, permanent hazard markers can be installed precisely at the natural limits of the hazard. Made from cement or other durable material, they are permanently in place, flush with the ground so that mowers can cut over them. They are marked with a detachable stake to make them highly visible from vast distances. These permanent markers along the hazards, just like the permanent distance markers on the tees, are in place forever until someone decides to change their location. At the end of the golfing season the detachable stakes can be taken in, but the permanent disk remains. At the start of the new season, the stakes are replaced in their permanent location.

For tournaments and special events the hazard margins are usually painted with red or yellow paint. The presence of the painted line takes the guesswork out of the decision as to whether a golf ball is in or outside the hazards. Many superintendents now paint hazards on a regular basis, a popular move that is much appreciated by ardent golfers.

OUT-OF-BOUNDS

At most courses the perimeter of the property is clearly marked with fences that serve as boundaries, thus making it easy to determine if a golf ball is in or out-of-bounds. In the absence of property fences, out-of-bounds is designated with white stakes. Such stakes should be placed on the property line. When there are no fences that serve as property boundaries, the property line must be determined from a registered survey. Once it has been decided where the exact property line is, it should be marked with white stakes. The possibility that the stakes may be knocked over and their location become obscure should be taken into account. It is advisable to use sturdy white posts or permanent cement markers that can easily be relocated if need be. When using permanent markers for boundaries or hazards, it should be clearly understood that the edge of the markers designates the boundary or hazard line and that the stake is merely a visual aid that helps the player determine where the ball crossed the line.

As with water hazards, the actual out-of-bounds line may need to be painted for important events or on a continuous basis, if desirable. Occasionally, out-of-bounds stakes may be installed to define the out-of-bounds between the play of two adjacent holes, as for example, in a dogleg golf hole. A better solution, if feasible, is to have a golf architect remedy the design and eliminate the need for an internal out-of-bounds.

Figure 15.1. Marking "Ground Under Repair."

GROUND UNDER REPAIR

Many times there are areas on a golf course in less than perfect condition which are slated to be repaired in the near future. Such areas should be marked as GUR (Ground Under Repair), as approved by the committee or its authorized representative, by using either a small sign, or preferably a painted white line, that distinctly outlines the limits of the work area. A dug-up irrigation leak may be GUR. So is a scar or a scrape caused by a maintenance vehicle. Dead turf caused by winter injury or summer heat stress is GUR. Any of these conditions and others may be marked GUR by order of the committee, or so declared by its authorized representative, who may be the superintendent.

For tournaments and important events, such areas are outlined with white paint by an official, or more often by the superintendent. It should be noted that GUR areas should rarely be painted beyond the fairway and the adjacent primary rough. Careful consideration should be applied in determining GUR. Landing areas and areas near putting greens should be the primary concern. There is a tendency on the part of overly ambitious club officials to paint any imperfection white, even if it is a hundred yards beyond the line of play. In such instances, superintendents should seek the assistance of the golf professional and work cooperatively for the benefit of all golfers.

Grass clippings that are left in piles to be picked up later are considered GUR and golfers once again get to move their ball, if it is in or close to the pile. Grass clippings, poorly spread in the rough, can provide unplayable lies, but no relief is granted. No wonder greenkeepers often become unwitting victims of a golfer's misfortune.

It is a good idea for key maintenance staff to carry along a GUR sign or a can of white paint on their vehicles. Less than perfect areas can be marked on the spot and scheduled for repairs. In fact, all GUR areas should become part of the maintenance schedule and checked off when they have been repaired.

CASUAL WATER

Casual water by definition is "any temporary accumulation of water on the course which is visible before or after the player takes his stance and is not in the water hazard." Golfers may take free relief from temporary accumulations of water on the course, as long as that accumulation is not part of the hazard. Such water is considered to be of a temporary nature and referred to as casual water. A player's golf ball can then be moved to drier land.

If casual water is a continuing problem on the golf course, the causes should be explored. Invariably such conditions are drainage related and should be addressed. Casual water during the heat of summer can lead to scald, the actual cooking of the grass in freestanding water that is heated by the sun. This is not an unusual condition and is totally preventable by the simple expedient of pumping the excess water away.

OBSTRUCTIONS

When maintenance equipment interferes with the play of the game, the players once again are entitled to relief. Be it mowers, tractors, or maintenance carts, such items are collectively referred to as moveable obstructions. The moveable obstructions do not only refer to maintenance equipment, they can also be a pile of lumber scheduled to be used for the construction of a shelter, or a skid of fertilizer destined to be applied to a fairway.

Superintendents should strive to make sure that such conditions are indeed temporary. If the pile of lumber, the skid of fertilizer, or the set of gang mowers are left in the same place for the major part of the golfing season, someone may very well decide that they have become permanent obstructions and a whole new set of rules will apply. Permanent obstructions are bridge abutments, rain shelters, irrigation controllers, etc.

LOCAL RULES

Local rules are supplementary rules to the rules of golf to deal with abnormal conditions. Local rules may apply to newly planted trees which need to be protected from erratic golf swings. The local rule will state that relief may be taken from staked trees. Similarly, at the start of the season when conditions are less than perfect, club officials will decree that "winter rules apply" and golfers will happily move their ball to an elevated lie on a tuft of perfect turf, only to sky their shot. Such is fate and misfortune on the golf course.

Local rules can also be instituted when major construction projects are under way on the golf course. A sodding job, a bunker renovation undertaking, the installation of a water line, all involve temporary inconvenience to golfers. Areas on the golf course that are under construction in this way should be declared as GUR. No fuss, no bother; golfers simply take their ball from these areas and drop them at the nearest point of relief, no closer to the hole, and carry on.

SUMMARY

If ever there is a case for the need of further education on the part of the greens staff, a seminar on the rules of golf as they affect maintenance should be highest on the list. Superintendents need to know the rules as they apply to their daily operations. They need to be able to advise their golfers on what rules apply and what type of relief is permitted. Superintendents need to work with their golf professionals to make sure that the course is marked correctly and consistently, so that all golfers can play by the rules enjoyably.

16 Trees

Whispering pines, waving palms, giant sequoias, flowering jacarandas, weeping willows, and many other kinds of trees line the fairways of the world's diverse golf courses. Yet some maintain that golf is a game for wide open spaces, and what's more, they have St. Andrews to prove it. Many other courses, built on landscapes that are not suited for their growth, are characterized by a scarcity of trees. There are many more that are proud of the trees that grace their properties and even include the names of trees into the names of their golf courses. To name but a few: Maple Ridge, Old Elms, Burnt Tree, Crooked Stick, Magnolia, Royal Poinciana, and perhaps most famous of all, Cypress Point!

Trees provide the setting for the game to be played to its fullest enjoyment. The shape of trees, the gnarly roots and strong trunks, the crooked branches, the towering heights, the whispering leaves, the cool shade, all combine to give trees an aura of permanency and at times an atmosphere that can be both forbidding and inviting.

When trees are too tightly spaced and encroach upon the playing ground, they tense the muscles of all but the most expert players, and cause erratic golf shots. Trees at a distance provide peace of mind, relax the body, and make one swing freely. Single trees, in the way to the green, are often best ignored; they are, as has so often been pointed out, mostly air anyway. On a bad golf day, trees can be therapeutic for a troubled mind. Who but the most self-centered, ardent golfer can possibly ignore the beauty of the flowering magnolias in the spring or the brilliant hues of maples in the fall? Such is the world we, as superintendents, live in and ply our skills to make a living.

Golf course superintendents have unique opportunities during the course of their working lives. At the beginning of their careers they often find themselves on properties that need help, golf courses that have been ignored and neglected. Trees are planted and looked after and the grass thrives. At the end of a lifetime, hard work and dedication have converted a barren plain into a veritable Garden of Eden. Birds sing in the trees, rabbits scamper through the bushes, and hawks circle overhead. There is a tremendous satisfaction in such an accomplishment, and few other professions provide opportunities to leave a legacy of those proportions.

Figure 16.1. Trees left unchecked will eventually obscure the view of the green at this spectacular golf hole on South Africa's east coast.

Figure 16.2. The presence of trees adds an element of peace and harmony to the golfing environment, precisely what golfers need who toil all day long in busy cities.

TREE SELECTION

It is best to check with the experts before deciding on what trees to plant. State colleges and research stations all have such information readily available. It is even better to visit neighboring golf courses and find out what trees grow best and where they are available. Check also with tree nurseries and learn about availability and planting times. A slack time for nurseries is often midsummer after the spring rush and before the fall planting season. That is a good time to examine their picked-over stock. Some real gems can be found among the discards: trees with crooked trunks and misshapen heads. Such "Charlie Brown" trees can be bought for next to nothing and will thrive under the watchful eye of the superintendent and the caring golf course environment. Keep in mind that perfect trees are often statuesque, much better suited for the straight lines of cemeteries than the free-flowing curves on the golf course.

There are many trees that have undesirable characteristics that make them unsuitable for golf courses in large quantities. Willows and poplars have extensive and fibrous root systems that spread well beyond the drip lines of these trees. Such roots become inevitably entwined in drains and stop the flow of water. In addition, both species are very brittle and even a minor wind storm will knock off many branches. As a result, the grass under and near willows and poplars needs to be cleaned constantly.

Certain types of maples, such as the Norway varieties, provide dense shade and make it difficult for grass to compete. A group of Norway maples, although attractive and fast growing, is earmarked by bare ground at the bases. Soft maples have objectionable roots that stick up aboveground and they can be just as dirty as willows and poplars. Ash trees are slow in the spring and make one wonder if they have died. Catalpas are even slower, frequently not showing leaves till June. The male species of the exotic ginkgo tree has a body odor problem that is objectionable.

Are there any trees that can be safely planted without arousing the ire of the golfers or the greens committee? We feel that there is a place for all trees. Certainly some trees are more desirable than others, but all have a place. It's just not a good idea to plant a ginkgo near the golf shop, a willow over the clubhouse septic bed, or a chestnut tree near the neighboring school yard.

Evergreens such as pines and spruces make for wonderful partitions and backdrops. After a number of years, a bed of needles will develop at the base of evergreens that titillates the nostrils and makes it unnecessary to trim the grass there. Beeches and maples are solid citizens in the forest but they produce leaves in abundance. The strong oaks last forever and keep their leaves into the winter, although dead and brown, long after the golfing season has ended.

The best selection of trees for any golf course includes a wide variety of many species. Those poor golf courses that only planted elms and had them knocked out by the Dutch Elm disease must have been terribly sorry that they did not include a few of the lowly poplars and willows. Golf courses that were solely planted with Austrian pines which have been decimated by the Diplodia fungus surely wish they had added some spruces and pines to their program. When disease strikes, it is always best to have a diversity of species, so that many will survive the devastation of an epidemic.

A TREE PLANTING PROGRAM

Not all golf courses are blessed with an abundance of native forests or widely spaced specimen trees. When, in addition, there are few inherent features such as streams and ponds or hills and dales, trees may need to be planted to separate the fairways, to screen the perimeter, or to give character to the holes. Groupings of trees break the monotony of an otherwise bleak landscape. Trees can be planted to accentuate the strategy of individual golf holes. Trees, small when first planted, are no hindrance but quickly grow up to become formidable obstacles. Trees planted in the wrong places can obscure vistas and views. Trees and tees almost never go together. Nor are trees a good idea near greens. Yet, a wisely planted tree can take the place of a bunker and does not need raking every day. For all these reasons and more, a tree planting program is a necessity, but it must be carefully prepared. Since in most cases the location of the trees affects the strategy of the golf holes, a qualified architect should be engaged. The plan prepared by the architect should show where to plant trees. The plan should be preserved, encased in glass or foil, and hung in a prominent place where it can stay for a while, because planting trees is a long-term project. Committees and functionaries should make a firm commitment to adhere to the plan.

THE TREE NURSERY

Planting baby trees in a nursery is a very satisfying occupation. Trees destined for the nursery can be as small as a few inches or as thick as the small finger on one's hand. They should be planted in fertile soil that can be watered when needed. It is best to plant the saplings in rows, a few feet apart. They may need to be protected with tree guards or stakes. Small trees grow quickly and may need to be transplanted after just a few years, or they will grow into each other. Planting small trees provides an opportunity to use a wide selection at very low cost. There is an opportunity to experiment with unusual trees in the nursery; to watch them grow and see how they adapt to local conditions. A nursery should be weeded regularly or treated with Glyphosate. Leaving the nursery unattended will result in the trees being overgrown with grass, and the nursery experiment will be a dismal failure. Using string trimmers or rotary mowers in small tree nurseries is not advisable. More trees have died from string trimmers than any other cause.

Trees should be moved from the nursery to their permanent locations according to the master plan and with the passing of time. Not all trees need to be moved at once. Leave a few, it's like insurance and money in the bank. If at all possible, the tree nursery should be located near the maintenance building. If a nursery is created in some out-of-the-way spot on the golf course, chances are that it will be out of sight and it will be forgotten and neglected. The advantage of having a tree nursery on site is that the planting can be done on short notice. Rainy days are ideal for transplanting trees from the nursery. The work may be messy, but its success rate is very high.

PLANTING TREES

For most trees there is a preferred planting time, but small trees can be transplanted with less pain than their bigger brothers and sisters. When the soil is moist and the buds on the shoots have not broken yet, that is an ideal time to transplant a tree. It will surely survive and grow if the following precautions are taken:

1. Preparing the hole that is to receive the tree is paramount. The old adage to dig a ten-dollar hole for a five-dollar tree still applies today. Make sure that the hole is twice as big as the root ball of the tree that will grow there. If the existing soil is particularly brutal, as is often the case on new golf courses, add some superior topsoil mixed with fertilizer.
2. Plant the tree to the same depth as it grew before, or even a bit higher. This is to encourage drainage. Freestanding water should not accumulate around the base of the tree. It will result in the tree having wet feet, a condition that will ultimately lead to its death.
3. Backfill carefully around the roots of the tree. Use good quality topsoil and stamp it down with the heel of one's boot. The earth around the tree must feel firm so that the tree is securely anchored and there are no air pockets in the soil surrounding the roots.
4. Create a well around the base of the tree. It is for water that will remain in place and gradually soak down to the roots every time the tree is given a drink. Newly planted trees are very thirsty at first and must be watered regularly. The well, meanwhile, will have to be leveled at a later date or surely some poor golfer will find an unfair lie. Heaven forbid!
5. Finally the tree must be staked to protect it from the elements and from people. Even small trees must be staked so they won't get run over. Larger trees may need more than one stake and even guy wires to secure them in position.

All of the above can be aided by the simple expedient of using a tree spade. Such contraptions come in all shapes and sizes and can be used for small trees but especially for very large trees. Tree spades like "The Big John" can move trees with a caliper of 10" and a ball of earth measuring 6–7 ft, weighing more than a ton. Several such trees planted in a group create an instant landscape or an instant hazard, depending on one's view. Trees that are planted with the large tree spade need postplanting care just the same. The spaces between the ball and the hole need to be filled with topsoil and tamped down with a two-by-four or a shovel handle. It is also advisable to create a well around the base of the tree for watering purposes. Large trees that are planted during the heat of summer need to be watered often.

Smaller trees will continue to be planted manually, because it is quick and easy. At certain times of years, deciduous trees can be planted with bare roots. Care must be taken that the roots are kept moist. An unusual planting method involves filling a hole with water, adding soil, manure, and fertilizer and mixing it thoroughly. The resulting slurry is used as a bath for all trees to take before being planted. A bare rooted maple that is dipped into such a mud bath finds its roots dripping with a concoction that contains all the essentials of life, and when now planted, is ready for certain growth.

DISTANCE BETWEEN TREES

It is important to visualize what the newly planted trees will look like once they grow up. They must be planted far enough apart so that they will not crowd each other. There must be sufficient space for mowers to get around to trim the grass. When trees are planted too far away from each other, they seldom do well. We believe that trees like company as they grow up, and that they survive better as a group than alone. As they mature, they can be thinned or transplanted.

Trees on a golf course seldom look good when planted in a straight row. Even along a fence line or perimeter, trees should be planted in an irregular manner, to create interest and to avoid monotony. Groups of trees should be made up of different species and be of varying sizes for the same reason.

TREE MAINTENANCE

Taking care of small trees is an easy task. They must be fertilized from time to time, watered if need be, and pruned to keep growth under control. Superintendents should carry along a small set of pruning shears to nip off branches that look out of place, or low branches that hit the roofs of golf carts. Pruning, however, is not a part-time assignment for the superintendent. Regular pruning of trees is part of the over-all maintenance operation and should be done on a timely basis.

As trees grow bigger, pruning becomes cumbersome, requiring the services of experts in the field. Deadwood must be removed and crossing branches eliminated. Wood chippers are used to pulverize the excess growth, and the bigger trees and branches are cut for firewood.

Many golfers do not take kindly to the cutting of trees, even trees that are past their prime or obviously dead or dying. Trees that were planted with good intentions originally may have lost their usefulness and become a hindrance. Such trees may at the same time have become "sacred cows" to many golfers, their removal a rallying cry to stop a project. Otherwise sensible people become quite sentimental and irrational when it comes to trees. To avoid these confrontations it is best to have a golf course architect on hand and let him make the final decision. As a last resort, take the trees down early in the morning or better yet, when the course is closed. Just make sure that the stump is obliterated and the scar sodded. Golfers rarely miss a tree, once it is gone.

Well-known American golf course architect Arthur Hills relates his involvement with the removal of hundreds of trees at the famed Oakmont Golf Club near Pittsburgh. An ambitious greens chairman had planted these trees many years before, when Oakmont was a barren field. Now these many trees had become overgrown and were crowding the fairways. It was Arthur's assignment to determine which ones should live and which ones were to die, but he managed to pass at least some of the blame onto the Oakmont's president, who quickly became known as "Chainsaw Smith."

Another story about tree removal involves golf course superintendent Richard Bator in the eastern United States. The trees on his course had encroached to such a degree around tees, greens, and fairways, that grass growth was sporadic, and drastic action was required. Bator cut down trees in the early morning or during the off-season. When asked by golfers what had happened to certain familiar trees, the response was always the same: thunder took it down or it was struck by lightning. His answer was the truth with a twist, because little did the golfers know that Bator carried two chain saws in his truckster; one was known as "Thunder" and the other was called "Lightning."

No responsible person likes heartlessly to take down the giants of the forests or specimen trees on the golf course. In most cases the trees that we planted many years ago eventually grow to maturity but for whatever reason are in the way and need to be removed. There are few that meet such a fate in comparison to the many hundreds or even thousands that we have planted in our days. For the golfers, the pain associated with the felling of trees can be lessened to a small degree by making the firewood available to those who need it.

LEAVES

Pretty as colors of the leaves may be in the fall, they cause tremendous problems for golfers who lose balls among them. Leaves are blown in piles or windrows. Leaves are swept into hoppers and hauled away to be composted or otherwise disposed of. The smell of burning leaves is now just a fond memory in the minds of grey-haired greenkeepers. The practice has slipped from the golfing scene just like hickory-shafted clubs.

On golf courses that are well known for their numerous trees, leaf removal is a big-time operation involving large machinery and several workers for weeks at a time. The highest order of priority is to keep the greens and surroundings clear of fallen leaves. Since leaves fall continuously but gradually, the greens may need to be cleared several times a day. The next order of importance is the landing areas, and after that the roughs, the bunkers, and the tees. It is an ongoing process not finished until the last leaf has fallen and is swept away. Sometimes there is help from a friendly wind that blows the leaves into a nearby forest or a stream whose current will carry the leaves away. Mostly it's just hard work.

Special attachments are available for rotary mowers, the large upfront varieties. Screens are placed inside the cutting units and these powerful grass cutters can be turned into very useful leaf mulchers. The fast rotating blades grind the leaves into tiny snippets that disappear between the grass blades. Mulching leaves in this manner quickly converts a leaf-strewn fairway or rough into a clean and playable turf. No doubt, once the snippets of leaves break down they will add organic matter to the soil.

Figure 16.3. Leaves are an annually recurring problem at northern golf courses. PTO-driven blowers are often used to clean the surface.

SUMMARY

When we were young and inexperienced we searched for fast-growing trees, and could not find any. As we grew older we began to realize that most trees are fast-growing trees, and that somehow trees grow bigger and stronger as we grow older and weaker. It was the Persian poet Omar Khayyam who stated many centuries ago that, "It is a wise man who plants a tree under whose shade he knows he will never rest." With that piece of wisdom in mind, we will continue to plant trees and on occasion, be horribly ruthless and cut down a perfectly healthy tree, but when we leave this earth there will always be a living legacy of our insignificant toil.

Landscaping

INTRODUCTION

A golfer on the way to the course receives a first impression of what is to come at the entrance to the grounds. This first impression often sets the tone for what lies ahead. A messy flower bed, a weedy lawn, or cracked pavement can be indicative of what the golf course or even the clubhouse will be like. Add a cool reception in the pro shop and some poorly cooked food in the grill, and no matter how well manicured the golf course, the stage has been set for a miserable golfing experience. That is precisely why golf club management is so much a team effort. All the components of the team must work together, like the gears in a well-oiled machine to produce a smooth running organization. Nowhere is such cooperation more important than at the entrance to the golf club. It does not need to be an elaborate rock garden with waterfalls cascading and fountains splashing. There is no need for statues, hanging baskets, or ornately trimmed bushes. The golfer in a rush to the first tee will barely notice such extravagances, but the subconscious will pick up the imperfections—the lawn not trimmed, thistles among the petunias, and trash on the pavement! Such blemishes are registered indelibly on the mind, only to be recalled when the putts don't drop and the service is slow.

TREES AND SHRUBS

Landscaping around the clubhouse is meant to dress up the buildings and to create a picture as pretty as a postcard. Everyone likes colorful flowers, showy bushes, and specimen trees. To arrange them to their best advantage is landscaping, and even the most modest clubhouse needs some landscaping to enhance its visual appeal.

Whereas on the golf course the emphasis is on the quality of the turf and the design of the holes, around the clubhouse there is an opportunity to show off un-

183

usual trees, flowering shrubs, rose beds, etc. Trees such as flowering crabs and Japanese cherries that would detract from the strategy of individual golf holes are ideal around the clubhouse. Tulip trees and gingkos are other specimens that fit into this category. Groupings of showy shrubs look magnificent on grassy banks near the locker room. In the shelter of the clubhouse buildings, plant material that would probably die on the golf course manages to survive when protected from wind and cold. Precisely because of the favorable clubhouse location, plant material will grow faster to maturity here than on the golf course. It is for this reason that one must at times be ruthless, and trim bushes and trees severely or even remove them completely. As with the trees turned sacred cows on the golf course, it is best to do this kind of work early in the day or in the dark of night, making sure that all evidence is removed before the golfers arrive.

The clubhouse grounds can be converted to a veritable botanical garden with a wide variety of plant material that is of interest not only to the golfers but to all visitors. Superintendents with a horticultural bend will find a perfect opportunity to display their knowledge on the grassy slopes that surround the clubhouse. Often trees are donated by members or are planted to remember deceased golfers. It is not unusual to tag trees with both their Latin and common name. This encourages visitors to stroll through the gardens and admire the beauty, and at the same time learn the names of plant material.

It is important to screen service areas with plantings that will hide the storage bins and the inevitable trash that accumulates. Groupings of dense evergreens give an immediate effect but deciduous shrubs can also be used to good advantage.

Visiting golfers need a place to drop off their clubs and a bag rack should be provided for this purpose. It is no sin to copy the design of the bag rack from a neighboring golf course. That is why superintendents carry cameras: to visit other golf courses, take photographs, and imitate new ideas.

FLOWER BEDS

To design the shape of a flower bed takes artistic ability, and unless the superintendent, the gardener, or someone else has specific knowledge of landscape design, it is best to engage the services of a landscape architect. Such a professional will prepare a plan showing the shapes and locations of all the beds, as well as features such as rock gardens and waterfalls. Often the trees are already in place by the time the landscape architect arrives. Most of these will be preserved and others added in prominent places. The architect's primary function is to create a plan with flowing lines that fits in with the existing buildings. Once the plan is in place, the superintendent and the gardener combine their talents and make the plan a reality.

It has been our experience that the need for quality topsoil in the flower beds is just as important as the soil under the grass on the golf course—perhaps even more so. Don't hesitate to dig out a new bed to a depth of two feet. Use the excavated material to build a mound or tee and then fill the flower bed with a topsoil that is rich in humus. Take a handful and hold it close to the nose; it should permeate the nostrils with the musty smell of animals and manure. Don't mistake black loam for quality topsoil. Black loam smells like the bottom of a bog where it came from and is liverish to the touch. Such material is not worthy of the name "soil" and it will never grow anything useful other than weeds.

Add lots of fertilizer to the new flower bed, particularly bonemeal in copious quantities. Don't hesitate to work in some manure but be cautious with certain kinds of manure. Too much horse manure can actually retard plant growth. For good measure add some triple ten fertilizer, and fork or rototill it in. Such a flower bed, high in fertility, will grow large plants with huge blossoms for years to come and will be the envy of neighbors and visiting friends.

Flowering Bulbs

In the springtime no garden is complete without at least some flowering bulbs. A show of tulips and daffodils always attracts attention. So does a border of crocuses and hyacinths. Large, grassy areas can be naturalized by planting bulbs in a random manner. How is this done? Simply by taking a handful of bulbs, throwing them over one's shoulder, and planting them precisely where they have fallen. Any other method invariably results in straight lines that are distracting and look artificial.

The grass between the bulbs cannot be cut without spoiling the naturalized appearance of the area. As soon as the bulbs begin to fade, it is time to cut the grass as well as the remaining flowers. Bulbs in flower beds are best left until the leaves begin to brown. This helps to store food inside the bulb below ground and assures plentiful blossoms next spring.

Annuals can be planted between the flowering bulbs first thing in the spring. This may look messy for a week or so but if the beds are carefully tended, the overall appearance will soon improve. Some people dig up the bulbs and store them till fall. We have found that it is best to leave the bulbs underground, thus assuring that no one will forget to plant them in the fall. Once bulbs are past their prime after two or three years, they can be dug up and planted on the golf course. Southern exposures along a tree line make for an excellent location. Their early blossoms will greet the golfers when they return to the course for their first game in the spring.

Annuals and Perennials

There are many annuals to choose from each spring and it takes some experience to make the right selections. It is important to select matching colors or the flower beds will resemble patchwork quilts. Instead, stick to just a few colors for best results. Individual beds often look better with just one kind of flower with perhaps a simple border planting. Obviously the height of the plant material is important, with the tallest specimens always at the back and the smaller plants in the front.

For immediate effect, plant the annuals close together. However, patient gardeners will allow for more distance between plants. Once the plants take root and receive encouragement, they will quickly fill in. Newly planted annuals need lots of water at first. Once they have rooted, they benefit from regular hoeing to break up the crusty earth and let in the air. Timely fertilizer applications are also essential, although beds constructed as described above will need very little in the way of nutrients for quite some time.

Perennials are the landmark of English gardens. Nowhere do perennials look richer and more profuse than in English country gardens near a Tudor manor or a Victorian mansion. There are a multitude of plants that blossom all season long and provide color and interest on a continuing basis. Study English gardens and implement what has been learned around the clubhouse. Keep in mind that English gardens were tended by hardworking, loving English gardeners. A perennial garden requires lots of attention, indeed devotion, to look its best.

Interested members can be recruited to help with the gardens. At the Toronto Ladies Golf Club the flower beds were designed by a talented member and nowhere are the beds as breathtaking as at this golf club. There is a profusion of lilies, hollyhocks, roses, impatiens, snapdragons, and sweet-smelling alyssums that grab the attention of visitors and members driving up the hill toward the pillared clubhouse.

PHOTO AREAS AND VIEWING OPPORTUNITIES

Golf courses are a favorite setting for weddings, anniversaries, and other important events. Such memorable occasions are often recorded in photos or on videos. The most suitable locations need to identified and enhanced. Visitors to the golf club also like to observe golfers in action. Perhaps there is an opportunity to provide a vista of the property from a high promitory. Such a viewing area should include a comfortable bench, possibly a table and some chairs.

ROCK GARDENS AND WATERFALLS

At exclusive country clubs the extent of the landscaping can become quite extravagant. We have observed the most elaborate rock gardens with cascading waterfalls and fountains spraying colored water, and even make-believe mountains spewing forth flaming gases. Impressive as such landscaping may be, we often wonder if the money would not be better spend on golf course improvements. At times it seems that the club's directors have their priorities mixed up. The vast majority of the club's customers come to play golf and not to look at an artificially created landscape. The real landscape of grass, trees, water, and sand is a piece of beauty seldom equaled in any other way around the clubhouse.

A GREENHOUSE AND A GARDENER

Any kind of extensive clubhouse landscaping will need the full-time attention of a gardener. There is the daily routine of watering and weeding, of trimming the bushes and the grass. The work is never-ending, with peak periods of activity in the spring, followed by regular routines as the seasons progress. Lawns need frequent cutting and fertilizing. The sprinklers must be set to ensure that both the grass and the landscape plants are watered properly.

A gardener's reputation depends entirely on the quality of the work that is produced. When the ladies "ooh and ah" as they admire a flower bed, when the men take pictures of the bushes, and when visitors want to know the names of plant material, then an astute gardener knows that the good work is being recognized.

Almost any professional gardener will want the convenience of having a greenhouse. It can be used to start new flowers from seed, to pot plants, and to create hanging baskets. The greenhouse is a perfect place to overwinter plants that might otherwise not survive. A greenhouse is a valuable addition to a gardening enterprise and no respectable clubhouse grounds should be without one.

SUMMARY

For many golfing establishments, the need for elaborate clubhouse landscaping is entirely superfluous. Their reason for being is to provide golf, and golf only. For many country clubs, the quality of the gardens is almost as important as the golf course. Such clubs go to great lengths to beautify their grounds, and a competent gardener is invariably the person who makes the clubhouse grounds shine. That all-important first impression starts with the appearance of the clubhouse grounds. It does not need to be elaborate, but it must be neatly tended.

18 Managing People

INTRODUCTION

When the workers arrive at the crack of dawn, or even before, they will all be assigned certain tasks, which will to a great degree determine the condition of the golf course. How they are organized and how they are managed will directly impact the golfers' enjoyment of their game for that specific day. As a rule, many of the decisions of who does what and who goes where have already been made the day before, but often there are last minute changes caused by the weather, the change of a function, or an event.

STAFF MEETING

In many cases the superintendent and the assistant will have a last minute meeting to decide the day's work. Often other key players also get involved. Then it is time for the superintendent to address the troops. Speaking to the assembled workers is much like giving a talk at a Turfgrass Meeting or Conference. It requires preparation and confidence. The assistant should be close at hand to help look after the details.

An address to the troops should start with general information about what kind of events are taking place on the golf course that day. Outings that are scheduled for the future can also be mentioned. Perhaps there is a major tournament in the offing and special preparations need to be made. During the opening remarks it is a good idea to single out one or two employees who have performed well the previous day or week and praise them in front of their peers. Such public praise is great for the morale of the crew.

Next, assign all individual routine tasks such as mowing, changing holes, and raking bunkers to specific crew members. Address them by their first name and make them feel that their task is important. Change the sequence of assignments frequently. If bunker raking is always the last job mentioned, the trapper will feel that bunker raking is least important, and the quality of the work may suffer. Start with the rough cutters one day and finish with the hole changers. Then turn the sequence around. If a certain worker has started earlier than usual, inform the rest of the staff what is taking place.

If a greens cutter is expected to be finished by midmorning, spell out the work that needs to be done for the remainder of the day. It is best that each employee knows what is expected all day long. It is even better that all employees know what everyone is doing. Therefore, be specific in spelling out exactly what is expected. Emphasize the need to repair ball marks to the greens cutters, and for the hole changers, remind them about the need for clean cups.

The address to the troops should not be a long one. Be precise and to the point. A long-winded chitchat quickly loses its effectiveness. Save the favorable comments from golfers to the last. That way the day begins with a positive note.

START UP THE ENGINES

While the crew receives its instructions, the mechanic or an assistant should put out all the mowers that will be needed that day and start up the machines to warm the motors. Right on the dot of the appointed hour, maybe earlier but never late, the operators mount their machines and are off. Stick around for a while, in case there is a breakdown. While the mechanic fixes the problem, the assistant or another pinch hitter is already on the way to fill in the gap.

CHECK AND CHECK AGAIN

About a half hour after the greens crew has left and is busy working on the golf course, it is time for the superintendent to make the rounds. Check the greens to make sure the mowers are cutting right and the lines are straight. Check a hole location to see if it is on a level spot. Pull up on a ball washer handle to test for soap and water, and pace off the tee markers and line them up with the center of the fairway. Stop and talk to the lonely trapper or help rake the edge of a bunker. It shows you care and sets an example at the same time. By all means pick up all trash, such as napkins and pop cans, as you travel across the golf course either by foot or on a cart. Praise the jobs that are well done and assist those who need help and additional training. A wave with the hand or a smile at a passing fairway mower or a rough cutter will do wonders for the morale and for the attitude of the workers. It is reassuring for the workers to know that the boss likes them personally and appreciates their hard work.

Occasionally stop and converse with the golfers. Don't intrude on their game when they are obviously engrossed in concentration but be approachable if they seem to want to talk. Listen to their concerns with undivided attention, even if you have heard their particular gripe a hundred times before. Apologize for work that may interfere with their game and explain the reasons for inconveniences. At all times present a congenial image, even when the grass is wilting and the machines are breaking down. Try to remember the names of your regular customers. It is much more pleasant to have an intelligent exchange with a person one can address by first name than an angry confrontation with a total stranger.

LOOK THE PART!

Whereas old-time greenkeepers wore collared shirts and ties and even jackets, the casual look seems to be universally acceptable today. But even when our golfers now wear blue jeans around the clubhouse and sometimes on the course, it still behooves the superintendent to look respectable. You will be treated in the manner that you dress. If the golfers cannot tell the superintendent from the workers, one should not be surprised that respect for the position will diminish. It is not necessary to make a fashion statement; simply wearing clean and functional clothes is sufficient. Many of the outdoors stores now sell clothes that are ideal for the superintendent. The cotton mixture material is durable and attractive. When golfing, a superintendent should look the part of a golfer, with a clean shirt and pressed trousers. For greens committee meetings, dress up in slacks and a jacket and possibly a tie. Many of the clothing items that are now sold through the GCSAA are ideal for superintendents to wear, and present a professional image.

COFFEE BREAKS AND LUNCHTIME

Few people are willing and able to work continuously without an occasional break. We all like to sit down from time to time, relax and have a coffee or a soft drink on a hot day. Our workers are no exception. Many will take along a thermos filled with coffee or tea and take a break under a shade tree or a bench on a tee. Others will visit the canteen on the golf course. A problem arises when all congregate at once near a halfway house or a snack bar. The overwhelming presence of a large group of workers tends to inhibit the golfers, who may bypass the canteen as a result.

Coffee breaks should be organized in such a way that they break up the greens staff in small groups that are spread out and don't interfere with the regular customers who frequent the canteen for their convenience. However, at lunchtime all staff is expected to return to headquarters and take a rest and a break. While they eat their sandwiches, the staff socializes and establishes bonds of friendship and camaraderie. Just before the conclusion of the lunch period, the superintendent or the assistant once again discusses the work assignments for the remainder of the day. Mostly this is just a rehash of what was already decided in the morning, but sometimes there are changes and the staff needs to be advised what is expected.

CHECK, CHECK, AND CHECK AGAIN

It is only by persistent checking on the workers that one can be sure that the work is being done. It is not necessary to interfere with the work of well-trained personnel, but by visiting and checking the progress, one shows an interest that is conta-

Figure 18.1. Look the part of the professional superintendent.

gious and leads to a higher quality performance and pride in the project. In addition, many of the little things that may be overlooked by otherwise diligent workers are noted and corrected by the timely visit of the master.

THE END OF THE DAY

At least for the hourly workers, the end of the day comes by mid-afternoon. All the machines and the operators make their way back to the Turf Care Center. It's wash-up time! Fuel tanks are topped off and equipment is cleaned and put away in an orderly fashion.

The floors are swept, the washrooms cleaned, and the staff room tidied.

It is best to appoint one or more persons on a weekly basis for cleanup and lockup duty. Prepare a checklist and have the person in charge make sure that everything is taken care of, put away, and locked up safely. It is time for everyone to go home except those few who are working overtime, perhaps the irrigation crew, the assistant, and almost certainly the superintendent. When all is peace and quiet around the shop there is a wonderful opportunity to get caught up on the administrative work. File the fertilizer or the chemical application report. Record all daily activities in a running log. Make telephone calls and get ready for meetings with committee members or other department heads. Relax for a while with a turf magazine, and then make one more swing over the golf course. Then it is time to plan the activities for tomorrow.

HIRING AND FIRING

To recruit and train a hardworking and dedicated greens staff is arguably the most important task that a superintendent must accomplish at the beginning of each golfing season. Of course, several of the greens staff are kept on year round. Others come back season after season, but a number of new workers need to be hired each new season. To buy a new mower or a tractor, one simply needs to obtain quotes and make a choice. To hire a new worker takes a lot more time and has the ultimate potential of being either a disaster or a great success. Machines can be returned for warranty if they break down or are unsuitable. Workers are human beings with feelings, who at times need to be scolded and praised, encouraged or dissuaded, as well as trained to be hardworking and devoted greenkeepers. The object is to hire carefully!

The Interview

There are many ways to advertise for help, and the want ads in the daily newspapers probably offer the greatest opportunity. Don't overlook local newspapers, bulletin boards in grocery stores, and word of mouth via existing employees. Some of the senior workers, with roots in the community, can spread the word that the golf course is hiring. Be wary of hiring family members of existing staff or the sons and daughters of golf club members. Never hire workers who are difficult to fire. The greens chairman's son falls into this category, and so does the manager's daughter. Stay away from these potentially difficult situations.

We prefer to hire people who live in the community so that they do not need to travel far to work. We like individuals who are active and play sports, but not necessarily golf. Such people are apt to be physically fit and won't need time off work to see doctors. The interview is conducted in a quiet place where there will be no interruptions from the phone or from people intruding. Usually there is another person present to make sure that all the questions are acceptable and that there cannot be any misunderstandings at a later time. It is not uncommon that for every person who is interviewed, at least three others have been screened out over the telephone or from submitted resumes as being unsuitable.

Picking the right person for the right job takes an uncanny ability that is learned after much practice and many mistakes. We have learned over the years through observation that the people we work for are often older and more conservative in their thinking than the rest of the population. Therefore we tend to hire people who fit into that mold. There is no place on the greens crew for activists and reactionaries. We want people who like working hard in the outdoors and with a smile on their face.

It is also worthwhile remembering that each new employee needs to be trained for several weeks or months. If, at the end of this training period the new recruit does not fit in and proves to be unsuitable, then we have wasted a lot of time and money and could cause grief to the unfortunate employee who did not measure up. Therefore, hire carefully. Don't make impetuous decisions. Check out the references, particularly the ones from other golf courses. It makes no sense to hire some else's problem. Better wait till the following morning before making up one's mind. Once a decision has been made, act promptly and bring the new recruit aboard as quickly as possible. Discuss the rules and regulations and have the new worker sign a copy of this document, so that there will be no misunderstanding about the conditions of employment.

The Training Process

If a new worker has been hired to cut greens, have one of the experienced hands or the assistant do the training. The nursery is a good place to start. Once some fundamentals have been mastered, a training video provided by a manufacturer should be shown. Now the time has come to take the trainee to an isolated green and make the first attempt to cut this green. In fact, it may need to be cut 2–3 times just to gain experience. There may be other greens on which the trainee can practice. The next day is time for solo flying, with the assistant lurking behind a nearby tree, keeping an anxious eye and waiting for disaster to strike.

Similar procedures are followed for fairway and rough mowers. Make sure that there is always a senior employee present to assist and supervise. Everyone needs to learn and we have to be patient with the newcomers. Unlikely as it may seem at first, they will eventually learn and turn into respectable workers. Some may even become superintendents on some distant day.

Hiring an Assistant

Once word gets out that a golf course is hiring a new assistant, the resumes, the phone calls, and e-mail messages will arrive in large numbers. Select 10–12 whose qualifications meet the job criteria and set up the interviews at least an hour apart. Try to arrange the interviews in a concentrated time period so that a decision can be made in a methodical manner. Use the following criteria as a basis of comparison, and score each applicant on a point basis. Tally the points and interview the top three for a second time.

Appearance: 15 Points

It is a fact that a favorable appearance increases the chances of success dramatically. Score a perfect 15 points for a Tom Cruise look-alike and 8 points for a well-dressed Rasputin.

Figure 18.2. Training operators—an essential element of an efficient staff.

Education: 15 Points

A Master's degree in agronomy is not necessary, but a Bachelor of Science ticket is worth 15 points; a four-week turf course, possibly 4 points, and a high school dropout does not score at all.

Experience: 15 Points

A few years on the greens crew at Augusta, followed by a stint as second assistant to a GCSAA past president should earn full points. Being in charge of the sand greens at Moosonee is worth 2 points.

Health: 15 Points

Downgrade body builders for being narcissistic, but put windsurfers, skiers, and scuba divers right at the top, followed by soccer and hockey players, in that order. Pool players and karaoke singers are a distant last.

Attitude: 15 Points

This is a difficult one to grade during an interview. Like laziness, it is almost impossible to assess. Yet without a positive attitude, all other criteria are meaningless. It is a good idea to check the references to find out about an applicant's attitude.

Maturity: 15 Points

Since an assistant will be a leader, we need a person who will command respect. We often think in terms of age when speaking of maturity, but we know of some very fine young people who act maturely in their late teens and early twenties. Others are still childish in their behavior when they are more than 30 years old. The degree of maturity that is desirable for the position is a subjective decision on the part of the interviewer.

Golfing Ability: 10 Points

We are suspicious of potential assistants with single digit handicaps. To maintain such a degree of golfing expertise requires much practice, which can only be at the expense of work. Similarly, an applicant who cannot break a hundred should take a greater interest in the game. A B-flight player would probably score highest in our calculations.

Check the references of the three applicants who score the highest and arrange for a second interview, at which time working conditions and salary are discussed in greater detail. During the interview, ask yourself the following questions:

1. Can I work and get along with this person?
2. Will this person take direction and follow instructions?
3. Does this person have leadership qualities and the ability to get along with the greens staff and the golfers?
4. Will this person represent our club respectably?

On the basis of such a thorough process, mistakes are rarely made and the new assistant will invariably work out well and become a valuable asset. The same process with minor alterations can also be used for mechanics, secretaries, and other key personnel.

Performance Reviews

Each worker and all key personnel should have a file detailing the history of employment. Part of the record-keeping process involves making timely notes in these files. Sick days, vacation periods, and lateness are all reported in the employee's docket. Any unusual occurrences that the employee was involved in should also be noted for possible future reference. In addition, once a year there should be a thorough performance review. Such a review should be in writing, and starts by listing all the positive accomplishments that the employee has had during the past season. In addition, shortcomings should be noted. Perhaps a worker has been lingering at the coffee table. Possibly a worker has developed an unpleasant attitude problem. The review is an opportunity to discuss drinking problems or antisocial behavior. By documenting such imperfections they become part of the record and serve as motivation for the worker to improve their performance. The document is discussed and agreed upon, and signed by both the superintendent and the employee.

Firing

To dismiss a person for unsatisfactory performance is a dreadful deed that must be done, ruthlessly sometimes, but done just the same. A new employee can easily be let go during the probationary period. Longtime workers who were excellent performers at one time but have developed bad habits should be given every opportunity to improve. When no improvement is discernible, swift and drastic action is required. A severance payment based on the period of time the worker has been employed will sweeten the sting. The reason for firing never makes sense to the person who is being let go, but if the transgressions are well documented there is very little argument and the decision is irreversible. Never keep on, for an extended period, an employee who has been fired. It is better to cut out the rot with one swift twist of the knife and let the healing process begin. A crew cannot function to its optimum performance unless all participants, workers and managers alike, work as a team to the best of their ability. The rotten apples must be removed, and swiftly.

DEALING WITH SALES AGENTS

Sales agents can be a great help to golf superintendents, especially novice superintendents who need assistance and often have few friends to call on when they take a new position. Company representatives carry a wealth of information, but one should be reminded that their primary goal is to sell product. Modern technology makes searching for information much easier, and comparing products and prices can now be done with ease. We should not become totally absorbed by price. Service, the willingness to help a customer, is usually more important than the cost of the product, and is really the foremost consideration.

SUMMARY

Managing people involves building relationships with fellow human beings. It means getting work done, motivating the workers, and often delegating certain tasks to the assistants. One should always remember that workers are often not very well rewarded for the work they do on the golf course, and when they perform extraordinarily well it may be because they are treated with respect and kindness by the superintendent.

The Tools

INTRODUCTION

We remember the frustrations of a young superintendent whose directors spent all the profits of the operation on the clubhouse and there was never any money left to buy equipment for the golf course. He was a competent superintendent but he had no tools to do the job, and the golf course began to suffer as a result. In spite of valiant efforts on the part of the mechanic, one fateful day every mower was broken down and the grass could not be cut. An important tournament was scheduled for the weekend, but there were no mowers to trim and manicure the turf, and the golfers would not be pleased. At the last minute, in the nick of time, along came a finance man, a whiz with figures and an expert on leasing. An agreement was made in short order and the deal was signed: brand new mowers arrived that very same day and the course was cut to perfection just in time for the tournament. The day had been saved by a new method of acquiring machinery: leasing instead of buying; small monthly payments for several years instead of one large sum all at once. Many golf courses are now replacing their worn-out equipment by leasing new machines and by spreading the cost of acquisition over several years. Superintendents are overjoyed, because they have the tools to do the work.

TOOLS TO CUT THE GRASS

To determine the number of mowers that are needed to cut the greens on an 18-hole course, one should think in terms of running a shotgun tournament early in the morning during the fall. At that time of year there is often only one hour to cut all the greens, and it will surely take three riders and at least six pedestrian mowers. During a regular morning in the summer, two riders or four walkers would be sufficient. Yet it is so handy to have the extra units as backup machines, and for that late fall shotgun.

For the tees, two riders will be sufficient or double the number if walkers are used on the tees. If the golfers start early or if the pro shop runs many shotguns and crossovers, additional units may be necessary.

There are many different ways to cut fairways but no matter which way is preferred, at least two cutters are needed, and many clubs have twice that many. One should be prepared for emergencies and backup units can save the day, especially when important functions are scheduled.

All golf courses need at least one specialty mower and preferably two, for surrounds—around bunkers and tees. These hard-to-get-at areas, frequently with very steep slopes, require ingenuity and lots of experience to produce satisfactory results. Sturdy machines are needed with good climbing ability.

The roughs on most golf courses encompass the largest area and need the most machines to get the grass cut. Consider at least one set of gang mowers, either tractor-drawn or self-propelled. Two upfront rotaries are also essential, as well as several rotary walkers and string trimmers. The rough is a never-ending job and requires lots of attention and dependable machines to stay ahead of the fast-growing grass.

TOOLS TO CULTIVATE THE GRASS

Walking aerators are for tees and greens and larger, tractor-drawn machines are meant to do the fairways. Spikers and overseeders are important tools as well, to augment the aerators, and are also useful as a means of introducing seed into established turf. Verticut units are needed on greens and tees to thin the turf and are often also used to pulverize the cores after aerating. They can be employed for the same purpose on fairways. There are other means worth considering, such as core processors and drag mats. Much of the aerating equipment is used infrequently and many golf courses are contracting such work out, thus eliminating the need for investing in expensive equipment.

Topdressers are regularly used on tees and greens and every golf course should have at least one or two of these machines. Topdressing fairways is gaining widespread acceptance, but the larger units that perform these operations are cumbersome and expensive. However, on bent grass fairways they are now a necessity.

MAINTENANCE VEHICLES

The greens staff needs to get around to change holes and markers, to make irrigation repairs and fix bridges and benches, and a myriad of small chores. There are some fine personnel carriers equipped with hydraulic lift boxes and extra seats. A rule of thumb dictates that almost half the greens staff needs to be mobile. Therefore, one should count on between five and ten maintenance vehicles for an 18-hole golf course.

SPRAYERS AND SPREADERS

Most operations now require computer operated sprayers for tees and greens. Such units are usually self-propelled. If there is a necessity to spray on a regular basis, a backup unit is easy to justify. For fairways, many superintendents use a tractor to pull the heavy spray rig. Reliable fertilizer spreaders, both big and small, are needed to apply fertilizer to fairways, tees, and greens as well as in the roughs.

TRACTORS AND TRAILERS

It is easy to establish the need for four tractors to do miscellaneous work on an 18-hole course. At least one of these units should be equipped with a front-end loader and a backhoe can be put to good use on most any golf course. It is customary for golf course tractors to be equipped with turf type tires. Several small utility trailers are needed for construction work and cleanup chores.

TRUCKS

No golf course is complete without at least one pickup truck and most would like to have a small dump truck as well. The first is used for a runabout, both on and off the golf course. The latter becomes handy for construction work and in northern climates, equipped with appropriate attachment, as a snowplow.

IN THE SAND BUNKERS

At least two powered bunker rakes are needed to rake the 50 or so bunkers on an average 18-hole course. Where bunkers are small, they may be raked by hand. In addition, power edgers are needed to trim the bunkers.

MISCELLANEOUS EQUIPMENT

1. Most courses would not do without a sod cutter, and an essential component of the sodding operation is a self-propelled roller.
2. A trencher to install both irrigation and drainage pipe is high on the list of most superintendents' needs.
3. A wood chipper to grind up branches and twigs.
4. Leaf blowers and sweepers.
5. Mowers, grinders, and a generator.
6. Water pumps and a power washer.

SMALL TOOLS

Let a superintendent loose in a hardware store and there would not be a shopping cart big enough for all that is needed on the golf course and in the Turf Care Center. High on the list would be several quality chain saws, some line trimmers, a couple of hedge trimmers, and too many shop tools to mention.

GREENKEEPING TOOLS

Our profession requires certain specific tools that are needed to practice the ancient art of greenkeeping. The secrets of greenkeeping often involve such tools and one must learn to be proficient in their use. Such skills are learned from wise old men who in turn learned from their predecessors. The tools that are specifically greenkeeping tools include:

1. A sodding iron to lift sod and to make small repairs on tees, greens, and even fairways.
2. A turf doctor or a square hole repair tool. The turf doctor makes it possible for square pieces of thick sod to butt against each other for an instant playable surface. There is a round model as well, but it leaves small triangles between the plugs.
3. A Levelawn to work topdressing and aerator cores into the turf by pushing it back and forth. This tool is ideal for small areas and in between tee markers at the end of the day.
4. A dandelion rake with many small teeth to scratch the grass.
5. A large square-mouthed shovel, which can be used with an educated swing, to apply topdressing to small areas.
6. Whipping poles, formerly bamboo poles but now often made from fiberglass, to whip the dew off the green. It also comes in handy to clean spilled grass clippings from the apron.

AN INVENTORY

There is wide divergency between different golf courses and the tools that they use for maintenance. Peter Leuzinger, well-known superintendent at the 27-hole Ivanhoe Club near Chicago, kindly made his equipment inventory available to us. Readers will be amazed at the number of units that Peter has at his disposal, but they should keep in mind that Ivanhoe is an established golf course whose members demand superior conditioning and they don't want Peter to be lacking for tools.

Figure 19.1. The Turf Doctor Tool, invented in Australia
and part of the Magic of Greenkeeping.

Figure 19.2. Another Australian contribution to greenkeeping: the Levelawn.

	Replacement Cost
TRACTORS:	
Three towing tractors, two loaders, and a Ditch Witch with a backhoe	$149,500
TRUCKS:	
One dump truck and a 4-wheel drive vehicle	50,000
UTILITY CARTS:	
One Toro workman, seven John Deere carts, four Club Car carry-alls, two Ezgo golf carts, one Yamaha golf cart	103,500
MOWERS:	
13 Toro walk-behind greens mowers and 7 riding greens mowers that are also used for tees	175,000
Four fairway mowers	119,000
One Toro upfront rotary, three Howard Price rotary mowers, one Ford rotary mower, two National triplexes, and one Brouwer triplex	121,000
Five small Toro rotary mowers	3,500
BUNKER RAKES:	
Two Toro sand bunker rakes	24,000
SPRAY RIGS:	
Two 300-gallon sprayers and a 160-gallon Hahn sprayer	44,000
TRACTOR ATTACHMENTS:	
Trailers, spreaders, plows, blades, and a chipper	25,900
RENOVATION EQUIPMENT:	
Aerators, topdressers, overseeders, a sod cutter, and a power roller	102,100
MISCELLANEOUS GROUNDS EQUIPMENT:	
Pumps, trimmers, edgers, chain saws, and spreaders	13,285
MISCELLANEOUS SHOP EQUIPMENT:	
Welder, pressure washer, hoist, grinders, and two Otterbine fountains	23,250
TOTAL	$954,035

Almost a million dollars for equipment just to maintain the golf course. Superintendents should compare the inventory at their own courses with what Peter Leuzinger has at his disposal at the Ivanhoe Club in Chicago. Few will measure up to this vast array of machinery and tools, but if thoroughly completed the exercise will result in an accurate inventory. Cataloging the equipment will quickly show where there are shortfalls and where the emphasis should be when making capital investment. Most importantly, an accurate inventory is essential for insurance claims in case of fire.

SUMMARY

There are heroic stories of superintendents who make do with hardly any equipment at all. Most of these tales are spun by tightfisted owners in smoke filled barrooms. The reality is that greens specifically, and grass generally, cannot be cut satisfactorily nor maintained with broken-down old mowers held together by binder clips. There comes a time when the old junk needs to be pitched out and replaced by modern machines. Golf course owners and club committee people ought to realize that a new piano in the dining room does not cut grass and that the soft rug in the grill is less important than fertilizer for the greens in the scheme of things. There will always be clubs and courses that have their priorities mixed up, but only for a little while; ultimately, the golfers will vote with their feet, and go where course conditioning is uppermost on the list. Thus the frustrations of not having the tools to do the job are only temporary, but if there appears to be no end in sight, another golf course may be the answer.

20 The Turf Care Center

The maintenance facility at any golf course is the center of operations, where each day at the crack of dawn all important decisions are being made that determine the condition of the playing surface for that day. Staff arrives and is put to work. Machinery is started up, carts are loaded with fertilizer, and sprayers are filled with water and chemicals. The maintenance building is a beehive of activity all day long, but especially early in the morning, with workers scurrying in all directions and gradually leaving for their assigned tasks.

In 1973 we baptized our old maintenance barn at the Board of Trade Golf Club in Woodbridge, Ontario, the "Turf Care Center." It was an attempt to upgrade our status, a facelift with words, to gain acceptance as an important element in the framework of the golfing operation. At the time of the name change we also painted the old barn and made it more functional for storing equipment and making repairs. The name Turf Care Center was proudly displayed on the side of the building so that both golfers and passersby could easily see and become familiar with the new name and the new image. Later we added additional buildings to house the mechanics' repair shop and staff quarters, as well as a separate building for pesticide storage.

Our maintenance compound also includes a small bungalow which houses a comfortable office and overnight facilities for guests and staff. To complete the maintenance compound, there is a large turf nursery with varietal test plots and a tree nursery. The entire area is almost two acres. It is functional, has some character, and amazingly, the name has stuck. We may not have been the first to use the term Turf Care Center, but we have certainly contributed to the general acceptance of the term in the golf course maintenance field.

EQUIPMENT STORAGE

Seldom is a storage building big enough to hold all the golf course equipment, and provisions should be made to enlarge the main building or to add another one. If space is insufficient, there is no choice but to store some items outside, exposed to

Figure 20.1. Setting up a mower to cut perfectly is an expert's job.

the elements. Tractor-drawn implements such as tillers, graders, wagons, trailers, and large rotaries can be stored outside for short periods. Ultimately, to preserve the equipment, arrangements should be made to have a roof over all implements.

Many maintenance areas include an out-of-the-way place for castoffs and relics. This is often the most interesting place to spend some time, and no visit to another golf course is complete without snooping around behind the barn. All sorts of treasures can be found. The remains of old mowers that our predecessors used, tools no longer used, and worn-out reels and twisted carts. All such items are of special interest and speaks of our history and our roots. The best pieces should be salvaged and possibly restored to be exhibited at turfgrass conferences. Michigan State University has a fine museum of old golf course equipment and gladly accepts donations of such items. Another contact is the Historical Society of the GCSAA in Lawrence, Kansas. We remember making an unusual find behind the barn of the Royal Melbourne Golf Club in Australia during a visit in 1984. The log of a huge, century-old eucalyptus tree had been fashioned into a turf roller and was used to flatten the fairways when the golf course was built. It was an awesome roller and the only remaining testimony of the days of yore.

THE SHOP

The shop is where the mechanic makes his repairs and performs maintenance on all equipment. It is like a big garage, where equipment can be raised and lowered; a place full of drills and grinding wheels with air compressors and wash-up solutions.

There are workbenches and tool chests and bins full of parts. Vises and jacks, crowbars and sledges, saws, hammers, and wrenches, all can be found in the shop at precisely the spot where the mechanic can always find them. Such a place can easily become messy and disorganized and it takes a dedicated mechanic with the encouragement of the superintendent to maintain a shop that is clean and tidy. The distinction of being the cleanest shop in North America belongs to the Collier's Reserve Golf Course near Naples, Florida where Tim Hiers is the superintendent. Here one can literally eat off the floors that sparkle and shine. The machines are not just washed every day, they are also polished and look like floor models at an equipment show. There is indeed not a speck of dust anywhere, not on the windowsills, not on the tool benches, not on the shiny doorknobs, not on the clear window panes, and not even on the jaws of the vise. This particular shop is an inspiration, and one cannot leave there without making a resolution to imitate some of these practices at home.

The area where mowers are sharpened is often kept separate from the mechanics' shop, because of inherent dust problems. The same problem arises when painting or spray painting is done in the mechanics' shop. For both operations, special arrangements must be made that include adequate ventilation. Local building codes differ from one municipality to the next but must be consulted and adhered to.

WOODWORKING AREA

Carpentry work is associated with sawing, planing, and sanding. All of the operations are dusty and messy and should be done in an area that can be separated from the rest of the maintenance building. Provision has to be made for proper ventilation. It is difficult to be a golf course superintendent and not have some knowledge of carpentry work. Apart from repairs to benches, tables, signs, and markers, there will be signs to build or shelters to repair, and bridges and railings to construct. Inevitably there is a crew member on the greens staff with special aptitude for carpentry skills. Such a person should be encouraged, and placed in charge of the woodworking details.

CLEANUP AREA

When the workers return from their work on the golf course, there needs to be a place where the mowers and all other equipment can be cleaned and washed. Up until recently a wash-up area consisted of a large cement pad with a catch basin in the center. Clippings and all other residue were washed down the drain. We have become conscious of the effects that such methods may have on the environment. Clippings and bits of soil fortified with pesticide and fertilizer residues make for a potent mixture.

Fully aware that the accumulation of such residues can hardly be beneficial and more than likely detrimental, prudent superintendents have installed a pre-washup station, equipped with forced air. Air hoses are used to blow away all loose material that has gathered on the mower during a day's work. Only then is the mower washed

Figure 20.2. Washing off mowers after use is standard maintenance procedure.

off! Using forced air as an intermediary step drastically reduces the amount of solids in the wash-up water. Just the same, the bottom of the catch basin should be cleaned regularly and the smelly concoction at the bottom of the pit spread out over a large area or composted with leaves and sod and soil.

After the machinery has been washed, it should be dried and put away once the fuel tanks have been topped. There should always be time to clean and wash machinery, even if it means overtime. No one likes to start the next morning with a dirty machine. There may not be time for polishing and shining, but perhaps a rainy day will come along, and instead of sending workers home, consider keeping them around and shining the machines.

FUEL STORAGE

All sorts of government bureaucrats have become involved in prescribing rules and regulations for the storage of fuels in aboveground tanks. We doubt if many of these officials ever leave their desks to visit a golf course, but we know that fighting city hall is a useless exercise, and most of us obediently follow the rules.

By and large the fuel storage tanks must be stored in a bathtub arrangement of sufficient size to catch all the liquid in the unlikely event that a tank should burst and spill its contents. Another solution is to use tanks with double walls, much like the Titanic did to prevent it from being ruptured by icebergs. The tanks should be surrounded by strategically placed cement-filled steel pillars, to keep workers from inadvertently bumping into the tanks and causing a rupture and a spill. The rules and regulations in every state and province, and in most countries of the modern world, know no limits. These rules must be adhered to or risk heavy fines and even imprisonment.

PESTICIDE STORAGE

Self-contained storage units that meet all the requirements of government ordinances are now available. Although such buildings are functional and serve a useful purpose, they are seldom a thing of beauty. In fact they are usually quite ugly, and some superintendents may wish to construct their own building that can be functional and also blend in architecturally with the rest of the buildings.

A pesticide storage building should be ventilated 24 hours a day, so that noxious vapors can be whisked away. It should be heated in the winter so that liquids won't freeze. The floor should be enveloped in cement or some other leakproof material. In case there is a spill, the liquids will be contained. The pesticide building should be kept under lock and key at all times. The contents of the building must be kept on file and should be available to anyone who needs to see them. It is prudent to keep inventories at low levels in case of a mishap. A month's supply is in most instances quite sufficient.

WORKERS' LUNCHROOM AND LOCKER ROOM

On a cool day, when there is frost in the air and a dark sky is laden with snow, the staff room needs to be cozy and warm for the workers to have their coffee and eat their lunch. Such a room is a second home for the greens staff, a place where they change, eat, drink, and talk to their companions. There should be a place to shower and wash, especially for those who have been applying pesticides.

A staff room should be equipped with plenty of full-size lockers, with spacious tables and sturdy chairs. There should be a refrigerator, a stove, a long counter with a microwave, a toaster, and a hot plate. There should be a coffee or a tea kettle, and cold drinks for when it gets hot outside. One should always remember the need for hardworking people to eat well and in comfort. The human engine needs plenty of fuel to perform the rest of the day.

Who should clean the staff room, the lunchroom, the shop, and the washrooms? In large operations one person is frequently assigned this duty on a full- or part-time basis. Smaller operations often have several of the junior staff take turns. The lunchroom should be cleaned and swept immediately after lunch every day. The washrooms and the floors may need sweeping and washing more than once a day. The entire maintenance area should look presentable at all times, but especially the washrooms and the eating area. Cleanliness benefits all the workers whose home away from home is the Turf Care Center. It is not unusual for visitors to drop in unexpectedly, and no one wants to be embarrassed and feel a need to apologize.

We recall a young man from France who had come to North America to learn the art of greenkeeping. He had been with us for about a month and had progressed well in our program of training young aspirants, until one day just before quitting time, my assistant came into my office and informed me that Pierre had refused to clean the washrooms. Now it is customary for everyone on our greens staff to take their turn at cleaning the washrooms. Pierre steadfastly refused even after I called him into the office and asked him for his reasons. He replied: "Sir, I came here to learn greenkeeping, not housekeeping." I tried to make Pierre understand that good greenkeeping starts with good housekeeping, but he would have none of it and refused point-blank to clean the washrooms. We don't know whatever happened to Pierre, but needless to say, he did not complete his training program and until this day, we have not deviated from our belief that cutting greens, raking bunkers, applying fertilizer, and yes, cleaning washrooms, are all equally important and need to be done with the same degree of dedication by all greens staff.

THE MATERIAL STORAGE YARD

Every golf course uses a variety of materials such as sand, top soil, gravel, and several others. For ease of handling, these substances must be kept separate, and inventive superintendents have designed a system of sturdy walls that makes it possible to separate the substances. Invariably the common back wall is the strongest, because loaders push against it while scooping up sand or topsoil. The base of the storage yard is often cement but asphalt can be used equally well. The width of the individual bins should be at least 15 ft so that there is plenty of room for dump trucks to back in without danger of damaging the walls.

Some superintendents insist on covering the topdressing materials and the divot mix, so that these materials will stay dry and are always ready to apply. Some have gone so far as to store these materials inside the main storage building next to the fertilizer.

There is a tendency on the part of many superintendents to stockpile vast quantities of fertilizer in the belief that savings can be realized by buying in large quantities. No doubt the price per ton or per bag of fertilizer declines as the quantity increases. We have also noticed that an excessive fertilizer inventory often results in broken bags and spillage. At times the fertilizer will absorb moisture and become hard, and is impossible to spread. We advise practicing moderation and limiting supplies to immediate needs. Take care to clean up broken bags of fertilizer and spread them in the rough.

THE OFFICE

The office may just be a desk with a telephone in the lunchroom, or it may be an air-conditioned room with several desks for the superintendent, the assistant, and frequently one for a secretary as well. No matter how small the operation, there is a need for some degree of record keeping and if office equipment such as computers and calculators are used, a dust-free and ventilated environment must be provided. Although secretaries are commonplace at many golf course operations, the advent of the computer has forced many superintendents to become proficient in the use of a keyboard. In some cases a computer was thrust upon the superinten-

Figure 20.3. Storing materials efficiently at the Vintage Golf Course in Palm Springs, California.

dent when a new irrigation system was installed and regretfully, many such computers are used for that purpose only. A record of all operations needs to be maintained and the days of the handwritten journal are as distant in the past as a greens mower without an engine.

ESSENTIAL RECORDS

1. An inventory of all equipment and machinery must be maintained and updated on a regular basis. It is essential that all serial numbers are recorded, as well as the year and cost of acquisition. Consider also estimating the replacement cost, and have the mechanic record all the repairs that are made to all machinery.
2. Fertilizer and pesticide applications should be recorded in great detail, such as the rate and method of application, and the prevailing weather conditions. Also, maintain a current inventory of all materials.
3. A daily journal of all activities that are performed by the greens staff should be kept current. It is easy to fall behind when recording the daily events, and it is often a good idea to assign this task to a trainee or a student to do before or after work.
4. Maintain daily time sheets for every employee, and calculate the number of hours that are devoted to the various tasks and projects. Employee information should be maintained, and performance evaluations need to be recorded at least twice yearly.

5. Many superintendents now maintain budget information on spreadsheets. Frequently, purchases and the resulting invoices are recorded at the Turf Care Center, making it possible for the superintendent to provide current budget information on a timely basis.

Although specific software packages are available that are designed for golf course use, the information can easily be stored in the file programs of most any computer. It is, however, essential, no matter what system is used, that backup copies are made on a regular basis.

In addition to record keeping, the office at the Turf Care Center produces monthly reports and updates on the maintenance program. Such reports and memoranda are presented to the regular meetings of the green committee. It is not unusual for the superintendent to take minutes at the greens meetings and these should also be filed for future reference. Contributions to the golf club newsletter are generated in the maintenance office, and so are letters and all other correspondence.

MEETING ROOM

Ideally, there is a room in the maintenance building sufficiently large to accommodate the entire crew and then some. The purpose of this room is for the superintendent to address the troops before they set out in the morning. Such a room should be well lit and be provided with many chairs for the greens staff to sit on while the superintendent speaks. There should be a blackboard or a white board for writing and sketches. Unless the crew is excessively large, there is no need for a sound system. A room that can be darkened is a bonus since it can be used to show slides and training videos on rainy days.

We address our staff during several minutes preceding their starting time in the morning. Each person is mentioned by name and their work assignment specified, not just for the morning but often for the entire day. Now is a good time to single out individual staff members who have done extraordinarily good work. It is also opportune to pass along compliments from golfers and even complaints, but never criticize individual workers in front of their peers. It is best to make reprimands in privacy.

Occasionally there is a unique opportunity to expose the entire greens staff to an important visitor. We remember Dr. Joe Vargas paying us a consulting visit and treating our troops to a slide presentation at daybreak. According to Dr. Vargas, it was the earliest turf talk that he had ever presented. Always introduce visiting superintendents, traveling agronomists, and club officials to the assembled staff. It makes everyone feel important and helps boost morale.

SUMMARY

The modern superintendent certainly has become much more of an administrator than our predecessors ever would have thought possible. We must not forget our primary function, which is to grow grass for golfers. We need to become better managers of time so that we can also look after the administration of our maintenance facility in an admirable manner. We also need to embrace the new communication methods of the 21st Century. When the greenkeepers of North America united in 1926, now the GCSAA, they did so primarily to promote the exchange of information so that they could learn from each other. Not in their wildest dreams could they have imagined that the exchange of information between individual superintendents from all over the world is now instantaneous. What will happen to our industry and our profession during the next century is a scary thought. It is even scarier to be left behind.

21 The Seven Deadly Sins
Against Greenkeeping

There are seven deadly sins that golf course superintendents and greenkeepers must not commit at any cost. They are sins against the integrity of the profession. They are sins of ignorance, of neglect, and of omission. Any one of these sins reflects badly on the professional image of the person in charge. It has been our experience that superintendents rarely lose their jobs for reasons of professional inadequacies. More often than not, the reason for dismissal is a clash of personalities, a failure to communicate, or promises to perform that are not kept. In all instances the person involved may possess excellent greenkeeping skills, but lacks in basic abilities that are necessary to get along in life and to excel. Our mandate in this work is to deal primarily with the art and science of greenkeeping. All other endeavors are best left to experts in those particular fields.

THESE ARE THE SEVEN DEADLY SINS:

1. FERTILIZER BURNS ANYWHERE
2. POORLY ADJUSTED GREENS MOWERS
3. SCALPED PLUGS ON GREENS
4. A GREENS MOWER CUT INTO THE APRON
5. LETTING NEW SOD DIE
6. KILLING GREENS WITH KINDNESS
7. A MESSY GOLF COURSE

1. Fertilizer burns anywhere. Accidents can happen, but there is rarely an excuse anymore for burning turf with fertilizer. Modern fertilizers contain mostly slow-release type nitrogen, but that is no reason for failing to try these products in the nursery or in the rough first. Be completely confident that the material you are applying will not mark the greens, the tees, or burn

the fairways. To be totally safe, it is always best to water all fertilizers in thoroughly.

2. Greens mower out of adjustment. Possibly the cutting cylinder is not touching the bed knife, and the quality of cut is very poor. More often, one side of the mower cuts lower than the other. On triplex mowers it frequently happens that not all mowers cut at the same height.

3. Scalped hole plugs on the green. Dead plugs on a green can spoil the appearance of an otherwise perfect putting green. Dead plugs result when the hole changer does his work improperly and becomes careless. The old hole must be filled perfectly level with the surrounding putting surface. If the plug is too high, it will be scalped by the greens mower and turn brown. When the plug sinks below the putting surface, the indent will deflect putts. Sometimes a fresh plug will dry out and turn brown because of wilt. Smart hole changers carry along a water bottle to give a squirt to stressed-out plugs.

4. A greens mower cutting into the apron. Cutting into the apron is an ugly mistake that should not be tolerated at a professionally managed golf course. More than likely it happens on the cleanup pass, when an operator becomes careless and moves too quickly. At times it happens when a novice operator does not lift the mower in time and cuts into the apron.

5. Letting new sod die. Fresh sod from a nursery, newly laid, is the culmination of a construction job well done. The shapes and the alterations have been carried out to perfection. The new sod, rolled and staked and marked as Ground Under Repair, is the icing on the cake. Three days later it is brown and dead for lack of water because someone just forgot. Such advertising of a greenkeepers' incompetence is definitely a deadly sin.

6. Killing a green with kindness! It happens when topdressing, especially sand, is matted in on a hot afternoon with the green under drought stress. Invariably this results in death. It can also happen when a green is aerated under similar conditions. Applying phytotoxic sprays such as Diazinon, and liquid fertilizers, all mixed together, will surely kill even the healthiest green.

7. A messy golf course strewn with napkins, paper cups, and beer cans. There may be an excuse for brown grass; there is never an excuse for a messy, untidy golf course. Good greenkeeping equals good housekeeping. The superintendent should always set the example when it comes to housekeeping. Stop and pick up the litter. Collect it in on your cart and dispose of it in the waste containers. Show the golfers and the workers that cleanliness is next to godliness. Remember also that invariably a messy maintenance building is indicative of conditions on the golf course. It is almost impossible to maintain a clean golf course from a dirty barn. A messy golf course is possibly the worst deadly sin, because it is totally preventable.

Some superintendents have posted the deadly sins on the bulletin boards in the Turf Care Center for everyone to see. Employees are reminded every day about the deadly sins. They check on their coworkers and if another worker commits a deadly sin, they'll pounce on that worker.

THE SEVEN VENIAL SINS

Besides the seven deadly sins there are seven venial sins. These are sins of a less serious nature, but sins just the same, and they should be avoided.

1. Smelly ball washers are all too common, even on some of the finest golf courses. While it is practically impossible to check all the ball washers all the time, a program should be in place to thoroughly clean the ball washers. Soap and water will do just fine. An overly ambitious superintendent, as a result of attending our "Magic of Greenkeeping" seminar, added Javex to the water in the ball washers. The balls came out shiny clean and there was a nice fresh smell emanating from the ball washer, but several golfers splashed some of the liquid on their pants and shirts. The bleached stains were not appreciated.

2. Dirty putting cups ruin the look of an otherwise perfect green. After sinking a putt, retrieving the ball from a filthy cup is a most unpleasant experience. One does not need to be squeamish to resent sticking one's hand into a dirty hole. The cup changer, in his daily routine, should carry along a moist sponge and use it to wipe off the inside of the cup. In addition, cups should be changed once or twice a season. For special events a squeaky clean cup is mandatory.

3. Golfers take pride in their golf course and like to do their part in keeping it in fine shape. We must give them that opportunity, and we do it by placing divot boxes on the tees, especially the tees of the par 3 holes. While many golfers for whatever reason do not make use of the divot mix, many more do. To find an empty divot box on a tee is a black mark against the greenkeeper.

4. Golfers will blame anything for their poor scores, including faults that are committed by the greenkeeper. High on their list is a set of imperfectly adjusted tee blocks. It seems that when tee blocks are not set up straight for the middle of the fairway, the greenkeeper is to blame for a hook or a slice. On par 3 holes, golfers miss the green because the markers are pointing the wrong way. Superintendents should scrutinize the work of their greensmen frequently. A daily routine tends to become monotonous and mistakes are often the result.

5. All too often when a mechanical bunker raker leaves the bunker, the operator forgets to wipe out the tracks. The result is an ugly pile of sand mixed with debris and at times dragged onto the turf. This venial sin borders on being a deadly sin. In addition to erasing the tracks, operators should also make sure that there is a sufficient number of rakes in each bunker. No rakes in the bunker is an unforgivable oversight; so are rakes with broken handles and missing teeth.

6. Torn flags are unsightly. It is best to start the new season with new flags and change them at least once during the season. Keep additional flags on hand in case some are vandalized. A complete set of flagsticks, pins, and tee markers should always be on hand for emergencies. Thieves in the night have been known to steal all of those items. Be prepared.

7. Long grass around the base of trees is an advertisement of incompetence. Long grass never looks more sloppy than when it is allowed to grow in profusion around trees, signs, and fence posts. Such lack of trimming is unforgivable even on the lowest of the low budget courses. Time must be found to correct such untidiness. It can be done by occasional applications of Round-Up, growth retardants, or simply by regular trimming. The latter is the most expensive method but probably also the most appealing.

The seven deadly sins are serious omissions that must not be allowed to last or to recur on any golf course. Once a deadly sin has been committed, it usually takes some time to take corrective actions. Venial sins, on the other hand, can be quickly corrected. The list of sins should be prominently displayed in the maintenance building for everyone to see. Greens staff and the assistant should measure their course against all 14 sins committed against the art of greenkeeping.

THE SUPER SUPERS

In our travels all over the world and our visits with colleagues from many different countries, we have noticed that some superintendents stand head and shoulders above all the rest. These individuals possess special qualities that make them stand out. We have studied these individuals and prepared the characteristics that all invariably have in common. They are the Super Supers and following are their earmarks:

1. The best superintendents in the world are invariably great greenkeepers. They can grow grass where there was none before. Their greens are strong and not anemic. There is grass on their tees, and their fairways are healthy.
2. They are knowledgeable and well educated and remain that way by constantly expanding their wealth of know-how and information.
3. They maintain the best possible golf course within the limits of their budgets. They don't gripe about the lack of funds, but instead find ways of getting the job done anyway.
4. They are environmentalists! They love the animal and plant life on their golf courses and do everything in their power to enhance and promote it.
5. They are hard workers, always up early in the morning and on the job till the last employee leaves, and frequently come back in the evening or late at night. They work hard and play when there is time. They play golf respectably.
6. They have an excellent staff, knowledgeable and well trained, who work with the superintendent, not for the superintendent.
7. They are enthusiastic about their work and they inspire their assistants to follow in their footsteps. They encourage all to excel at whatever they are doing.

8. They are effective communicators. They instruct their staff both verbally and in writing. They make information available to their golfers regularly, and inform through newsletters and at meetings. They respond to letters, and always return phone calls.

9. They look the part and they exhibit a professional image. They wear jackets when it is appropriate and they look distinguished and neatly dressed at all times.

10. The Super Supers are active professionally. They serve in their professional associations. They attend meetings, conferences, and seminars. They stand up and speak when called upon. They are the counted ones.

Appendix A:
Job Descriptions

GOLF COURSE SUPERINTENDENT

Function

A superintendent's primary function is to maintain the golf course at a level that satisfies the golfers and to keep all expenses within the limits of an operating budget. A golf course superintendent is first and foremost a greenkeeper, who can grow grass where there was none before and who can prepare a playing surface that meets the demands of the game. A superintendent is proficient at managing people and machinery and in getting the job done effectively. Above all, a superintendent is aware that the land which comprises the golf course is a living habitat for all creatures and that it must be conserved for future generations.

Qualifications

The credentials of a superintendent are a combination of academic knowledge, technical training, and practical experience. Whereas there are some very successful superintendents with less than a high school diploma, it is now generally agreed that a post-secondary diploma from an accredited turfgrass school is a minimum requirement. There are many superintendents who have Bachelor's and Master's degrees in Turfgrass Science. Specific technical training is learned from seminars and specialized short courses. Experience is garnered under the tutelage of an established master in the art of greenkeeping. Such practical experience is passed on from old-timer to novice, and often includes secrets that can only be learned on the job.

Areas of Responsibility

Highest on the list is the golf course as the top priority in a superintendent's daily duties. The greens must be visually checked, as well as the tees and the fairways. Diseases, insect pests, and weeds must be kept under control. The grass must be cut regularly and to the satisfaction of the golfers, the bunkers raked, and the markers and pins changed in such a manner as to provide a pleasurable golfing experience.

With the heat of summer come the many pests that attack the grass. A superintendent needs to be vigilant to ensure the survival of the turf. During the busy golfing season, greenkeeping is a daylong occupation that knows no free weekends. Golf course maintenance is a service industry which requires a commitment on the part of the superintendent to serve and satisfy the customers.

In addition to the golf course, many superintendents look after the clubhouse grounds, swimming pools, and tennis courts. At the end of a busy day, there are administrative duties such as record keeping and report writing chores that need to be taken care of. There are meetings to attend with the manager and the golf professional as well as the greens committee. The superintendent also has to deal with commercial suppliers of materials and equipment.

Deploying a large number of workers efficiently is essential to get the work done. The greens staff is hired very carefully, trained thoroughly, and their performance checked repeatedly. The work for the staff must be scheduled to keep everyone busy all the time. Some responsibilities can and should be delegated to the assistant. Golf course workers, under the direction of the superintendent and the assistant, must be well motivated, work diligently, and be trained to be considerate to the golfers. Workers who do not measure up to the accepted standards must be dealt with promptly and effectively.

Recently the superintendent's position has taken on an extra dimension: to present an image in the community of being a friend and a steward of the environment. Present-day superintendents demonstrate through their actions that they care about the land they have been entrusted with. They are in essence, and at all times, the ultimate conservationists.

The superintendent presents a congenial image, neatly dressed and groomed, and is always willing to answer questions and to share knowledge in a professional manner. A superintendent is a somewhat competent golfer who plays regularly and fraternizes with neighboring colleagues.

Specific Skills that are Required

A superintendent should know how to operate all machinery and equipment in the maintenance building and be capable of teaching this skill to others. A thorough knowledge of pesticides and fertilizers is essential. Being familiar with the irrigation system is paramount, since grass will not survive without water.

A thorough understanding of the needs of the golfers and the demands of the game is essential. A superintendent should know the rules of golf as they pertain to the maintenance of the course. A superintendent should play golf regularly and have an established handicap.

In addition to being a competent greenkeeper, a superintendent needs to possess administrative skills to deal with the business aspects of golf course management. From time to time a golf course superintendent is expected to address meetings and to present reports and budgets. The contemporary superintendent understands and knows how to use computers.

Professional Development

No one can operate in a vacuum, and least of all a superintendent in today's rapidly changing world of golf. Superintendents must belong to and participate in regional, national, and international professional associations. Attendance at seminars, conferences, and field days at universities where turfgrass research is conducted is essential. A superintendent should visit with colleagues to compare maintenance practices and to play golf.

A superintendent needs to attend refresher courses in turfgrass management, and constantly learn new computer skills. In their formative years, superintendents should attend a Dale Carnegie course or belong to the Toastmasters organization. Participation in community groups is highly recommended.

What it Means to be a Greenkeeper!

Longtime golf course superintendent Paul Voykin at the Briarwood Country Club near Chicago has this to say about our profession:

"Were I not a greenkeeper, I would miss the soft warm rains that fall on the turf that I grow. I would miss the white snow that covers the golf course in late fall for the first time, melts away, and then softly comes again. I would truly miss all the challenges of nature that go with my profession; the hot sun of summer heat and the salty sweat of humidity on my brow. I would miss the pleasure of admiring turf manicured and maintained under both good and adverse conditions and knowing that I had a hand in keeping the verdant picture that way. I would miss her many gifts to us greenkeepers, the trees changing in the seasons and the flowering shrubs in the spring. I would miss the daisies and the other wildflowers that grow in the roughs, and I would miss the wood thrush calling its mate in early morning. I would miss the honest faces of commercial friends calling on me and old greenkeepers advising me. But most of all I would miss getting up each early morning and playing the endless chess game of man against nature or perhaps, more truthfully, trying to work with nature and relishing the achievement, the satisfaction and the pleasure that come once in a while each season when, just for a short time, I have won the battle."

Summary

A superintendent is always a greenkeeper at heart, who loves to work out of doors and can't wait to get to work every morning. A superintendent is committed to provide the best possible course for the golfers. The superintendent goes home at night after a long day's work, secure in the knowledge that because of his efforts, the world is a better place to live in.

ASSISTANT GOLF COURSE SUPERINTENDENT

Function

To assist the superintendent in all areas of responsibilities with regard to the maintenance of the golf course. The assistant should at all times function as an extra set of eyes, ears, and legs for the superintendent. The ultimate objective of both the superintendent and the assistant is to provide the best possible playing conditions within the limits of the operating budget.

Education

- A post-secondary degree in turfgrass science or a related field, or at a minimum, a diploma in turfgrass maintenance from an accredited institution.
- A valid pesticide license, where applicable.
- Attendance at a human relations course such as a Dale Carnegie program or the Toastmasters organization.
- Membership in professional associations.
- Continuing education by attendance at turfgrass conferences and seminars.
- A valid operator's license (if applicable) for chainsaws, string trimmers, and other such tools.

Areas of Expertise

- Total familiarity with the operation of the pumphouse and the irrigation system. Ability to troubleshoot and repair all parts of the system.
- Total familiarity with the chemicals and fertilizers used in turfgrass maintenance, knowledge of rates of application and calibration of sprayers, etc.
- Recognition of the correct mower settings and mowing patterns, ability to make adjustments to cutting heights and cutting quality.
- Ability to pick the right person for the job, to select suitable people for particular jobs, and to motivate the staff.
- Knowledge of the game of golf and the rules of golf, and ability to play golf reasonably well.

- Ability to write reports and attend meetings at intervals. Confident and conversant with all areas of golf.
- Ability to expertly handle most pieces of equipment required for maintenance.
- In conduct and deportment, the assistant should at all times reflect the image one wishes the greens staff to assume.

Responsibilities

- The hiring and firing of the greens staff is the primary responsibility of the superintendent. The assistant may be involved in the preliminary screening of new staff and reports on the performance of new staff to the superintendent.
- The assistant arrives at work well before the majority of the greens staff, not only to set an example, but also to take care of any early emergencies.
- The assistant will meet with the superintendent to plan the work for the day.
- Work assignments and daily tasks are handed out by the assistant and the superintendent to individual members of the greens staff, most often in a joint session.
- The assistant and the mechanic help with getting machinery started and getting work going expediently.
- When not involved in an actual project, the assistant will go out on the golf course and check on the performance of the crew as well as the condition of the course and the turf.
- The assistant will help the crew members and, by example, show how the work needs to be done to perfection.
- The assistant trains new crew members in the operation of machinery and various other tasks on the golf course.
- The assistant, with the superintendent, helps organize the crew in such a manner that all workers are busy and that the work gets done efficiently.
- The assistant never hesitates to participate physically in the work on the course.
- While working with the crew, the assistant keeps an eye on the grass, checks for disease, weeds, insects, and any other imperfections, and reports all findings to the superintendent.
- An assistant should converse intelligently with golfers and members on and off the course.
- An assistant should habitually check on inventories to ensure that materials and supplies are available when needed.
- An assistant must possess some business acumen and computer literacy in order to carry out various office tasks related to budgeting and accounts payable. Specifically, the assistant should be able to work with spreadsheet programs such as Microsoft Excel and word processing programs like Microsoft Word or Word Perfect.

Summary

The assistant's background and on-the-job training should be of such quality as to enable him or her to take complete charge of the golf course during the absence of the superintendent. In fact, should the superintendent resign from the job or suddenly become ill or die, there should be no hesitation on the part of the greens committee to place a well-trained assistant, with proper credentials, in complete charge of the maintenance operation. To reach this level of competency is the goal in training an assistant.

GOLF COURSE MECHANIC

Qualifications

In addition to several years of work experience, the golf course mechanic should be either:

- licensed
- certified via training programs
- possess a diploma in mechanics from a recognized institution.

Continuing education by attendance at seminars, workshops, or training programs is mandatory. The golf club should provide the mechanic with his own set of tools and must hold a valid driver's license.

Expertise

The golf course mechanic should be competent in the following fields:

- small engine repairs
- tractor engine repairs (gas and diesel)
- hydraulics
- welding
- electronics
- grinding and sharpening of reels and bedknives
  operation of most equipment required for golf course maintenance.

Responsibilities

The mechanic is responsible for:

- preventative maintenance, repairs, and set up of all equipment and licensed vehicles used by the crew at the Turf Care Center
- fabrication of new or alterations to existing equipment

- maintaining an adequate inventory of parts and supplies
  keeping the shop in a clean and respectable manner
- overseeing the assistant mechanic.

The mechanic reports directly to the superintendent or to the assistant superintendent. Some overtime may be necessary in addition to the normal 40 hour work week.

Summary

Essentially, the mechanic ensures that the equipment is in a safe and operational state, enabling the greens department to provide the best possible playing conditions within the limitations of the operating budget.

GOLF COURSE SPRAY TECHNICIAN

Function

The spray technician will work under the supervision of the superintendent and the assistant. The main areas of responsibility will be the application of pesticides and fertilizers, as well as some regular maintenance duties.

Education

The spray technician will have a strong background in disease identification, insect technology, weed identification, and nutrient deficiencies as they apply to turfgrass maintenance.

- Must be either working toward or already have a post-secondary education (degree or diploma) from a reputable institution.
- A valid Pesticide Applicator's License is a necessity.
- Continuing education by attendance at seminars and conferences related to spraying and/or pest control for golf courses is essential.

Areas of Expertise

- broad knowledge of the identification and life cycle of the diseases, weeds, and insects that invade fine turf
- familiarity with pesticides and their phytotoxic characteristics
- operation and calibration of all equipment used for spraying and fertilizing
- knowledge of pesticides, their mode of action, and residual effects
- knowledge of fertilizers and their phytotoxic characteristics.

Responsibilities

The spray technician is responsible for:

- The total commitment to safety precautions and measures related to pesticides and spraying, not only for oneself, but for others.
- Regularly checking the golf course for pest and nutrition related problems, and reporting all findings to the superintendent or the assistant.
- All spraying and fertilizer operations on the golf course under the direction of the superintendent or assistant superintendent.
- Filing accurate reports and records of all operations, which includes application rates, spreader settings, weather conditions, pest symptoms, and quantities of materials used.
- Keeping an up-to-date and accurate inventory of all pesticides and fertilizers, and reporting any shortfall to the superintendent or the assistant.
- All spray operations are done in a completely safe manner, preferably ahead of the golfers.
- At times, the spray technician will also be involved in the application of wetting agents and biostimulants.

Summary

Essentially, the spray technician is responsible for carrying out all spraying duties as directed by the superintendent or the assistant. When not occupied with spraying or fertilizing, the spray technician will perform regular golf course maintenance duties with the rest of the greens staff.

IRRIGATION SPECIALIST

Function

The irrigation specialist works under the supervision of the superintendent and the assistant. The prime responsibility is the operation and repair, and at times, making additions to, the irrigation system. The objective of the irrigation specialist is to ensure the system is totally functional any time irrigation is necessary.

Education

- Must be either working toward or already have a post-secondary education (degree or diploma) from a reputable school related to turfgrass maintenance.
- Sufficient on-the-job training to troubleshoot, repair, and operate all parts of the irrigation system.
- Continuing education by attendance at seminars and conferences related to golf course irrigation.

Areas of Expertise

- basic knowledge of hydraulics relating to volume, pressure, and flow
- knowledge of soil/water relationships and turfgrass water requirements
- total familiarity with the pumping stations as related to golf course irrigation
- able to repair and operate all types of sprinkler heads, piping networks, and control systems
- basic knowledge of design and installation of irrigation systems
- knowledge of electronics and computers required to operate and repair modern irrigation system components
- ability to recognize dead or dying turf caused by wilt.

Responsibilities

The irrigation specialist is responsible for:

- Ensuring that the irrigation system is totally functional when it is needed.
- Troubleshooting and repairing all parts of the system as needed.
- Checking the turf for drought stress symptoms, taking immediate remedial actions.
- Making recommendations to the superintendent on the programming and scheduling of nightly irrigation.
- Adding and/or changing the design of the current system when required to do so by the superintendent.
- Ensuring that all heads are not only turning on, but functioning properly and distributing water evenly.
- Ensuring that all heads and repaired areas are level with the surrounding turf so they do not interfere with golf.

Summary

The irrigation specialist is required to have the watering system in constant operating order when watering is required. Considering the size of the system and the many heads and controllers involved, the position of irrigation specialist is very critical and should be a year round position.

GARDENER

Function

The gardener will work under the supervision of the superintendent and the assistant. The gardener will be responsible for the maintenance of the flower beds, clubhouse lawns, parking lots, and halfway house in a manner which best reflects the needs of the golf club. Being a gardener is a very important position since people's first impressions are made when arriving at the clubhouse.

Education

- a post-secondary education (degree or diploma) from a reputable school related to horticulture
- a valid pesticide license and other applicable permits
- continuing education by attendance at horticulture-related seminars and conferences.

Areas of Expertise

- broad knowledge of annuals, perennials, shrubs, trees, and other woody plants including size, shape, time of flowering, seasonal colors, hardiness, and planting locations
- familiarity with common weeds, diseases, and insects
- operation of equipment necessary to prepare/maintain flower beds and lawns
- operation and programming of irrigation controllers
- knowledge of pesticides and fertilizers pertaining to landscape plants.

Responsibilities

Late Winter/Early Spring

- In discussion with the superintendent, determine the annuals and perennials required for the flower beds.
- When the snow has melted, begin initial cleanup around the clubhouse. The gardener should concentrate on cleaning up damage done by the snow plow, and in the flower beds in close proximity to the clubhouse.

Spring

- Responsible for preparing the beds for planting of annuals. He or she will then be responsible to for purchasing the plants required, and ensuring that the beds are planted at the proper time.
- The gardener must ensure that the clubhouse lawns are neatly trimmed and any garbage or debris is removed from the clubhouse area.

Summer

- General maintenance of flower beds (weeding, watering, fertilizing), clubhouse lawns, and halfway houses. The gardener must make sure any garbage or debris is removed from the clubhouse area on a daily basis.
- The gardener will be expected to help the greens staff on the golf course when required.

Fall

- Remove annuals killed by frosts.
- Clean up the beds and prepare them for spring flowering bulb plantings.
- Planting of spring flowering bulbs.
- Final winterization of flower beds.

Summary

The gardener is encouraged to be self-motivated and to maintain the gardens, clubhouse lawns, and halfway houses to the highest standard possible. However, the gardener must consult with the superintendent and assistant superintendent concerning plans, to ensure that everyone is satisfied before proceeding.

GENERAL GREENS WORKER

Function

A general greens worker will work under the supervision of the superintendent, the assistant superintendent, or any other designated person. The greens worker will be responsible for the maintenance of the golf course grounds, which includes the cutting of various areas as well as topdressing, aerifying, divoting, and any other general maintenance work that may be required.

Education

- A general greens worker should have a grade 12 high school education and a valid driver's license.
- It is necessary to be able to write brief messages and to follow written instructions.

Areas of Expertise

- drive a maintenance vehicle
- drive a tractor
- operate several different types of mowers
- operate string trimmers.

Responsibilities

- work proficiently under the direction of supervisors, and complete assigned tasks within given time limits
- work safely and take care of machinery and tools

- at the conclusion of the work period, clean up tools and equipment
- the occasional application of pesticides is part of the duties of a general greens worker.

Summary

The objective of the general greens worker is to help provide the best possible playing conditions for the golfers.

Appendix B:
Inverness Golf Club
Palatine, Illinois
Maintenance Program, 1997

OBJECTIVE: TO ACHIEVE THE BEST POSSIBLE PLAYING CONDITIONS WITHIN BUDGET

It is our mandate to provide pleasurable playing conditions for all our members and their guests and ensure the survival of the golf course, not just for a day or a week, but for an entire season and for many seasons to come. To that end we have to follow practices that are agronomically sound and good for the grass. We strive to implement practices that will result in a near perfect playing surface but also want to make sure that our greens, tees, and fairways survive the rigors of our cold climate in the winter, and especially the heat and humidity of the summer. It is often a fine edge between what is good for the golfers and what is good for the grass. We try to cope with and handle all the unknown variables that may affect our course. The following pages outline our practices, based on knowledge and experience that have made us successful in the past and enable us to be successful again in the future.

GREENS

During the regular season, May through September, the greens are cut every day of the week with the exception of Monday (unless there is a holiday or special event day, in which case Tuesday might be the exception), for recovery purposes. We cut with walk-behind mowers and vary the direction of cut each day. The height of cut is between 5/32 and 9/64 of an inch, which is constant throughout the season. We generally provide a green speed which is acceptable to our members.

It takes three people 2 1/2 hours to cut all 19 greens.

TEES

The tees are cut three times per week. The height of cut on the tees is 1/2 inch. We have one individual whose duty it is to clean the tee areas and remove the tee markers. Either the mower operator or the person cleaning the area puts the markers back in position.

It takes one person 2 1/2 hours to cut all the tees on the course and another person 2 hours to clean the tee area and replace the markers.

FAIRWAYS

We generally cut the fairways three times a week. The schedule varies from Monday, Wednesday, Friday or Tuesday, Thursday, Saturday, depending on weather and course activities. Fairways are cut at a height just over 1/2 inch and the direction of cut varies each time to avoid wheel marking and tire tracking. The collars and approaches are normally cut on the same days. All clippings are collected on the fairways, collars, and approaches.

It takes two people 6–7 hours (depending on the amount of clippings and number of golfers) to cut all the fairways on the course.
It takes one person 2 1/2 hours to cut all the collars and approaches.

INTERMEDIATE

There is a step cut between the fairways and the roughs. This cut is about 6 ft wide and cut with an out-front rotary mower. The step cut is mowed two or three times per week, depending on the time of year.

It takes 1 person 2 1/2 hours to do the step cut.

DEW REMOVAL

We remove dew by dragging the fairways, greens, and sometimes tees with a high-pressure rubber hose between two motorized vehicles. This procedure starts at the green and dragging continues down the fairway toward the tee on each hole. This procedure is done most days during the summer season. We achieve a better quality cut when the dew is removed and we are convinced that removing the dew has reduced the number of pesticide applications.

ROUGHS

The largest area to maintain is the roughs. We have almost 80 acres of rough that are cut with two different types of mowers. One man operates the tractor that has a seven-gang mower. This tractor cuts the largest portion of all the roughs. We also use a pull-type rotary mower which has three five-foot units that are used periodically in place of the gang mower. When necessary, we use up-front rotary mowers to cut grass. A fly mower is used around the bunker faces that are not easily reached with the bank-type mower.

Our objective on the roughs is to cut all 80 acres once a week, except when we are delayed by rain. It is difficult to cut roughs on weekends because weekend golfers are less tolerant of noise and the interruptions caused by maintenance equipment than weekday golfers. Just the same, from time to time, especially on long weekends, we need to bring in staff on Saturdays and Sundays in order to get caught up.

BUNKER MAINTENANCE

The sand is raked daily in all 41 bunkers. We try to create a smooth, firm, surface, although the latter is difficult during dry times. The operators report when they encounter thin sand on the bunkers. Once this determination is made, sand is then added to them. The edges of the bunkers are edged mechanically throughout the summer.

It takes two people 3 hours to do all the bunkers.

HOLE CHANGING AND MARKERS

During peak season, the hole on the green and markers on the tees are changed daily. The location of the hole is changed daily, with six of the holes in the forward position and an equal number of holes either in the back or in the middle of the greens.

The hole changers often also change tee marker placement.

It takes 3 hours for one or two people to change all the tee markers as well as the holes on the putting greens.

DIVOTING

Filling divots is done periodically. We use a mix of sand, soil, humus, and seed.

Divot boxes are provided on par 3 holes. Green staff regularly restore divots that golfers forget to repair.

Divoting is a job done in the afternoon or late morning when other tasks have been completed.

TOPDRESSING

We topdress twice a year, which creates a level putting surface. We use a mix of sand, soil, and humus for this procedure. Topdressing is done in the morning, after the greens have been cut so that they are dry. Topdressing is performed by four people and takes 5 hours.

AERIFYING

Aerification of the tees is scheduled both in the spring and fall. The greens and fairways are aerated once during the fall season.

We have the ability to aerate 18 greens in one day under normal conditions. The tee areas can also be aerated in one day. Fairways often take many days to complete.

After the aeration process, the cores are ground up, and then a steel drag mat is used to work the soil back into the holes left after the coring of greens, tees, and fairways. We often combine seeding with aerification and use bent grass to thicken the existing turf.

VERTICUTTING

We verticut the greens to thin the grass, which allows the blades to stand upright. The mower blades operate in the vertical plane and sever the creeping stolons. The verticutting process provides for a better, grain-free putting surface.

We verticut greens two to three times a year, depending on the severity of the thatch buildup. Mowing the greens with walk-behind mowers that are equipped with groomers also helps to thin the grass. The daily use of groomers is determined by the superintendent.

FERTILIZING

Our fertilizer program varies, depending on the need of the grass. Usually in the spring, nitrogen is applied at a rate of 1 pound of nitrogen per 1,000 sq ft on the greens, tees, and fairways. This application includes a small amount of phosphorous and a half-pound of potash. Some areas are fertilized more often than others. The greens receive the most applications, followed by tees, then fairways. The rate of application varies according to the amount of growth, which is dependent on weather conditions. As the rate of growth decreases, the need for applications of fertilizer increases. To prevent burning of the grass as temperatures increase, the amount of nitrogen applied is reduced. Typically in the fall, fertilizer is applied to ensure a green turf in the spring. Fertilizer programs are the result of years of experience and knowledge that enables one to make the decision as to when and how much to apply during the growing season.

APPLYING PESTICIDES

We treat the grass with pesticides to control insects and to prevent disease caused by fungi. Pesticidal control is done mainly when there is an apparent need. If the course is in good condition there is no need to apply pesticides. Pesticides are applied if a problem exists, and only as a last resort. Keeping the course healthy often eliminates the need for a pesticide application. If an application is necessary, it is done when the course is not in use by golfers, and applied at low rates. Our operators are licensed to apply pesticides and use every precaution to apply the treatment in a safe manner.

IRRIGATING

Water is an essential element in the process of growing grass. Our irrigation system is automatic and runs off a computer in the maintenance shop. The computerized system is very flexible and gives us several advantages such as controlling the amounts, location, and time of watering.

Most golfers prefer a dry terrain. The hot summer months make this a challenge. In the summer the roots have a tendency to become short and can die quickly without ample water. However, too much water encourages disease in localized moist areas. In extremely hot conditions, a light vaporizing mist will cool the plants.

DRINKING FOUNTAINS

Three portable drinking fountains are checked, cleaned, and refilled with ice, water, and paper cups daily.

HAZARD AND GROUND UNDER REPAIR MARKINGS, OUT-OF-BOUNDS STAKES, AND YARDAGE MARKERS

All hazards are painted with an appropriate color of paint, using the "Rules of Golf" as a guide. Ground under repair is marked with white paint and refreshed as needed during the golfing season. White out-of-bounds stakes are placed along the boundaries of the golf club in areas where the club property is not defined by fencing. Sprinkler heads are marked with yardage tags to the center of each green. There are also brass plates to mark 100, 150, and 200 yards in the middle of each fairway. Tees have brass plates which designate the hole number and yardage.

MEETINGS

The grounds and green committee meets in the spring of each year, and then on an as-needed basis during the year. The green superintendent attends all meetings and submits a capital budget of anticipated expenditures at the beginning of each fiscal year. There is also a heritage committee which is responsible for the oversight of major course improvements. This committee consists of five longstanding members of the club. The green superintendent is also a member of this committee.

MAINTENANCE FACILITY

The facility consists of three buildings and a small greenhouse. One of the buildings houses a pesticide storage unit. We also have an EPA-approved aboveground encased concrete field storage tank. This unit holds two 500-gallon tanks, one for gasoline and one for diesel fuel.

The mechanic and his part-time assistant have a repair shop in one of the buildings. The same building houses the office and the kitchen. The other two buildings are used for equipment and irrigation storage.

The greens staff starts the day in the office building. Starting times vary with the season. Every morning starts with a brief meeting between the superintendent and his assistant, and later both meet with the general staff. This is to give out the daily assignments for each individual. Adjustments can be made after the morning break, as the day progresses, or weather conditions change. Most of the staff works a regular eight-hour day. A coffee break is taken in the early morning, and lunch before noon. On weekends and holidays we work a three-hour shift.

Seasonal staff consists of approximately 13 employees, which may include one or more turf interns. Our full-time staff consists of the superintendent's assistant, a mechanic and an assistant, a foreman, and a tractor driver. These people are responsible for the repair of equipment, including refurbishing ball washers, tee markers, benches, signs, and numerous other golf course accessories. Their responsibility also includes plowing snow, and ice control of the clubhouse drive and parking lot. We wind down the busy summer season with an employee party and include the greens committee and several other club members.

We strive to keep the area as neat as possible, but as one can well imagine with the various activities that occur in the maintenance area, doing so is a constant challenge.

Prepared by: Michael Bavier, Golf Course Superintendent

Appendix C:
Toronto Board of
Trade Country Club
Woodbridge, Ontario
Maintenance Program, 1997

OBJECTIVE: TO ACHIEVE THE BEST POSSIBLE PLAYING CONDITIONS WITHIN BUDGET

It is our mandate to provide pleasurable playing conditions for all our members and their guests and ensure the survival of the golf course, not just for a day or a week, but for an entire season and for many seasons to come. To that end we have to follow practices that are agronomically sound and good for the grass. We strive to implement practices that will result in a near perfect playing surface but also want to make sure that our greens and tees and fairways survive the rigors of our cold climate in the winter and the heat and humidity of the summer. It is often a fine edge between what is good for the golfers and what is good for the grass. We think we can walk that tight rope without falling most of the time. The following pages outline our practices, based on knowledge and experience that have made us successful in the past and will give us the best chance at being successful in the future.

GREENS

During the regular season, May through September, the greens are cut every day of the week, with one day off, either Monday or Friday, for recovery purposes.

Every second day the cleanup pass is omitted in an attempt to prevent the buildup of the dreaded Triplex Ring Syndrome. Several greens are cut regularly with a walk-behind or pedestrian mower. This lightweight mower is easier on the grass and encourages the buildup of a grass mat. The height of cut on our greens mowers is 3.35 mm, which does not vary from spring to fall. We like to provide a green speed of approximately 9 ft on the stimp meter. On the off day the greens are dew-whipped around the cup.

It takes three people 4 hours to cut all 50 greens.

TEES

The tees are cut three times per week, which is difficult to do when there is a three-day weekend. The height of cut on the tees is 7 mm. The hole changers put the tee markers aside to speed up the mowing process. The mower operators put the tee markers back where they belong.

It takes two people 5 hours to cut all the tees on three courses.

FAIRWAYS

We generally cut the fairways on one course every day, while the other course receives a rest, except for weekends, when fairways are rarely cut. We now have the capability, because of an extra mower we purchased, to cut the fairways on 27 holes during a morning shift and stay mostly ahead of the golfers. This will result in the fairways being cut more often and will provide a tighter playing surface. We are concerned about the development of thatch on the fairways, which shows as soft, spongy lies. For that reason, the fairways are verticut at least once during the season. The South Course fairways are cut during the afternoon and on weekends. The collars and approaches are cut with one of our older riding greens mowers at the same time that the fairways are being cut.

It takes four people 4 hours to cut all the fairways on one course.

INTERMEDIATE

There is a step cut between the fairways and the roughs. It is a swath about 10–12 ft wide, cut with an old hydraulic set of self-propelled gangmowers. We make the step cut three times per week.

DEW REMOVAL

As has already been mentioned, the greens are dew-whipped on mornings when they are not cut. This year we plan to drag the fairways with a rubber hose between two carts as a means of dew removal. We plan to have the necessary equipment in place by July 1st. Dew removal, apart from providing dry grass for golfers to play on, has an important side benefit: dry grass is less prone to disease. If we could postpone or eliminate just one pesticide spray, the whole operation would be worthwhile and quickly pay for itself

ROUGHS

By far the largest part of our effort goes into maintaining the roughs. We have almost 200 acres of land that are cut with one kind of rough mower or another. We employ two men to operate our two tractors and five gangs and they do the largest portion of all the roughs. Both the tractors and the cutting units are as old as the golf course. It is a marvelous example of our overall efficiency. In addition, we use several other people with mowers to keep the rough sufficiently short for play:

- a Kubota tractor with rotary mowers, mostly for holes #2 to #9 on the West
- a marvelous new, large upfront Toro rotary that literally eats the grass and helps all the other machines, especially in large wide-open areas where it is most efficient
- a smaller version of the above for between trees
- a John Deere reel type mower for around tees, greens, and bunkers
- two young people with line trimmers, Flymos, and rotary mowers to do the bunker faces and grassy hollows and everywhere else where nobody can get

Our objective on the roughs is to cut all 200 acres twice a week, except when we are delayed by rain. It is difficult to cut roughs on weekends because weekend golfers are less tolerant of noise and the interruptions caused by maintenance equipment than weekday golfers. Just the same, from time to time, especially on long weekends, we need to bring in staff on Saturdays and Sundays in order to get caught up.

BUNKER MAINTENANCE

The sand in the bunkers is raked daily in all 120 bunkers. We try to create a smooth, firm surface, although the latter is difficult during dry times. The operators report when they encounter thin sand, and such bunkers are topped up. The edges of the bunkers are treated with Round-Up, a grass killer, and not edged mechanically. Golf course architect Arthur Hills has determined that it is best that way.

It takes two operators to do all bunkers in 4 hours. During the week we will often use one operator to rake bunkers all day long. On weekends we always have one operator on each course and do the South Course after that.

HOLE CHANGING AND MARKERS

A rule of thumb dictates that the hole on the green and the tee markers on the tee are changed every 250 golfers. This, in effect, means that we do this chore every day.

The location of a hole is changed in accordance with a plan that reserves the best places for weekends and Tuesdays. On all other days we use the rest of the greens, which in essence means that there will be some difficult placements on the off days. One of the reasons that our greens continue to winter so well, year after year, is that we are such sticklers about using the entire green for hole placements and by so doing spread the wear, and at times suffer the wrath of irate golfers.

The hole changer is assisted by a second person who concentrates on tee maintenance and also repairs divot scars and ball marks. These two workers also check the ball washers, the washrooms, and pick up the trash, adjust the ropes, and report anything unusual to the supervisors.

It takes four people 4 hours to change all 45 holes and tee markers as well as the holes on the putting green.

DIVOTING

Filling all the divots is a time-consuming job taking loads of a specially prepared mix, as well as almost a ton of seed. Yet it is at the same time one of the most important functions that we perform. Every handful of divot mix represents a very small, unique opportunity to introduce a new superior bent grass to our landscape. By the end of the season all these divots, combined, cover quite a large area that otherwise might very easily have become *Poa annua*.

Divot boxes are provided at all par 3 tees. In addition, greens staff regularly repair divots on the par 3 holes that golfers forget, and all the other tees are repaired as well. We also fill in the divots on landing areas on the fairways. At times we use divot mix to top off irrigation trenches that have sunk.

Divoting is a job done in the afternoon or late morning when all the other operations have been completed.

TOPDRESSING

It is impossible to create a perfect putting surface without regular topdressings. We have been using a special sand for this purpose since 1973 and there have been no ill effects. The greens on both the East and the West are generally dressed every other week, usually on Mondays. The dressing is so light that by the time it is matted in and watered in overnight, the next morning's cutting removes all visible side effects. But what a difference it makes to the health of the green and its smoothness. All ball marks left unrepaired by thoughtless golfers will have been filled in. After a topdressing, a green looks better, feels better, and putts better; knowledgeable golfers know this and encourage their superintendents to topdress.

Topdressing is done in the morning, after the greens have been cut so that they are dry, and the sand is left to dry. Once dry, it is matted in with a steel mat or a brush. Preferably, irrigation water or regular rainfall is used to help wash the sand into the turf. After that, the surface is cut and is nearly perfect. The same process is repeated on the tees. We would like to topdress some or all fairways but don't have the resources or the machinery at this time.

Topdressing is done by four people and completed during the morning before lunchtime. On the South Course we occasionally topdress with a sandy topsoil to alleviate a unique hydrophobic condition that tends to exist during the summer months.

AERIFYING

On average, 250 golfers two-putt every one of our 50 greens every day of the week from April till November. All that foot traffic causes severe compaction, and if we did not aerate from time to time, the grass would die or turn into *Poa annua* very quickly.

We schedule a once-a-year aeration for all greens on both the East and West Course greens during the last week of July or the first week of August. At that time we use the 1/2" tines, and as a result, this severe operation affects putting for up to 10 days afterward. Aside from this major aeration, we aerate several selected greens during the balance of the season with minitines. This latter process leaves small holes that hardly affect putting. Both processes are done in conjunction with overseeding with bent grass. We also employ the Toro Hydroject, which is a painless way of aerating underground without disrupting the surface. By no means does the Hydroject replace hollow tine aerating.

Tees are also aerated during the midsummer week, as well as beyond that time frame when needed. Aerating fairways is a very big undertaking because of the large acreage involved. We like to aerate at least one course during June and early July. From mid-July into September it is not a good time for aerating fairways. The turf is too weak at that time and the aeration actually will harm the grass. The second course is usually done during October.

We have the ability to aerate 18 greens in one day under ideal conditions without breakdowns. Aerating tees is no more complicated than aerating greens, but fairways are very time-consuming. It takes several hours to complete the fairway on a typical par 4 hole. After aeration, the cores need to be pulverized and worked into the turf. The process is magical from an agronomic point of view. The grass grows with renewed vigor after an aeration.

VERTICUTTING

This is a process that is meant to thin the grass. The mower blades operate in the vertical plane and sever the creeping stolons and roots of the grass. The grass mat stays thinner and the buildup of thatch is lessened.

We verticut only occasionally because thatch is not a serious problem at the Board, except for fairways where we have to be vigilant.

FERTILIZING

A program based on many years of experience and attendance at conferences and meetings is in place that dictates when, where, and what is applied to the grass to promote optimum growth. Our policy is to avoid having the grass become overly lush. Instead, we like the turf to be lean. It is better for the health of the grass, and as a coincidence also makes for a better playing surface. We have our special secret of applying an organic concoction on the grass during November that virtually guarantees healthy greens in the spring.

SPRAYING WITH PESTICIDES

We treat the grass with pesticides to control and prevent diseases caused by fungi and insects. In addition, we need to eliminate and control weeds from time to time. Our approach to pesticide treatment can be compared to the human body's method of practicing preventative medicine. A healthy body, just like a healthy grass plant, needs very little medicine. We do everything we can to grow healthy plants, and spray only as a last resort. Spraying is usually done when there are no golfers around, but this is not always possible. The dangers of exposure to pesticides are vastly exaggerated by activists. No human being has ever died from pesticide poisoning on a golf course. Just the same, we take all possible precautions because we know pesticide applications are an emotional issue and we want our golfers to know that we care about their well-being. At the same time, golfers should realize that we cannot grow grass without pesticides altogether.

Aside from the fact that all our operators are fully licensed to apply pesticides, we also use the most sophisticated computer operated machinery. Our equipment makes it possible to pinpoint our treatments, and as a result we use very minimal amounts.

IRRIGATION

Without water we would not be able to grow grass, and without grass there would not be golf as we know it. Our 24 year old system is still functioning remarkably well, although frequent repairs are needed. Our coverage is less than adequate, a fact that is difficult to prove during the spring of 1996. It is in the technology where we have fallen behind the times. Our controllers are old-fashioned and not connected to a computer. Our system is scheduled for a refit in 1998 and 1999. We have to make do in the mean time.

The plant is operated by a technician and an assistant. Between them, they keep the system functional. After a severe winter, it takes several months to make the system completely operational and trouble-free. By that time, fall is here and we no longer need supplemental water.

Our philosophy is to keep the golfing terrain as dry as possible so that golf is pleasurable. In July and August when grass roots are short and plants die quickly when not watered, that can be difficult. It is a razor's edge operation: the line is ever so thin between abject failure and glorious success. We keep trying, and succeed most of the time.

WASHROOMS AND DRINKING FOUNTAINS

The washrooms are checked and cleaned three times daily, twice by the greens staff and once by the rangers. The drinking fountains are checked and cleaned weekly. The rangers also check both, and report malfunctions.

HAZARD STAKES, BOUNDARIES, GROUND
UNDER REPAIR, etc., etc.

Yellow, red, and white stakes are placed in their respective places in accordance with a plan approved by the Golf Committee. The stakes are checked regularly by one of the assistants and kept in place as required. GUR is marked for special tournaments and events but not all the time. Ongoing repairs are usually marked with a GUR sign or roped off. A white stake is in the middle of most fairways at exactly 150 yards from the center of the green. In addition, a blue stake is often used at precisely 200 yards from the center of the green and a red stake at the 100-yard mark. There are also yardage tags on many sprinkler heads. When no tag is available, the correct yardage is painted on the sprinkler with white paint.

MEETINGS

The superintendent and at times the assistant attend all meetings of the green committee. There are about nine meetings annually. The superintendent takes the minutes, distributes them, and keeps these on file.

THE TURF CARE CENTER

Our maintenance shop, office, and storage barn are under three different roofs but arranged in such a fashion that the resulting compound is quite functional. The lean-tos are in a bad state and need to be repaired soon. At the Turf Care Center we make most of our equipment repairs under the supervision of our full-time mechanic and his assistant. The mowers are sharpened and adjusted here on a regular basis. Tee markers are painted, signs repaired, and a myriad of other small chores carried out.

All the greens staff start their day at the Turf Care Center at daybreak each and every day. Every morning starts with a meeting between the superintendent and his assistants and the general staff is briefed for 5–10 minutes before starting time in a general session. This briefing takes place in the staff room. The important criteria is that everyone knows what they are supposed to be doing and what everyone else is doing during the entire working day. There should be no surprises, but there are frequently adjustments as the day progresses and weather conditions change.

Most staff work a regular 8-hour day with a half hour lunch break. Coffee breaks are allowed in the morning, and the greens staff generally takes these breaks in the halfway houses or at the Turf Care Center. Many staff are required to work overtime, especially the assistants. During the week we start work at exactly 6:30 a.m., but we are all here long before then. The Turf Care Center generally closes by 5:00 p.m. On weekends and holidays we start at daybreak and work till noon, although the supervisors are here much longer. It is difficult to get work done on the weekends because many golfers don't want us around.

The senior year round staff meets monthly or more often to discuss our operations and how we can improve. Two members of the greens staff are also part of the Board of Trade Safety Committee and they are charged with the responsibility of making sure that we work safely and have no accidents.

We like to keep the Turf Care Center just as clean and as tidy as we do the golf course, but it is a constant struggle. We host a green committee social and a barbecue at the Turf Care Center. We also organize a staff party, and last year in August, a barbecue attended by over 150 people was held to raise money for turfgrass research. Our buildings are in full view of the golfers and also the people that drive and walk on Clarence Street. We don't mind being watched, because we take pride in the work we are doing.

Prepared by: Gordon Witteveen, Golf Course Superintendent
            Cory Janzen and Gary Stairs, Assistants

Appendix D:
General Information for
All Employees, 1997

TORONTO BOARD OF TRADE COUNTRY CLUB, TURF CARE CENTER

Please make sure that our office has the following:

1. Social Insurance number
2. Completed tax deduction form
3. Name, address, and telephone number
4. Name of next of kin in case of accident
5. Bank account number for pay deposit.

Hours of Work

1. The regular work week consists of five 8-hour days. During the golfing season some staff will be required to work on weekends and holidays. During the off-season some staff may be required to help with snow clearing.
2. During both the golfing and the off-season some staff may be required to work overtime.
3. During the golfing season, starting time is 6:30 a.m. There is a 15-minute coffee break at approximately mid-morning and a one-hour lunch period at 11:30 a.m. The afternoon work period is only three hours, and there is no coffee break.
4. We expect all employees to arrive at least ten minutes prior to starting time to discuss the work assignments and the events of the day.

5. Anyone arriving late for work will be responsible for cleaning the catch basins. Repeated lateness will result in dismissal.

6. At the end of the work period we allow ten minutes for wash-up of tools, machines, and yourselves. You must not leave the Turf Care Center until quitting time.

In the Morning

Before leaving the Turf Care Center in the morning be sure to have your hard hat with you. Also take your rain gear when there is a possibility of rain. Too much time is wasted in the morning making several trips to your locker or having to come back once you are on the course. We like our employees to be prompt and we like them to be on the way to their various tasks when the hour strikes. It is very important to be ahead of the golfers in the morning. Once behind, one rarely catches up.

Overtime and Weekend Hours

1. We encourage our employees to finish their assigned tasks, even if it means working a short time past quitting time.

2. We may request you to work overtime when important jobs must be completed. Working overtime when asked and accepting the assignment will benefit an employee.

3. Weekend hours begin at daybreak and last for about 4–5 hours.

4. The duties for weekend work are generally outlined on the blackboard at the main shop.

Lunch

1. You are encouraged to bring your own lunch. Some of our employees buy their lunch in the village, but we prefer you to stay around the Turf Care Center during lunch hour.

2. Consumption of alcohol will not be tolerated during working hours or lunchtime. Be sober when you arrive at work. Any infraction of this rule will result in instant dismissal.

3. You are encouraged to participate in lunch hour activities, such as baseball, basketball, and practice chipping and putting.

4. Being a better-than-average euchre player is commendable.

Breaks

1. Breaks are 10–15 minutes in length. During the summer season there is only a morning break. A break is a privilege and not a right.

2. If you are near the Turf Care Center, take your break there. If you are at the Turf Care Center, do not go to the halfway house for your break.

3. Do not abuse the halfway house privileges. It is not a place for green staff to congregate during break time and by so doing cause inconvenience to members, who, after all, are paying customers.

Take your break to fit in with your work schedule and take it at the halfway house nearest your work area.

Dress

1. Hard hats are a government requirement and must be worn when you are in areas where you are prone to be hit by golf balls.
2. Dress for the weather. It may be quite chilly in the morning, even during the summer. Bring gloves, especially when you are cutting greens.
3. Rain gear, pants, and jackets are provided, but you must bring rubber boots. If it looks like rain, take your rain gear out on the course with you.
4. Shorts may be worn by both males and females, but not short-shorts.
5. Golfers may not remove their shirts, and certainly not around the clubhouse or in the halfway houses.
6. Men may not wear tank tops, and women may not wear tube tops.

We like our employees to be clean and neat in appearance, at least at the start of the day.

Equipment and Machinery

1. You are expected to take care of our equipment and machinery and to treat it as if it were your own. We will not tolerate abuse.
2. Check the oil and fuel before machinery is taken out. Fill up with fuel before lunch and at the end of the day before storing the machinery.
3. Know the difference between gasoline, gas and oil mix, and diesel fuel. When in doubt, ask the mechanic.
4. Machines, carts, tools, etc., must be cleaned at the end of each day. Make sure to remove grass clippings from the reels.
5. Most machines function best at low throttle and at low speed. Never drive at excessive speeds. The only time you are allowed to move fast is when you are on your own two feet!

The Environment

1. You are expected to act responsibly with regard to the environment.
2. From time to time you will be asked to apply pesticides and/or fertilizers to our turf. These tasks are always performed under the direction and supervision of a licensed operator.
3. You will be instructed in all the proper procedures with regard to fertilizers and fungicides and other hazardous materials.

4. Help to ensure that pesticides and fertilizers are not applied to streams and ponds.
5. Make sure that no hazardous materials enter catch basins.
6. Report any spills of hazardous materials immediately to a supervisor.
7. Be conscious of waste. Conserve, reduce, and reuse.
8. Help keep our property tidy and clean. Never hesitate to pick up other peoples' refuse.

Turf Care Center Maintenance

1. Each employee has a responsibility to help keep the main storage barn, the shop, the lunchroom, and the washrooms clean and tidy.
2. You will be asked to clean the washrooms from time to time. If you have reservations about such tasks, let us know now, so we can hire someone else.
3. Each employee will be asked to be on Lock-up Duty for at least one week during the season. A schedule will be posted.
4. Remember senior staff does the onerous tasks during the winter season. Junior staff does them during the summer.

The Telephone

1. The telephone is a business telephone and not for personal use.
2. Do not have your friends and family call our number and expect us to take messages.
3. If you must use the phone, in emergencies only, always ask first.
4. Never, ever, make long distance calls without permission.

Absenteeism, Days-Off, and Holidays

1. If for any reason you cannot make it to work, phone us before starting time. Not having our number is no excuse.
2. If you are late, and did not let us know, you are in trouble. If you are late a second time, you are in serious trouble, and if you are late again, don't call us. Go look for another job.
3. If you need a day off, ask the superintendent. We are approachable.
4. Please make doctor or dental appointments for the afternoon, since the morning is the most important part of our day and that is when we need you the most.

Rates of Pay

1. Your rate of pay was determined at the time you were hired.
2. Raises are unlikely in the present economy.

3. Statutory holidays are paid days off, provided you work the day before or the day after.
4. You will be paid time-and-a-half after 44 hours during any week.
5. Payday is every second Friday, and your pay will be deposited into your account by our office.
6. Check your pay stub for mistakes and report them to the superintendent or the secretary.

Channels of Authority

1. The golf course superintendent is in charge of the entire maintenance operation. In most instances you will receive your instructions directly from him.
2. In addition, you may, from time to time, receive instructions from the assistant or from the maintenance supervisor.
3. The chief mechanic is responsible for all equipment, and his instructions on machine operation must be followed.
4. The irrigation specialist is responsible for the operation of the watering system. Leaky sprinklers, broken pipes, and other malfunctions must be reported to him.
5. The secretary is responsible for administrative duties, and when there is no one at the Turf Care Center, the secretary will direct employees.
6. Other senior staff will have responsibility over work crews, and their instructions must be followed.
7. Summer staff should listen to advice from senior staff in order to do assigned tasks properly. Advice is given to prevent mistakes and more importantly, to avoid injury.

Members and Guests

1. Our whole operation is geared to pleasing our customers because they pay the fees that make it possible for us to earn our pay.
2. At all times be pleasant, friendly, and helpful to the golfers.
3. Try to avoid interrupting their game, but if you must, do so with a smile and a wave of the hand.
4. There is a delicate compromise between the needs of the golfers and the need to get the work done.
5. If a problem develops, never argue with the golfers. Apologize, even if you think you are right, and refer the matter to the superintendent or the assistant as soon possible.
6. Sexual harassment by golfers, country club staff, or fellow greens staff will not be tolerated. Report such incidents immediately to the superintendent.

Golfing privileges are strictly governed by established rules and regulations as specified elsewhere. Please remember that such privileges are earned and that you do not have an automatic right to play golf here.

General

The foregoing rules and regulations apply to all employees of the Board of Trade Greens Department. If you have any questions or complaints please do not hesitate to bring them to our attention. Our objective is to have a satisfied, cohesive crew striving to maintain the golf course in superior condition. Each employee must take pride in a job well done. Remember, each task is important, no matter how insignificant it may appear to you. Collectively our good work provides an outstanding golfing facility on which happy golfers play.

Index